Geographies, Genders and Geopolitics of James Bond

D1287152

Lisa Funnell • Klaus Dodds

Geographies, Genders and Geopolitics of James Bond

palgrave
macmillan

Lisa Funnell
Women's and Gender Studies Program
University of Oklahoma
Norman, OK, USA

Klaus Dodds
Department of Geography
Royal Holloway, University of London
Egham, UK

ISBN 978-1-349-84881-2   ISBN 978-1-137-57024-6   (eBook)
DOI 10.1057/978-1-137-57024-6

Library of Congress Control Number: 2016958108

Printed on acid-free paper

This Palgrave Macmillan imprint is published by Springer Nature
The registered company is Macmillan Publishers Ltd.
The registered company address is: The Campus, 4 Crinan Street, London, N1 9XW, United Kingdom

ABSTRACT

Geographies, Genders, and Geopolitics of James Bond discusses the representational geographies of the Bond film franchise and how they inform our reading of 007 as a hero. This book offers a new and interdisciplinary lens through which the franchise can be analyzed and explores a range of topics that have been largely, if not entirely, overlooked in Bond film scholarship. These topics include: the shifting and gendering of geopolitical relations; the differing depiction and evaluation of vertical/modern and horizontal/pre-modern spaces; the use of classical elements in defining gender, sexuality, heroic competency, and geopolitical conflict; and the ongoing importance of haptics (i.e. touch), kinesics (i.e. movement), and proxemics (i.e. the use of space) in defining the embodied and emotive world of Bond. This book is comprehensive in nature and scope as it discusses all 24 films in the official Bond canon and theorizes about the future direction of the franchise.

ACKNOWLEDGEMENTS

This book is the product of a shared passion for watching, understanding, and analyzing James Bond. But without the love, support, and patience of our families, we would not have been able to complete it. As a result, we dedicated this book to our families.

Lisa Funnell needs to thank her family for their unwavering support and encouragement. She must thank her dad, Lorne, for introducing her to James Bond and sharing his love for the series. She is also grateful to her mom, Mary, for indulging them as they wore out the James Bond VHS tapes that they regularly watched over Sunday dinners. Finally, she is thankful to her brother Dave, her sister-in-law Caren, and their wonderful children Tailor, Harrison, and Daniel for their excitement about the book especially since this one has colorful pictures! You are an unending source of love and laughter in my life!

Klaus Dodds thanks his family, Carolyn, Alex, and Millie, for their enduring patience with an unrelenting interest in James Bond. But it all started many years ago. His passion for Bond is rooted in the 1970s and 1980s, and watching Roger Moore–era films on multiple occasions with his brother Marcus. Outside the family, the students attached to GG3067 Geopolitics on Film at Royal Holloway, University of London have always been great audiences to try out material.

We are incredibly grateful to the generosity of our colleagues and friends for your support on this project. We extend a warm thank you to Drs. Peter Adey, Michael Boyce, Sean Carter, Jason Dittmer, Nick Jones, Nick Vaughan-Williams, and Robert Weiner for reviewing an early draft of the manuscript. Your insightful comments helped to strengthen the arguments in our book. We also must thank Karl Schmidt, the Digital Media Lab Manager of the Film and Media Studies Program at the University of Oklahoma, for helping us select and configure the screen shots featured in our book. We are grateful to James DiStefano, Managing Editor of the *Journal of Popular Film and Television*, and Kathy Jackson, Assistant to the Editor of the *Journal of American Culture*, for your interest in our research and support in its publication. Finally, we must thank Chris Penfold and Lina Aboujieb from Palgrave Macmillan for your interest in our project and guidance throughout the publication process.

We also extend our thanks to the University of Oklahoma for funding this project. Financial support was provided by the Office of the Provost, Office of the Vice President for Research, College of Arts and Sciences, and Women's and Gender Studies Program at the University of Oklahoma.

Additionally, we are thankful for receiving permission to reproduce selections from the following copyrighted material.

An earlier version of Chap. 2—"The Haptic Geographies of James Bond's Body"—appeared as Funnell, L. and Dodds, K. (2015) "The Man with the Midas Touch": The Haptic Geographies of James Bond's Body. *Journal of Popular Film and Television* 43.3: pp. 121–135. Reproduced with the permission of Taylor & Francis.

An earlier version of Chap. 3— "The Anglo-American Connection"— appeared as Funnell, L. and Dodds, K (2015) The Anglo-American Connection: Examining the Intersection of Nationality with Class, Gender, and Race in James Bond Films. *The Journal of American Culture* 38.4: pp. 357–374. Reproduced with the permission of John Wiley & Sons.

CONTENTS

LIST OF FIGURES

CHAPTER 1

Introduction

James Bond is an iconic action hero who is defined by his social locations (i.e. who he is) and the actions he takes in a vast array of geographical places (i.e. what he does and where he conducts his missions). On the one hand, James Bond enjoys a high degree of privilege given his membership to every significant dominant social group in the West: he is a white, cis-gender, middle-class, heterosexual, able-bodied, and British man who has enjoyed a private school education and attended Cambridge University. He can move, act, and perform; gain access to places, spaces, and resources; and use his intersectional and social capital in ways that most people cannot. It is this privilege that makes Bond such an attractive character with worldwide appeal. On the other hand, the missions he completes define Bond's masculinity. His performance in the field, and his ability to seduce and sexually satisfy multiple women in each film, is critical to consolidating, what Robert Connell would note as being, his "hegemonic masculinity" (2005, p. 37). His heroic competency is demonstrated and validated through his actions, which work to secure the geopolitical interests of Britain and its Western allies (and particularly America). For James Bond, where things unfold is integral to how things unfold (Purse 2011; N. Jones 2015a).

While action cinema generally trades in visual spectacle and physical mastery, the human and physical geographies of those environments being mastered is often taken for granted by audiences and critics alike. What is often overlooked in the discussion of Bond's heroic identity is

© The Editor(s) (if applicable) and The Author(s) 2017
L. Funnell, K. Dodds, *Geographies, Genders and Geopolitics of James Bond*, DOI 10.1057/978-1-137-57024-6_1

the fact that his character is also strongly defined by political and physical geography—the places, spaces, and very material contexts within which he operates including air, rock, snow, wind, and water. For example, in an interview with *Variety* magazine, Marc Forster, the director of *Quantum of Solace* (2008), hinted at the aesthetic significance of this relationship as he aspired to connect the four elements— earth, air, fire, and water —across his film (Thompson 2008, 11). The film's plot revolves around a plan to secure water resources in the Bolivian desert with a dramatic finale involving a hotel engulfed by fire. But *Quantum of Solace* also involves an array of overseas locations including three in Latin America (Chile, Mexico, and Panama) and extensive filming in Italy and Austria in addition to London. The film opens with a dramatic car chase as Bond and his pursuers glide through a marble quarry sending dust into the air. Following the opening credit sequence, the action moves to the famous Sienna horse race, and Bond is seen running across rooftops, squirreling through tunnels, and falling through a glass cathedral dome. The elemental (in the form of rock and mineral derivatives such as marble and clay) make Bond's escape both materially possible and aesthetically desirable, and his accidental suspension in the air via a rope attached to the scaffolding increases the dramatic tension of the scene. Later in Bolivia, the earth and air play a connected role as the contours of the subterranean desert environment makes Bond's escape possible by allowing him to descend into it via a parachute from a plane plummeting to the ground.

These material geographies are not unique to *Quantum of Solace*. Across the film franchise, Bond is defined as much by gender and geopolitics as he is by his interaction with elemental, resource, and political geographies, and the intersection of these aspects lies at the heart of our book, *Geographies, Genders, and Geopolitics of James Bond*. As a field of study, geography is more than the creation and analysis of charts and maps (although maps, globes, and scale models are frequently featured in Bond films to highlight geopolitical relations as well as the villain's desire to redraw these boundaries). Instead, geography is an expansive field that explores space, place, scale, materiality, emotions and affect, and human and environment interactions. When combined with film studies, film geography and popular geopolitics offer critical lenses through which scholars can examine the ways in which physical and human environments are conceptualized; often gendered but also intersected by age, race, class, and sexuality amongst other social locations; and depicted in mainstream culture, which in turn influences social-spatial discourses and practices. Film geographers, for more than 30 years, have argued that film is an assemblage of textual and extra-textual processes, objects, agents, and sites and spaces (Cresswell and Dixon 2002; Lukinbeal and Sharp 2014). Film, as a geographical practice, explores the process by which spaces are framed and shaped while evoking and provoking the experiences of living—both moving through and remaining firmly in place. Geographical environments and landscapes in film provide rich content for analysis, and arrays of distinct places are associated with particular film genres, including the imperial spy thriller (e.g. *The Thirty Nine Steps* 1915 novel and later 1935 Alfred Hitchcock film) and the blockbuster action and spy film (e.g. the Harry Palmer series in the 1960s).

As recent Bond and Bourne films demonstrate, the city environments of Berlin and Moscow are capable of evoking Cold War geographies of division and intrigue. A wintry Moscow seems particularly complicit with this framing, as ice and snow play their part in contributing to a chilly geopolitical aesthetic. Spies and assassins shiver, sludge, and skid through the decaying urban infrastructure of the former Eastern bloc. And Bond's visits to Berlin, Bratislava, and Moscow always occur in winter and/or at night, suggestive perhaps of a Cold War geopolitical nostalgia for a form of "cloak and dagger" spying rather than a more contemporary era punctuated by mass surveillance and cyber-terrorism.

For his part, Bond represents a highly idealized vision of Britain as he travels the world on government-sanctioned missions in order to safeguard their geopolitical interests. In 1970, writer Raymond Durgnat famously described Bond as a "one man Suez taskforce" and "The last man in the British Empire's superman XI" at a time when political elites were still smarting from the humiliating withdrawal from the Suez Canal zone in 1956 (Durgnat 1970 qtd. in Parker 2014, p. 74). The ways in which Bond travels to and interacts with different places, spaces, and people conveys powerful messages about Britain's geopolitical self-conceptualization and the relative worth of other nations and people by comparison. As James Chapman, a British historian of James Bond, asserts,

[Bond] represents a nationalist fantasy, in which Britain's decline, as a world power did not really take place. One of the ideological functions of the Bond narrative is to construct an imaginary world in which Pax Britannia still operates. Thus Britain is presented as being in the frontline of the conspiracies directed against western civilization. (2000, p.4)

Britain's relationship with the United States as signified through the friendship of Bond and CIA agent Felix Leiter bears little resemblance to the material realities of that "special relationship" in practice. Instead, the Bond films, much like Ian Fleming's novels, position Britain as a great power with persistent extra-territorial reach and influence even in the midst of decolonization and Cold War geopolitical reordering.

While a small number of academic works have been published on the international and representational politics of James Bond (see Bennett and Woollacott [1987], Chapman [2000], Lindner [2003], Black [2005], Dodds [2003, 2005, 2014] Funnell [2011a, 2015a, b, c]), little attention has been directed towards their interconnection or the role that geography plays in defining this relationship and spatially representing threat, danger, insecurity, and safety. In comparison, *Geographies, Genders, and Geopolitics of James Bond* focuses explicitly on the more than representational geographies of the Bond films, by addressing how Bond is shaped by embodied, material, and even elemental encounters with humans, objects, and earthly forces such as ice and fire respectively. The book is also attentive to other geographies as well. Although the Bond films were produced by Eon Productions based in Pinewood Studios (located outside of London), they are also American films funded by United Artists. The Anglo-American provenance of the franchise helped to shape the production, distribution, and consumption geographies of the films. For example, Soviet audiences rarely saw the Bond films during the Cold War, and if they were watched, they were seen by a relatively small group of privileged individuals in so-called closed shows (Bahun and Haynes 2014, p. 25). For the Soviet authorities, Bond was too Western, bourgeoisie, and physically and sexually attractive for local audiences. He was (and is) a man who has clearly enjoyed a good life, consuming champagne and fine food including Soviet caviar, in addition to possessing a plethora of consumer goods and mobilizing advanced technology. As a result, there are geographies of both absence and presence that one can trace in relation to who was able to watch the Bond franchise during the Cold War. The content and marketing of the Bond films have distinct geographies as well. In 2013, Chinese authorities finally gave permission for the release of *Skyfall* (Mendes 2012) in the mainland after changes were made to the explicit Chinese references in the film. In the official Chinese version, Bond's archrival Raoul Silva is no longer tortured by Chinese agents and references to the dirty politics surrounding the handover of Hong Kong to China in 1997 were removed. Ironically, the film sees Bond travel to

Shanghai and Macau as part of his mission to discover the whereabouts of a lost computer disk. The insertion of a Chinese component to his mission was a deliberate attempt by the franchise to appeal to (mainland) Chinese audiences,[1] who comprise the most lucrative film market next to the United States.[2]

This book, while mindful of these productive and consumptive geographies, addresses the more than representational geographies of the Bond film franchise and how it informs our reading of James Bond as a hero. It offers a new and interdisciplinary lens through which the franchise can be analyzed and explores a range of topics that have been largely, if not entirely, overlooked in Bond film scholarship. These topics include: the shifting and gendering of geopolitical relations; the differing depiction and evaluation of vertical/modern and horizontal/pre-modern spaces; the use of classical elements such as earth, air, fire, and water in defining gender, sexuality, heroic competency, and geopolitical conflict; and the ongoing importance of haptics (i.e. touch), kinesics (i.e. movement), and proxemics (i.e. the use of space) in defining the embodied and emotive world of Bond.

This book is comprehensive in nature and scope as it discusses all 24 films in the official Bond canon and theorizes about the future direction of the franchise.

GEOGRAPHIES, GENDERS, AND GEOPOLITICS OF JAMES BOND

In his book *Goldeneye*, Matthew Parker explores how Fleming's visits to Jamaica shaped the imaginative and material geographies of his Bond novels. Parker argues that "all roads lead back to Jamaica" in terms of making sense of how, why, and, critically, where Bond's origins lie (2014, p. 6). Fleming's first encounter with the former British island colony was in 1943 when he was invited to attend a naval conference involving Britain and the United States. As a naval officer working for the Admiralty during the World War II, Fleming was involved in naval planning, which included imagining outlandish schemes to misdirect and confuse German naval forces operating in the Atlantic Ocean, the North Sea, and the English Channel.

After the war, Fleming purchased a property in west Jamaica and it was here that his career as a novelist materialized. In Goldeneye, he found a place to escape from the British winter from which to write and imagine a post-war world. His stays in Goldeneye were sensuous affairs, and Fleming writes with passion about his daily swims in the warm waters of the Caribbean and the pleasure he took from the garden and wildlife that inhabited the property and surrounding area (Parker 2014, p. 6). It is perhaps no surprise that his secret agent, James Bond, is comfortable and competent in onshore and offshore tropical environments. He is also sensitive to and appreciative of the natural environment—again reflecting Fleming's experiences including scuba diving with the famous French diver Jacques Cousteau in April 1953 (Fleming 2015, p. 32). Bond is rarely if ever depicted killing animals and/or destroying landscapes unless they are intimately connected to the success of a mission. Jamaica was Fleming's favorite home and the island features strongly in his novels (*Live and Let Die, Dr No, Thunderball,* and *The Man with the Golden Gun*), and, notably, in the first Bond film, *Dr. No* (Young 1962).

From his home in Jamaica, Fleming's novels in combination with his journalistic/travel assignments outline an imaginative geography of the post-1945 world that is nostalgic while forward-looking. Both Fleming and his secret agent enjoyed travelling and only the novel *Moonraker* is entirely based in southern England. Travel provides opportunity for Bond to undertake a variety of missions from the United States and Japan to smaller island states of Jamaica, Seychelles, and Bermuda. While Bond never travels directly to Africa and South America, his worldwide encounters are rarely uneventful. They provide opportunities not only to be immersed in "exotic" spaces and cultures, but also encounters with other people and places that sometimes serve to bring to the fore Britain's changing role in the world. In *You Only Live Twice*, Bond is to be found reflecting on how Britain had been "bled pretty thin by a couple of World Wars" (1964, p. 81), while retorting to his Japanese counterpart Tiger Tanaka that the country still had the ability to project itself around the world.

Three of the Bond novels were set in the United States (*Diamonds are Forever, Goldfinger,* and *The Spy Who Loved Me*) and Fleming's depiction of the Anglo-American connection was riddled with ambivalence. Fleming's novels and journalistic accounts of the United States contain admiration for technological prowess and, in President Eisenhower's terms, the American military-industrial complex, but there are also traces of disgust and displeasure at consumer culture, criminality, and currency. In *Diamonds are Forever*, Bond is shown to be uncomfortable in urban America, and not just Las Vegas. Taken together, Fleming's America is defined by its cultural and geopolitical excess, and while not unique to this former British naval officer and journalist, it plays a pivotal role in his novels. While his CIA sidekick, Felix Leiter, is the 'good American', the country and its inhabitants appear uncooperative, surly, and even jealous of Bond's fieldwork skills.

The novel *Dr No* and its film adaptation convey this ambivalence for the United States in how and where it grounds itself in the former British colony of Jamaica. Bond is read, seen, and heard reminding the literary and/or film audience that the mission is unfolding on 'British territory'. In the film, Leiter remarks to Bond that "You Limeys can be pretty touchy" about the territorial sovereignty of the island. While Fleming might assert the sovereign authority of the United Kingdom in the British Caribbean, he also acknowledged that the sovereignty in question was graduated rather than absolute. In the novel, the villain buys a smaller island off of Jamaica ostensibly so that guano could be harvested and exported. In reality, the investment program is a ruse to establish a secret radio station designed to interfere with the tracking of US rockets off Cape Canaveral. In *Live and Let Die*, Mr. Big takes over Surprise Island, close to Jamaica, and enrols Jamaica into his drug-related empire. In both cases, it is clear that British sovereign power is not sufficiently adept at administrating and monitoring the activities of others, be they Chinese or American criminals and villains. But as Dr No reminds readers, the British are shown to be willing to cede sovereignty to their American allies when they agree to let the US authorities annex part of the island in the name of protecting biodiversity.

Fleming's imaginative geographies of the post-1945 world, shaped by his experiences of living in Jamaica but travelling more widely in North America and Asia, were remarkably versatile.[3] While Goldeneye might have struck some as a marginal place to view the world, it played host to a prime ministerial visit by Winston Churchill and a recuperative stay by an ailing Anthony Eden, in the aftermath of the turmoil of the Suez Crisis. As an island-state agitating for independence, Jamaica was a productive space to think about and plot how a British agent might work with American personal and forces, while negotiating a Cold War context shaped by anxieties about communist insurrection; the influence of Cuba, China, and the Soviet Union; and the resource and strategic potential of the British Caribbean. Villains, in Fleming's world, were quick to point to British vulnerabilities in this changing world order. As Hugo Drax tells Bond in *Moonraker*, "[You are] too weak to defend your colonies, toadying to America with your hat in your hands" (1955, p. 208).

Drax's stinging retort helps to further identify the filmic geographies of Bond. Fleming's novels appear in the 1950s and 1960s, a time of great geopolitical change. Bond's world is shaped by the intersection of Cold War and colonial geographies. Through his relationship with his CIA counterpart, Felix Leiter, the reader is able to bear witness to how these geographies and geographical relationships become manifest. Bond and Britain offer access and facilitation to the colonial spaces of the Caribbean and Asia in return for American technology, investment, and military muscle. The transition from novel to film was critical in cementing the physical geographies and geopolitics of James Bond.

The final element influencing our interest in the geographies of Bond is more embodied and sensual in nature. The geopolitical environments that Bond encounters are ones that are lively, emotional, and felt. This is established in the opening pages of Fleming's first Bond novel, *Casino Royale*, when he describes the physical and sensual awareness of Bond:

> [Bond] explored his present physical sensations. He felt the dry, uncomfortable gravel under his evening shoes, the bad, harsh taste in his mouth and the slight sweat under his arms. He could feel his eyes filling their sockets. The front of his face, his nose and antrum, were congested. He breathed the sweet night air deeply and focused his senses and his wits. He wanted to know if anyone had searched his room since he had left it before dinner. (1953, p. 3)

From the outset, Bond is conceptualized as a sensual spy who relies on his touch and feel to navigate his way through missions.

In a similar way, the filmic Bond's touch and feel is vital to early mission success, whether it be navigating the coastal waters off Jamaica in *Dr. No* or the backstreets of Istanbul in *From Russia with Love* (Young 1963). The cinematic Bond is depicted as an agent who immerses himself in his work. He will use his physical and sexual prowess to his and Britain's advantage, and his skills ranging from accomplished card player to pilot and diver are frequently put to strategic use in a variety of temperate, tropical, underwater, aerial, mountainous, and urban environments. His body and demeanor, while not without their limits when it comes to sheer endurance, are renewable resources to be exploited time and again for the sake of his mission. The sites and spaces of literary and filmic James Bond are proving grounds, places to match and, vitally, exceed the competencies and resources of his rivals and villains.

Bond's ability to immerse in a variety of social-spatial worlds is linked to a wider circuit of expectation and privilege. While Bond can express affection and camaraderie for local helpers such as the Cayman Islander Quarrel (*Dr. No*) and his son Quarrel Jr. (*Live and Let Die* [Hamilton 1973]), he is addressed as "Commander" by them both and they exhibit deference to his judgment. Bond's geopolitical world is one peopled with white professional Anglo-American men (Leiter, Q, and M [1962–89, 2012–15]) battling enemies and adversaries, defined and counter-posed by ethnic, racial, sexual, and class-based registers. Bond rarely battles against people who look and sound like him. When he does, in the cases of Alec Trevelyan in *GoldenEye* (Campbell 1995), Elliot Carver in *Tomorrow Never Dies* (Spottiswoode 1997), and Moon Tan-Sun/Gustav Graves in *Die Another Day* (Tamahori 2002), the inference is clear that his adversaries are traitorous and fraudulent white men who did not enjoy 'conventional' family lives. In the case of Trevelyan, his father murdered his mother before committing suicide leaving Trevelyan orphaned and to be raised by the state. As a child, Carver was disowned by his father, a British media baron, and subsequently raised by foster parents in Hong Kong. Finally, although Moon Tan-Sun was raised by his military father to be colonel in the North Korean armed forces, he fakes his death and sets up a new identity in the West as Gustav Graves, using pioneering gene therapy. Here, the prevailing geopolitical context of tension with communist North Korea is made freakish by direct reference to the both the racial and facial transformations of Graves. While other Bond films have used aberrant bodies to depict deviant ideologies and practices (for example, the East German super-man Eric Kriegler in *For Your Eyes Only* [Glen 1981]), it appears particularly egregious in *Die Another Day*.

Our book also explores how gender and its intersection with sexual orientation strongly shapes the depiction of women as both allies and adversaries. When lesbian women—both actual and assumed—make an appearance they are either capable of being seduced by Bond (e.g. Pussy Galore in *Goldfinger* [Hamilton 1964]) or represented as sexually unattractive adversaries (Colonel Klebb in *From Russia with Love*) who at times compete for the affections of the Bond Girl. The gender politics of James Bond continue to attract a plethora of critical commentary but arguably the gender geographies of the franchise receive less explicit reflection in much of the academic and commentary style literature. For the purposes of our investigation, we draw attention to several dimensions including the gender geographies of the office and field, the hegemonic masculinity of James Bond, and, finally, the intersectional geographies of gender, race, and sexuality.

The gendered distinction between the office and the field is hugely important to the Bond narrative. After an opening pre-title sequence that begins with Bond being seen through the barrel of a gun, as initiated in *From Russia with Love*, the film turns to Bond's arrival at Universal Exports/MI6. The long-standing figure of Miss Moneypenny, as the private secretary of M, is highly significant in shaping the gender geographies of Bond. While their encounters range from overtly flirtatious to collegial companionship, Moneypenny's demeanour and orderly office environment help to set up a context in which men such as Bond are shown to belong to the field and where British or local female field agents, while they can be occasionally depicted as competent (e.g. Paula Caplan in *Thunderball* [Young 1965]) or out of their depth (e.g. Caroline in *GoldenEye*), are usually disposable in terms of the mission's overall success. The sorts of women who appear to thrive in the field are frequently American and later Chinese/Russian agents who prove their worth to Bond, or Bond Girls who pose no threat to Bond's competencies in the field (e.g. Stacey Sutton in *A View to a Kill* [John Glen 1985]).

Bond's relationship to women in the bedroom and in the field is of course vital to his hegemonic masculinity. Those sites and spaces, ranging from the most intimate to the most dangerous, provide testing grounds for Bond to perform for himself and others. How he performs is critical, as is the judgment of others. While M might admonish him with regard to his treatment of women, his/her deliberate strategy of using seduction and sex to obtain secret information or secure access to the hench people themselves is a crucial element in his continued success. It also bolsters his heroic and hegemonic masculinity since few men can match him. Rarely are Bond's adversaries shown in an intimate setting. If anything the bedroom, as in the case of Franz Sanchez in *Licence to Kill* (Glen 1989), becomes a place to punish a romantic rival rather than actually perform sexually. Sanchez is never shown making love to his girlfriend.

The geographical and ideational consequences of Bond's hegemonic masculinity is that there are some things that the villain cannot be seen to do. The most obvious and important is that Bond's adversary is never allowed to have sex. The male villains can kiss their girlfriends and they can touch their female partners, but they are not allowed to perform in the bedroom. (The exception is Francisco Scaramanga in *The Man with the Golden Gun* [Hamilton 1974] whose intimate scenes with Andrea Anders

draw attention to his positioning as Bond's parallel and villainous counterpart in the film). But on the whole, there are almost no intimate geographies to their life-worlds. They can represent mortal threats to Bond
but they never represent a sexual threat to him; in fact, it is Bond who is
positioned as a sexual threat to the villain. Time and again, Bond 'steals'
the villain's girlfriend or seduces the female staff attached to his enterprise.
Even his close male companions are rarely shown to have personal/famil-
ial lives, and when they do, such as Leiter marrying Della in *Licence to Kill,*
it ends in tragedy. After Della is murdered, Leiter joins Bond as a widower
but he is never shown thereafter to have any romantic interests. The bedroom is thus Bond's privileged space for the performance of hegemonic
masculinity—it fits into a broader picture of his kind of spy-craft being
rooted in seduction, double-dealing, and defection, and not bureaucracy
and conventional work patterns.

But Bond's hegemonic masculinity is not unchanging. It is capable of
shifting and mutating depending on geographical and geopolitical contexts. The net result is to enable Bond to retain power over other men and
women. The 'tough-tender' Bond in the Daniel Craig era is indicative of
this shift in the way in which Bond's masculinity plays out in particular
environments. In *Casino Royale* (Campbell 2006), Bond's comforting of
Vesper Lynd in the shower after staving off an attack in the stairwell by
two hench people is significant in the film's narrative. Bond's identity as
a protector is restored after Lynd's successful 'skewering' of his character
and background while enjoying an intimate meal with Bond in a train
carriage. Later the intimate physical torture endured by Bond provides a
backdrop for his restoration and resurrection. He is shown to be still capable of making love to Lynd and in the aftermath of her death he resolves
to finish the mission (which continues into *Quantum of Solace*).

The final area we highlight is the intersectional geographies of gender,
race, and sexuality. The gender geographies of Bond are rarely devoid from
other registers and the manner in which they shape encounters and experiences in an array of sites and spaces. Bond's relationship with May Day is
one such example in *A View to a Kill.* Having first set eyes on her in Paris,
while attempting to pursue her up the Eiffel Tower, Bond can only gasp in
amazement at her spectacular parachute jump from the top of the structure. His pursuit by car is ultimately unsuccessful and if anything reveals
the limits of an aging Bond played by Roger Moore. As if recognizing the
unlikely scenario that Bond could ever overwhelm May Day in a combative
encounter, Bond's relationship with her is consummated in the bedroom

(where she dominates him in bed) while there are references throughout the film to her 'freakish' height and strength. She is the first black love interest since Rosie Carver in *Live and Let Die*, a hapless CIA field agent who is killed by the villains for treachery. As a result, May Day is only the second black woman who has served as a love interest of Bond[4] and it is striking that her superior strength and fitness in the field are ultimately buried underground, as she saves Bond's life from a large explosion in a mine. Her self-detonation is vital to Bond's credibility as a capable field agent, which he subsequently gets to demonstrate by fighting his archrival at the top of the Golden Gate Bridge in San Francisco.

Finally, our book foregrounds geopolitics and is inspired by critical geopolitical literature that has explored the role of imaginaries in projecting and portraying international politics. Bond's imaginative geopolitics is one shaped by colonial, Cold War, and post–Cold War contexts on the one hand but also complicated by transnational and global actors, processes, and structures on the other. The Bond films in the 1960s, unlike Fleming's novels, do not position the Soviet Union as the premier threat facing the UK and its allies. A transnational network (SPECTRE) is the primary menace, and one capable of building strategic alliances with criminals and drug dealers for the purpose of wielding influence and power. *Thunderball* outlines the scale and geographical extent of SPECTRE and its activities, after earlier missions where Bond has foiled its plans in the Caribbean and Turkey.[5] Operating out of a secret meeting space in Paris, the location of the SPECTRE executive is finally revealed to be inside a building run by an international refugee resettlement agency. The audience, by following the movements of SPECTRE agent Number 2 (Emilio Largo), is taken into the secret world of the organization where he is asked to update the executive committee about the plan to steal nuclear weapons from NATO bomber planes. Before he can do so, Number 1 (Blofeld) asks for an update on SPECTRE's activities, which involve 'Red China' drug deals in the United States, blackmail of a Japanese double agent and French nuclear scientists, and a consultation fee for a UK train robbery. A large world map to the rear of the room is shown to be directly in front of Number 1 and his partially hidden yet elevated position from the main body of the SPECTRE committee further emphasises his global oversight.

The SPECTRE meeting in *Thunderball*, against the backdrop of a large world map and an obscured leader, could be juxtaposed with an early scene in *Dr. No*. After the local agent has failed to make routine contact with London, one of the radio operators working in the MI6 building alerts his superior that the intelligence network in Jamaica might be a source for concern. As with the SPECTRE meeting, a world map is shown adorning one of the walls and the room is filled with radio operators making connections with agents all over the world. But there is a key difference between the two maps. The world map that is to be found in the SPECTRE committee room has no international boundaries marked on its surface. There is a Mercator projection of the world in which the continents and islands are depicted in white while black-coloured seas and oceans surround them. The world map in the British room, however, is quite different. It shows the countries and empires of the world and international boundaries are detectable. In so doing, the films juxtapose two geographical imaginations—a world composed of sovereign territorial states and a world beyond states where international boundaries do not need to be represented. Bond, as a British agent, has the task of both working across boundaries like SPECTRE while at the same time as upholding the boundaries of Britain and its imperial portfolio. Bond affirms the territorial sovereignty of the state while acting to erase it as and when it suits his purpose and by extension Britain. It is perhaps not for nothing that villains have a habit of pointing out to him that he is not so different from them; he might serve a different master but he is at times indifferent to the prevailing geopolitical order.

This book also highlights the intertextuality of the geopolitics of James Bond. The Bond films deliberately and knowingly connect to others in the franchise—indeed, the overlaps are considered an important part of the narrative progression of Bond. So audiences watching *On Her Majesty's Secret Service* (Hunt 1969), for example, would see references to the Sean Connery Bond films of the 1960s, which suggest a continuation of the Bond character even though a new actor (George Lazenby) is featured in the title role. Such allusions include the character of Bond as spy, his relationship with women, the role and significance of technology and gadgets, the use of violence and its connection to mission completion, and finally, the placement of objects such as maps and globes, and the role of sites and spaces (e.g. M's office and 'exotic' locations such as Brazil, Egypt, and Thailand). Bond returns to some 'exotic' places more than others (e.g. there have been three mission visits to Turkey), and there are still areas of the world where Bond has not reached yet (e.g. Antarctica).

Skyfall, the third film starring Daniel Craig as James Bond, is profoundly intertextual, as audiences discover that Skyfall is Bond's childhood home in Scotland. As Bond and M battle against a disgruntled former MI6 agent intent on terrorizing London and MI6 itself, audiences are given insights into his childhood, especially in the aftermath of the death of his parents. The film is intensely geopolitical in the manner in which it reflects upon the relationship between terror, cyber-espionage, and Britain's place in the world. Right at the start of the film, the focus is on tracking down a disk encrypted with secret information about UK spies. Bond's quest, however, is both physical and virtual. He needs to recover the top-secret disk while at the same time he struggles to discover how the villain has cyber-hacked into MI6's computer networks. Travelling from Istanbul to Hong Kong/Shanghai and finally returning to London/Scotland, this Bond film is unusual in showing London's vulnerability to terrorist attack and Bond and MI6 battling against the evil genius without any help from their US allies.

The narrative arc explores the personal trajectories of Bond, M, and the arch-villain Silva. But the film also addresses the role of loyalty and revenge in the covert world of the field agent, as well as the capacity of men and women to 'bounce back' from trauma (Dodds 2014, p. 118). While Bond's resilience is made possible by a combination of luck and support from his boss M, Silva's resilience provokes revulsion from M, even though she abandoned him to Chinese operatives when the UK gave up their hold on Hong Kong in 1997. M's deliberate geopolitical amnesia ended up provoking Silva to take his revenge on her and MI6 while inadvertently showcasing a world that is no longer about Bond's mastering of a gadget here and there but rather one composed of critical infrastructure that can be manipulated by an adversary armed to the teeth with computing power instead of bombs and missiles.

As feminist political geographers note, the body is productive of geopolitics and Bond's body is an important site in and of itself. Bond's body, including his scars and injuries, acts as a living archive of previous missions and provide evidence of his continuing relevance in a changing world (for example, Dixon and Marston 2013). Silva's body has also been injured but his face in particular is depicted as grotesque. He shows M his physical deformation while imprisoned in a giant specimen jar-like prison. While Bond's ability to touch and feel objects and people is crucial to mission success, adversaries are not granted that privilege. Bond Girls desire his touch while villains fear it. But Bond's body is fundamentally privileged in this geopolitical audit. A feminist geopolitical sensibility would ask us to be alert to the bodies that are positioned as vulnerable or even disposable. Bond's love interests frequently bear the brunt of his calculative strategies.

They are the ones who get fatally injured, tied up, and left exposed by an approach that often relies upon him emphasizing his physical and sexual prowess and taunting adversaries in the process. Silva's touch, while hugely effective when it comes to the computing keyboard, is positioned as repugnant when it comes to (sexually) caressing Bond and Severine.

Bond scriptwriters, moreover, understand that Bond fans enjoy and expect those intertextual references. This is most evident in the Craig-era films. For instance, the death of Strawberry Fields in *Quantum of Solace* recalls the murder to Jill Masterson in *Goldfinger*. In *Skyfall*, Bond transports M in the classic Aston Martin DB5 originally featured in *Goldfinger*. And the train sequence in *Spectre* (Mendes 2015) references *From Russia with Love* through Bond's fight with Mr. Hinx as well as *Octopussy* (Glen 1983) and other Connery- and Moore-era films[6] via the white dinner jacket worn by Bond. Most dramatically, *Casino Royale* is a prequel that reboots the title character and takes him back to the Caribbean, where some of the earliest films were located like the inaugural *Dr. No*. In the film, Bond is depicted twice emerging from the sea in a bathing suit while a woman watches him from the shore. These scenes not only reference the introduction of quintessential Bond Girl Honey Ryder in *Dr. No* but also reverse the traditional gender roles of 'the gaze', thus signaling a change in the representational politics and heroic model of masculinity governing the Craig-era films (Funnell 2011a, p. 466–68). Moreover, *Casino Royale*'s introduction of a new Bond, played by a blonde-haired Daniel Craig, provoked initial skepticism amongst some journalists and fans who were unhappy that the new actor to play Bond looked 'different'.[7] In the story, Bond is shown carrying out his first kill and eventually obtaining his revered 'Double 0' status. Mindful of a post–9/11 geopolitical environment, danger and insecurity are shown to have a more mobile quality as a new terror-business organization (Quantum Network) adroitly moves money, terror, and influence via cyber-networks and secret partnerships, just like SPECTRE was shown to be able to do in the 1960s films.

Our three terms, geographies, genders, and geopolitics bring to the fore an innovative way of reading and engaging with the James Bond franchise. More broadly, we make the case that the intersection of film studies, gender studies, geopolitics, and geography is a productive way of thinking about how film evokes experiences of inhabiting, moving through and staying put in a world, in Bond's case, made unsafe by agents, objects, and structures imperiling Britain and its allies and their collective interests.

THE BOOK'S MISSION

Geographies, Genders, and Geopolitics of James Bond offers a detailed analysis of the textual and visual geographies of the Bond film franchise. The second chapter explores how James Bond is both conceptualized and depicted as an embodied agent. Bond's body is complicit with geopolitics, as are the men and women he encounters. We address how his body is a territory onto which his missions unfold. Bond might be a 'blunt instrument' but he is also capable of being sensuous and affective. He is touch-orientated and his feel for people, objects, and situations is an essential element to this success in a range of sites and spaces, stretching from the bedroom to the most extreme geographical environments. Chapter 3 builds on our examination of Bond's bodily geopolitics by examining how his relationship with American agents is crucial to mission success. His long-standing relationship with CIA counter-part Felix Leiter is clearly significant but so is his ability to master American sites and technology as well as women and particularly American Bond Girls. His intuition, touch, and movement allow him to emerge as the dominant/superior figure, even if the infrastructural resources of MI6/Britain bear little comparison to his allies and adversaries such as the Soviet Union, China, and SPECTRE.

Chapter 4 explores the shifting representations and embodied encounters with the Soviet Union/Russia. Given the Bond film's initiation in the 1960s, the cartographies of the Cold War play an important role notwithstanding the transnational organization SPECTRE. Bond encounters Soviet agents, technology, objects, practices, and sites and spaces throughout the 1960s, 1970s and 1980s. He learns to seduce Soviet women, navigate through Soviet environments, master Soviet objects such as tanks and planes, and work with their spies and spy masters if the mission demands. The Soviet Union, and latterly post–Cold War Russia, are depicted in the Bond franchise as unreliable and unsafe spaces. Even if Bond can form personal and intimate relationships with Russian women (and some men), he has to navigate through a country that cannot control its objects or people, which threaten national and international security. Unlike their British counterparts, the loyalty of Soviet and Russian characters is depicted as fragile and liable to be corrupted in favor of criminal and terroristic organizations.

Chapter 5 addresses the 'Asian city' as elemental to the geographies of James Bond. It explores the differing depictions of Asian cities and urban landscapes noting two fundamental distinctions. First, a division is drawn between the developed and cosmopolitan cities of East Asia (like Tokyo, Hong Kong, and Shanghai) with the lesser developed urban spaces of South and Southeast Asia (such as Bangkok, Udaipur, and Ho Chi Man City). While the former is defined by their vertical development, technological advancement, and nighttime color, the latter are defined as being horizontal, chaotic, and pre-modern. The second distinction is in the ways that Bond demonstrates his fieldwork skills. While Bond's high-tech encounters with the local resources in East Asia emphasize their social and geopolitical equitability with Britain (as both allies and threats), his destructive street-level encounters in South and Southeast Asia demonstrate a sheer disregard for these spaces and their corresponding nations. The franchise presents the impression that South and Southeast cities can easily be exploited with little geopolitical ramifications.

Chapter 6 explores the elemental in the Bond films focusing specifically on resource conflict. While the success of Bond's missions often depends on his ability to negotiate and navigate the elemental, he also encounters these elements as an agent of Britain who works to safeguard their geopolitical interests. Through the figure of Bond, Britain is placed at the center of the gold exchange standard, African blood diamond trade, and the energy crisis of the 1970s. And in the Brosnan- and Craig-era films, Bond inserts himself into international conflicts over oil and water. Resource management is clearly gendered as women are both associated with the elements/resources and control access to them. As a result, the narratives have patriarchal significance as they convey the impression that Bond's colonial masculinity is needed to maintain global order over the (feminine) elements.

Chapter 7 explores the gender and geopolitics of mobility, and the messages conveyed about power, access, and management through Bond's movement (or lack thereof) in a range of physical and social spaces. On the physical level, Bond operates in a variety of physical environments from the villain's lair to national monuments to construction sites, and the destruction/preservation of individual sites and spaces has particular narrative and geopolitical significance; although Bond has a 'license to destroy', he uses it strategically. In addition, Bond is a mobile hero who uses various modes of transport—trains, planes, automobiles—which are often coded as feminine and his mastery over them has patriarchal significance as it confirms his libido-based heroism. On the social level, Bond operates in a variety of social environments from tourist traps like the carnival and circus to highbrow spaces like the members-only (and often high-limit) casino and opera. While Bond successfully navigates his way through both, he is more comfortable in the latter as they are defined through physical means and cultural codes. Although Bond possesses the social and cultural capital required to access these spaces, he is not one of them as he acts, more often than not, on behalf of Britain rather than for himself.

The final chapter considers what we term 'heartland geopolitics'. It reflects on the importance of London in the Brosnan- and Craig-era films in which the threat and safety of the nation are operationalized through the city's infrastructure and inhabitants. While London has a fleeting presence in the early Bond films, it works to anchor Bond and the interests that he serves later in the franchise while giving place to the long-standing relationships that sustain him (e.g. with colleagues Moneypenny, M, and Q). Until *The World Is Not Enough* (Apted 1999) and most notably *Skyfall*, London and the MI6 building were safe spaces untroubled directly by the planning and plotting of villains and evil geniuses. SPECTRE might be involved with criminality (e.g. train robberies in the UK) and villains might steal things from Britain (e.g. bomber jets) but they were rarely able to get close to the country's population and infrastructure. Bond's success depends upon him stopping the threat posed to Britain and neutralizing anyone who might be approaching British territory and overseas interests. Bond's role in protecting and serving the 'heartland' is both abstract and personal. He serves 'Queen and Country' but he also protects those close to him, especially M and Moneypenny. In the Judi Dench–era, a female M further hardwires the gendering of the heartland. Men such as Bond protect the nation state while women like M are associated with it and are thus in need of protection even if they are Bond's superiors. In *Skyfall*, the feminizing of the heartland is made explicit narratively and visually. The film conveys the impression that by protecting M, Bond is safeguarding Britain and enabling her to 'finish the job'. Although Bond ultimately fails in this regard, the death of M helps to deepen his commitment to Queen and Country.

Our afterword offers a few final thoughts about the implications of the Bond franchise's long-term engagement with spies, surveillance, and terrorism. As one of the most successful forms of popular entertainment, the Bond franchise continues to demand our attention as to the way it represents and engages with the threats posed by criminal syndicates and cyber-terrorism while exploring and even justifying the need for surveillance and spying by the liberal democratic state. In Bond's world, accountability and oversight get in the way of 'finishing the job' and as the latest film *Spectre* suggests, having agents prepared to confront danger in the real as opposed to virtual world is still absolutely necessary.

NOTES

1. For a detailed discussion, see Langfitt (2015).
2. For a detailed discussion, see Curtin (2007).
3. As a former journalist, he had visited Russia some years earlier in the 1930s.
4. Halle Berry who plays Jinx Johnson in *Die Another Day* is multiracial and Naomie Harris in *Skyfall* does not sleep with Bond.
5. Dr. No only gives Bond some insight into their territorial footprint and one grounded in his experiences of a Chinese connection.
6. Connery's Bond wears a white dinner jacket in *Goldfinger* and *Diamonds Are Forever* while Moore's Bond wears one in *The Man with the Golden Gun* and *A View to a Kill*.
7. Similar 'concerns' are being raised about particular actors, like Idris Elba, who are rumored to be in the running for the coveted role of Bond in future films. These comments both subtly and overtly focus on Elba's race and draw attention to the way in which whiteness has long shaped the identity and social privilege of Bond.

CHAPTER 2

The Haptic Geographies
of James Bond's Body

James Bond is a body-focused spy whose physique and touch communicate powerful messages about identity and power in the franchise. This is clearly relayed in the inaugural novel *Casino Royale* in which Bond is very attentive to the importance of his body to mission success. Fleming writes,

> After a cold shower, Bond walked over to the Casino. Since the night before he had lost the mood of the tables. He needed to re-establish that focus which is half mathematical and half intuitive and which, with a slow pulse and sanguine temperament, Bond knew to be the essential equipment of any gambler who was set on winning. (1953, p. 40)

The emphasis on Bond's body was heightened when Fleming's novels were adapted into films, and the casting of Sean Connery, an ex-bodybuilder, for the title role was significant in conveying an almost animalistic virility.[1] Scholars such as Laura Marks have explored how film appeals to the senses since it cannot technically represent smell, touch, and taste.[2] Unlike literature where internal sensations can be described in vivid detail, film is a visual media in which internal thoughts, feelings, and sensations are expressed externally and usually through the body (unless there is a voice-over narration). As the Bond films transitioned generically from spy thrillers to action films,[3] they have increasingly focused on the body of Bond as the locus of his identity and film-making practices have played their part in sustaining that transition.[4] Moreover, action is a body-focused genre that is defined primarily through the sheer excess of visual spectacle. One only

© The Editor(s) (if applicable) and The Author(s) 2017
L. Funnell, K. Dodds, *Geographies, Genders and Geopolitics of James Bond*, DOI 10.1057/978-1-137-57024-6_2

has to think of how the opening shot of Bond striding across the screen with a sense of purpose before turning and pointing his gun towards the viewer is emblematic of his kinesthetic and proprioceptive qualities. As noted by Yvonne Tasker, narrative elements in action films are often "subsumed within the spectacular staging of action sequences employing star bodies, special effects, artful editing, and persuasive music" (2004, pp. 6–7). Filmmakers, including those associated with the Bond franchise, have proven adept at using close-up body shots, focus alteration, and sensual imagery to appeal to touch. Thus, it is important to explore the representational and body politics of the Bond franchise and the messages being conveyed through Bond's touch and feeling.

This chapter examines the significance of Bond's body and haptic encounters across various situations, spaces, and contexts. Our discussion of the haptic geographies of James Bond focuses on how his body is defined as being fit, sensual, technical, memorializing, and calculating, as well as the ways in which his body changes in accordance with shifting generic and gendered codes in the franchise. Bond, as M noted in *Casino Royale*, might be a "blunt instrument" but his apparent bluntness should not obscure something equally fundamental: he is a touch-oriented and sensuous secret agent. Without that touch and without that feel, he would be a 'dysesthetic instrument' (i.e. someone who has lost their sense of touch), and ultimately less likely to serve Queen and Country with any great distinction.

Haptic Geographies of James Bond

Haptics or touch is a primary form of non-verbal communication. Touch not only conveys different social messages but it also takes place in particular social contexts and carries with it definite notions of power.[5] In the Bond films, Bond's body operates in different environments like the office, bedroom, and the villain's secret lair (see Chap. 7), and his haptic encounters in each space communicate powerful messages about this identity and role in each film. We use the term 'haptic geographies' to explicate how the sensuous experiences of touching and feeling manifest themselves in sites and spaces and the awareness of those moving through those environments.[6] As a spy, Bond has had to learn through experience and training: to be aware of his body and its relationship to the wider world, to monitor what his body is capable of (and what it is not), to assess and act upon non-verbal clues, and to consider how his ability to touch and feel can be crucial to mission success. In the opening pages of *Casino Royale*, Bond visually inspects his hotel room after a night of gambling at the casino. As Fleming writes, "Doing all this, inspecting these minute burglar alarms, did not make him feel foolish or self-conscious. He was a secret agent, and still alive thanks to his exact attention to the detail of his profession" (1953, pp. 6–7). However, in the film *From Russia with Love*, Bond is shown to be carefully examining his hotel room in Istanbul using his touch (in addition to sight) to investigate a picture, phone, ceiling light, and mirror in order to discover if the room is 'bugged'. As he 'feels' his way through the room and performs this evaluation, the familiar James Bond theme music plays, building to a climax when he discovers that the phone in his room has been tapped. In his account of *Sensuous Geographies*, Paul Rodaway identifies a "haptic matrix" and argues for an appreciation not only of touching but also of being touched, and for reaching out as well as positioning oneself within reach.[7] In this scene, lasting little more than two minutes, Bond illustrates well how he uses his 'heightened senses' to careful effect. But his touch is not infallible, as the film never shows him inspecting the alternative room he was offered after complaining to the hotel management that his original accommodations were 'unsuitable'.

One reason why James Bond outlives his adversaries and thus continues to operate as an effective 00 agent is his haptic qualities. He is a man acutely aware of his own body and its relationship with others. He enjoys a keen sense of movement and is able to swim, run, climb, crawl, scramble, and fight with considerable aplomb. He understands the need to position his body in ways that appear both physically and sexually dominant but is also discreet when he needs to hide himself or placate his superiors. All of this occurs in particular sites and spaces that are, on the one hand, shaped and governed by social rules/conventions such as M's office, the hotel lobby, and at formal dinners, and on the other hand, are composed of non-human elements that Bond can utilize with considerable distinction. On numerous occasions, Bond has saved his own life as well as the lives of others by using his innate capacity to improvise with unlikely sounding objects such as an electric fan in *Goldfinger*, which he throws into bathwater in order to electrocute a potential assailant who is on the verge of shooting him. His capacity to survive depends, over and over again, on his touch-oriented and sensuous body.

The Fit Body

The body of James Bond is presented as the ideal of masculinity and is diegetically contrasted with the physique of the arch-villain in order to reaffirm his physical superiority as hero. This approach was first utilized in the early Bond films in order to convey the impression that Bond was fitter than his primary adversaries. From *Dr. No* onwards, Bond's body has been an essential element contributing to mission success. In the vast majority of films, there is at least one scene in which Bond appears shirtless or with an open button-down shirt, which showcases his slender but toned chest; he might be seducing a woman, getting dressed after a sexual encounter, or engaging in some form of leisure activity like tanning by the pool. He is also depicted with a 'well-dressed body'—one that is equally at home in swimming trunks as it is dressed in a dinner jacket and suit. While others have noted Bond's conspicuous consumerism,[8] our interest is in exploring how the franchise sought to convey a sense of physical fitness in association with fashion and other artefacts of consumer culture.

In the Bond novels, Bond is often pit against a villain with an exaggerated physique. In *Live and Let Die*, for instance, Fleming describes the body of Mr. Big in the following way:

> It was a great football of a head, twice the normal size and very nearly round [...] Curiously, there was nothing disproportionate about the monstrous head. It was carried on a wide, short neck supported by the shoulders of a giant [...] the total impression was awe-inspiring, even terrifying. (1954, pp. 60–61)

While the bodies of the filmic villains are not as exaggerated and oversized, Bond's fiercest opponents in the 1960s do have a noticeably larger body mass and some can even be described as overweight and at times oddly dressed. In *Goldfinger*, Auric Goldfinger does not appear shirtless as he plays cards by the pool but his round stomach appears to protrude though the buttons of his golden shirt, which fits him snugly. His large and powerful hench person, Oddjob, also moves slowly and cumbersomely in a formal suit, but his ability to use his bowler hat as a weapon is essential given his limited range of mobility. However, as Bond discovers through closer encounters, Oddjob is extremely strong. Naturally, Bond is able to defeat both men using his fitness and agility while attempting to disarm a nuclear bomb (in the case of Oddjob) and bringing a wayward plane under control (in the case of Goldfinger). Similarly, Emilio Largo in *Thunderball* does not appear shirtless, but his rounded figure is emphasized when he wears a black form-fitting diving suit. While his hench person Vargas is notably slender, he is shown to be the literal opposite of Bond. As Largo says to Vargas within Bond's earshot, "Vargas does not drink. Does not smoke. Does not make love. What do you do, Vargas?" Both men offer visual and sensual contrasts to Bond who appears competent and confident, conveying the impression that Bond is fitter, physically and sexually, and thus is more inclined to be victorious over his opponents.

Bond is also presented as being a younger and more vital hero. Although Bond is in his late thirties and early forties, he never comes across as being too old to engage in physical action or seduce a beautiful woman, however younger she might be than him.[9] Even a visit to the health farm Shrublands in *Thunderball* sees Bond not only seduce one of the care-workers but also identify a person of criminal interest. In comparison, many of his main adversaries appear noticeably older than him, which sends the message that they are past their physical and sexual prime. For instance, villains like Goldfinger, Brad Whitaker in *The Living Daylights* (Glen 1987), and Frank Sanchez in *License to Kill* have receding hairlines and this works to age them over Bond. Moreover, Sanchez who is a comparably younger villain, is never shown making love to his girlfriend but rather taking revenge on other men who display interest in her. In addition, Karl Stromberg in *The Spy Who Loved Me* (Gilbert 1977), Aristotle Kristatos in *For Your Eyes Only*, and Elliot Carver in *Tomorrow Never Dies* have grey hair that ages them at least a decade over Bond. Emilio Largo also has grey hair and the age difference between him and his kept woman Domino Derval is so great that he tells people that he is her 'guardian' (rather than, say, 'escort') in order to save face. This naturally renders Bond a more suitable romantic match for Derval and the film illustrates this point by having them first meet in bathing suits underwater in the Bahamas. And like all villains, these men rely heavily on their hench people (and their collective touch) to do most of the physical labor in their films, and this further contributes to the impression that they, the evil geniuses, are incapable of matching Bond on a physical, let alone sexual, level.

Bond is also presented as being able-bodied and he is often contrasted with a villain who has a physical impairment that limits him physical and/ or socially (as he is perceived as being 'freakish'). The villain in *Dr. No* has metal claws for hands and has difficulty holding onto objects. He is better at crushing objects, like Kananga's bodyguard Tee Hee who uses his mechanical right arm equipped with a pincer to deadly effect in *Live and*

Let Die. Emilio Largo is missing an eye and has to wear an eye patch over it. In *The World Is Not Enough*, Renard suffers from congenital analgesia, a rare condition in which a person cannot feel pain or indeed any sensation. This renders Bond more capable of pleasuring Elektra King. LeChiffre in *Casino Royale* has a malformed tear duct that causes him to sporadically and uncontrollably cry tears of blood that stand out against his notably pale complexion. Raoul Silva in *Skyfall* experienced facial disfiguration when he attempted to kill himself with a cyanide tablet; he wears a palette in his mouth to hide the deformity. And in the final scenes of *Spectre*, the face of arch-villain Ernst Stavro Blofeld is injured, leading to the (iconic) vertical scar across his right eye that extends from his forehead to the bottom of his cheek. In all of these cases, Bond as an able-bodied and sensual man (see the following section) is contrasted with a villain who suffers from a visible physical impairment, which is assumed to also be detrimental to their libido. Bond is not subject to the social stigma that is often associated with the loss of a body part or its function; rather his body shape and associated scars function as a living record of his physical plights, confirm his masculinity in action, and serve as sources of fascination for the many lovers who have caressed his body.

Unlike the primary adversary featured in each film, Bond fights various hench people who frequently possess abnormal/unhuman strength and/or abilities. For example, Jaws appears in both *The Spy Who Loved Me* and *Moonraker* (Gilbert 1979) with metal teeth that can cut through metal and bone (Fig. 2.1).

May Day, featured in *A View to a Kill*, is an abnormally strong woman, which the film suggests might be the result of genetic experimentation along with her lover and arch-villain, Max Zorin. Xenia Onatopp in *GoldenEye* has the ability to suffocate her opponents with her thighs (underlining the sexual frisson of these scenes) while Mr. Stamper from *Tomorrow Never Dies* is the muscular protégé (who can feel no pain but still experiences pleasure) of a doctor who tortures people for a living. Finally, the depiction of the brawny but silent Mr. Hinx in *Spectre* who kills his targets by pressing his thumbs into their eye sockets is reminiscent of classic Bond strongmen like Oddjob and Jaws. Bond films convey the impression that hench people who possess super-human abilities and are genetically or mechanically altered are somehow cheating when they face Bond. Audiences are left with this impression of Eric Kreigler's artificially enhanced body in *For Your Eyes Only*. His extraordinary strength and powerful grip, however, prove fatal as Bond uses them against Kreigler

Fig. 2.1 *Moonraker* (Eon Productions et al. 1979)

who he pushes to his death after he picks up a large stone to throw. In each case, Bond's normative body is contrasted with these unnatural and genetic anomalies. This works to position Bond's fit body as the ideal in comparison with his opponents who are too effete and/or weirdly strong by comparison. His adversaries may be stronger or smarter but their bodily excesses and detriments prove to be their downfall.

The Sensual Body

The body of James Bond is also presented to the audience as highly sensual. Bond's heroism is rooted in the lover literary tradition, which produced "many of Britain's most glamorous national heroes" (Hawkins 1990, p. 29). These "brilliant, witty, urbane, cultivated, and sensitive" men fought for a higher cause while safeguarding the women they loved (Hawkins 1990, pp. 29–30). The inaugural *Dr. No* established Bond's reputation as a man who 'radiated' sexual magnetism. As such, his ability to excite, seduce, and sexually satisfy women serves as a visual and haptic signifier as of his libidinal masculinity—he makes women swoon (such as Penelope Smallbone in *Octopussy*) and his sensual touch proves electrifying (as Miss Moneypenny exhibits in *Dr. No*). Throughout the Bond series, women are affected by his charm and virility, even those decades younger than him. The teenage skater, Bibi Dahl, in *For Your Eyes Only* is smitten on first meeting Bond in Italy, and after hugging Bond she warns him, "I could eat you up alive." Jeremy Black notes that Bond's sensuality also functions as a tipping point in the films as he is able to align women with his mission and moral plight (2005, pp. 107–109). Bond sleeps with numerous women in each film from primary characters like the Bond Girl to secondary figures who appear fleetingly in roles such as hotel receptionists and chance encounters in bars and casinos. Moreover, the Bond franchise clearly demarcates good from bad women via domestication:

> In order to be presented as a 'good' character, the Bond Girl is expected to submit to the will and libido of James Bond, forfeiting her own liberated sexual identity for a domesticated one. By comparison, women who embrace their liberal sexualities and refuse to adhere to the 'Bondian' standard of normative femininity are presented as 'bad' and are violently punished. (Funnell 2011b, p. 201)

Through his serial seduction of women, the franchise not only defines the heroic identity of Bond but also shapes the impression of the women with whom he sexually interacts, and the manner in which he seduces them. Even Pussy Galore in *Goldfinger*, who the film subtly suggests is a lesbian, cannot resist his charms, however forcefully imposed.

During these lovemaking scenes, the films send messages about how audiences are supposed to read these haptic encounters. On the one hand, there are a number of scenes that emphasize Bond's connection with a particular woman. While the sexual act might not be shown on screen— we usually see the foreplay and the aftermath—the soundtrack often signals the type of heightened emotions being experienced. For instance, *Octopussy* features a romantic soundtrack that uses the melody from the title track "All Time High." This creates the impression that Bond is making love to a woman rather than simply having sex with her. On the other hand, there are scenes in which Bond engages in coitus with a female villain and a musical score is notably absent. This occurs in *GoldenEye* in which Bond's haptic encounter with Xenia Onatopp is coded differently. During their conversation and foreplay, there is no music playing, which suggests that this interaction might not end the way that Bond expects. When Onatopp begins suffocating Bond with her legs—a sexually charged image that is presented through an aerial (or bird's-eye view) shot and enhanced by Onatopp's manic screams—the tone of their encounter changes and Bond spends the remainder of the scene trying to dislodge himself from her deadly (sexual) grip.

The Bond films also convey messages about what is considered to be appropriate touching. While Bond can sleep with multiple women in each film, sexually liberated and debauched women are judged harshly for their sexual appetites and desires. Women who challenge Bond's status as a sexual aggressor are typically presented as 'bad' women who need to have their characters and their touches tamed. In *Thunderball*, Fiona Volpe is depicted as a black-widow assassin who uses her body and sexuality to forward her agenda (much like Bond); she disarms her targets with her sensuality and then kills them. During her haptic encounter with Bond, she not only dominates him in bed but also ridicules him afterwards. Volpe states,

> "But of course, I forgot your ego, Mr. Bond, James Bond, who only has to make love to a woman and she starts to hear heavenly choirs singing. She repents and then immediately returns to the side of right and virtue. But not this one!" All at once, Volpe rejects domestication, challenges the notion of ideological repositioning, and unrepentantly proclaims her status as a "bad girl" in the film. (Funnell 2011b, p. 202)

In the Bond franchise, sexually aggressive women like Fiona Volpe, May Day, Xenia Onatopp, and Elektra King are coded as deviant and thus require (social and sexual) repositioning. After they reject Bond's attempt at domestication following their haptic encounters with the British spy, these women are killed off in their films since they threaten the traditional gender roles and representational politics that have long structured the series.[10]

The Bond franchise also uses sexuality to contrast the (hetero)normativity of Bond with the sexual aberrance of his opponents. In the early Bond films, homosexuality was perceived and presented as a form a sexual deviance. This problematic impression worked to equate homosexuality with notions of criminality and moral impropriety, and thus rendered these villains in the franchise more deplorable. For instance, in *From Russia with Love*, Bond competes with lesbian Rosa Klebb for the affections of Bond Girl Tatiana Romanova. Klebb's caressing of Romanova in the former's office is depicted as unwanted and exploitative given Colonel Klebb's military ranking. This is elaborated on more fully in the novel when Fleming sets the meeting between the two women in Klebb's apartment. After discussing the mission, Klebb exits the room only to return wearing lingerie and explicitly propositioning Romanova: "Turn out the top light, my dear. The switch is by the door. Then come and sit beside me. We must get to know each other better" (1957b, p. 86). A fearful Romanova flees the apartment, running "wildly off down the corridor with her hand over her ears against the pursuing scream that never came" (1957b, p. 86). While the novel ends with a confrontation between Bond and Klebb, the film adjusts the narrative to include Romanova who walks in on the conflict and chooses Bond over her lesbian suitor, killing Klebb in the final scene of the film.[11] In *Diamonds Are Forever* (Hamilton 1971), Bond battles against two gay couples. He defeats bodyguards Bambi and Thumper, who the film subtly suggests are lesbians, by submerging them in a pool and kills the gay assassins Kidd and Wint in the final scene of the film. The latter play a more central role in the narrative and are depicted as 'freakish' homosexual killers who take pleasure in using their touch to kill people in unusual ways (e.g. via scorpion sting). Homosexuality is linked to notions of criminality when the pair is depicted holding hands as they walk away from one of their victims. Moreover, the manner in which Bond kills Wint—by placing a bomb between his legs and tossing him overboard—conveys a troublesome message of the triumph of heteronormative masculinity over seemingly 'deviant' homosexual men. More recently in *Skyfall*, Silva makes sexual advances towards Bond, which work to further vilify him, thus rooting the Craig-era films in the problematic representational politics of the Connery-era films. Homosexual characters in the Bond franchise are consistently positioned as having the wrong kind of touch.

The heterosexual qualities of Bond are a staple feature of the franchise even if other scholars have read Bond in a more explicitly camp manner, with his penchant for tailored suits, martinis shaken not stirred, and his ambivalent attitude towards women; Bond might lust after women but he seems happiest in the company of men. Bond's homosocial nature and his deep affection for men is most powerfully relayed in Fleming's novels in which Bond expresses the warmth he feels towards his male allies, such as Felix Leiter ("Bond looked affectionately at the Texan with whom he had shared so many adventures" [1959, p. 257]), M ("Bond sat down and looked across into the tranquil, lined sailor's face that he loved, honoured and obeyed" [1957a, p. 106], and Darko Kerim ("He was the rare type of man that Bond loved, and Bond already felt prepared to add Kerim to the half-dozen of those real friends whom Bond, who had no 'acquaintances,' would be ready to take into his heart" [1957a, pp. 137–38]). The novels also clearly distinguish Bond's male allies from his female conquests. In the novel *Goldfinger*, Pussy Galore is depicted as a criminal and lesbian who directly challenges Bond's libidinal masculinity by winning the affections of Tilly Masterson, the woman with whom Bond is working. The film, however, only subtly suggests that Galore is a lesbian and presents her as a pilot who initially resists Bond's charm and touch as a matter of professional practice (i.e. she does not mix business and pleasure). Bond's eventual 'seduction' of Galore in a barn is more akin to sexual assault as she does not consent verbally and she tries to push Bond away from her. Although she eventually 'succumbs' to his touch (by force), she still retains her professional persona; she helps Bond defeat Goldfinger by leading a flying operation designed to lull her former boss into a false sense of security at the Fort Knox gold complex. Bond's touch has been successful in so far as he has seduced her but she is not represented as a sexual conquest per se.

In addition, the depiction of Bond's frequent haptic encounters with women is contrasted with images of villains who cannot or do not sleep with women. For example, arch-villain Ernst Stavro Blofeld who appears across numerous early Bond films—*From Russia With Love, Thunderball, You Only Live Twice* (Gilbert 1967), *On Her Majesty's Secret Service* (*OHMSS*), and *Diamonds Are Forever* —is more interested in petting his white pussy cat than seducing the multitude of (white) women who appear in his films and eventually sleep with Bond.[12] In *OHMSS*, moreover, the older 'butch' female villain Irma Bunt stands in sharp contrast to the swooning young women Bond encounters at Piz Gloria. In *For Your Eyes Only*, the villain Kristatos is infatuated with his teenage skating protégé Bibi Dahl but does not (or perhaps cannot) seduce her. His affections are deemed inappropriate when compared to Bond who rejects Dahl's sexual advances deeming her to be too young (or a child). In *The World Is Not Enough*, Renard is unable to sleep with the licentious Elektra King since he lacks the ability to feel physical sensations. Instead, it is Bond who is able to sexually stimulate and satisfy King using his sensual touch and a bucket of ice.

Thus, the sensual body of Bond forwards powerful messages regarding his heroism and normative masculinity as defined through his haptic encounters and diegetic comparisons with other characters in his films. Perhaps, Goldfinger was the most perceptive of all the villains Bond has ever faced, when he threatened to castrate him with a laser beam, and Pussy Galore the most perceptive Bond Girl/conquest when it came to directing Bond's touch towards saving her from being associated with

Goldfinger's fiendish plans to blackmail the United States. Despite the danger, Bond is able to talk, scheme, fight, and/or sleep his way out of any unpleasant situation. But on occasion he does require help, like in *Casino Royale*, when it is obvious that LeChiffre would have tortured him to death and in the process destroyed his male sex organs. Even after this terrible ordeal, Bond proves that he is able to make love to Vesper Lynd, which works to further cement the power of his libidinal and normative masculinity. He has not lost his loving touch.

The Technical Body

James Bond also possesses a technical body as he engages with his surrounding environment and displays a mastery over technology, nature, and even outer space. He demonstrates his vast and intuitive knowledge of technology by using his technical touch to skillfully remove the solex agitator in *Man with the Golden Gun*, deactivate a bomb in *Octopussy*, and bring a wayward plane under his control in *Tomorrow Never Dies*. However, Bond's intuitive understanding of technology is something that evolves over the course of the franchise and parallels his changing relationship with Q, the inventor who develops all of Bond's spy technology. In the Connery-era films, Q is presented as being more knowledgeable about technology than Bond. He often provides Bond with detailed tutorials on how to use the gadgets he has created. In *Goldfinger*, Q's instructions for the modified Aston Martin are so long and detailed that the scene fades out to suggest that a great length of time has passed. Years later, when Q reveals the modified Lotus Esprit in *The Spy Who Loved Me*, Bond drives off without listening to Q's instructions and is able to use all of the gadgets expertly including transforming the car into a submarine (Jones 2015b, p. 209).

Bond's mastery of technology is also clearly gendered. This is notable in the film *Tomorrow Never Dies* when a much older Q introduces Bond to the new BMW 750iL. The car is defined by two key features. First, the operational computer has a female voice since Q believes that Bond would respond more attentively to a woman than a man, and this component works to strongly gender the car. Bond even uses feminine pronouns to describe the car when he says "let's see how she responds to my touch."[13] Second, the car can be driven by remote control and Bond is far more adept at operating the vehicle than Q. Bond not only demonstrates that he has a greater technical touch than the car's inventor, but this touch is notably gendered suggesting a link between Bond's mastery with technology and supremacy in the bedroom. The car is later destroyed in a violent conflict in a car park in Hamburg but not before Bond has used the extraordinary technology to effectively neutralize some adversaries dispatched by Elliot Carver.

Throughout the series, Bond drives cars with hi-tech modifications that allow him to easily out-maneuver his opponents. The Bond brand has most strongly been shaped by the Aston Martin, which makes appearances in numerous films throughout the series including *Goldfinger*, *The Living Daylights*, and *Skyfall*. His relationship with various models of the car— using the vehicle for his mission and then disposing of it—takes on gendered connotations (given the gendering of cars within car culture) and arguably mirrors the relationships he has with women in his films. In fact, cars play a key role in defining Bond's relationships with women. Bond's strongest female allies and adversaries often demonstrate their comparability and/or compatibility to him through driving. But their touch is represented in rather different ways. Bond is saved by Japanese agent Aki driving her Toyota 2000GT in *You Only Live Twice*, but Bond marvels at the car's advanced technology rather than at Aki's driving skills. Other Bond Girls get to perform their roles rather more dramatically: Anya Amasova saves Bond by driving a van into Jaws in *The Spy Who Loved Me*,[14] Melina Havelock drives Bond out of trouble in a yellow Citröen 2 CV in *For Your Eyes Only*,[15] Wai Lin physically maneuvers her body while handcuffed to Bond on a motorcycle in *Tomorrow Never Dies*,[16] and Camille Montes picks up Bond and helps him evade capture in *Quantum of Solace*.

However, Tracy di Vicenzo arguably demonstrates the most superior driving skills. She first appears in *OHMSS* driving a Cougar Eliminator, a popular muscle car of the era, as she speeds past Bond on a coastal road. This peaks Bond's interest and initiates his wooing of her. Later in the film, she saves Bond from Blofeld and his hench people by picking him up at an outdoor ice skating rink and driving through a stock car race, impressing Bond who is in the passenger's seat (Nepa 2015, p. 190). When they finally seek refuge in a barn, Bond proposes to di Vicenzo as she has clearly demonstrated her comparability and compatibility to him. Moments after they marry, however, she is killed in a drive-by shooting while sitting in the passenger's seat. The film ends with a shot of Bond clutching her lifeless body while sitting in the driver's seat of the car. Had she been driving (and controlling her own destiny), she might have survived the ordeal but the price to be paid by Bond would have been certain death.

Additionally, many of Bond's strongest female adversaries are proficient drivers of automobiles. In *Thunderball*, Bond first encounters Fiona Volpe on the open road when his silver Aston Martin DB5 is being pursued by an assailant in a black car. Before Bond can respond to the attack—as he has only opened the center console to reveal the control panel for the gadgets in his car—Volpe zooms in on her BSA Lightening motorcycle and blows up the pursuing car, much to Bond's surprise. She then speeds away to a remote location where she ditches the bike by rolling it into a lake where it sinks. Through this encounter, Volpe is set up as a wildcard who continuously challenges and undermines Bond's heroic and libidinal masculinity in the film. Thirty years later, Bond initially meets another hench person, Xenia Onatopp, on the open road while driving the very same Aston Martin in *GoldenEye*. This time, the hench person challenges Bond to a race and the pair drives at break-neck speeds along a winding mountain road before Onatopp spins out. Much like Volpe, Onatopp is depicted as being wild and reckless (through her driving), and her challenge to Bond on the roadway anticipates her positioning as a sexual and mortal threat to Bond in the film.[17] The Bond films forward the impression that women drivers need to be brought under Bond's control (and domesticated) via his sexual touch; if that does not work (i.e. if they remain Bad Girls and do not transform into Bond Girls), they will have to be killed off in their films.

The Memorializing Body

Bond also possesses a memorializing body. Given the episodic nature of the franchise, there is limited intertextual referencing across the films especially when compared to other action series in which sequels allude to characters and events that have taken place in previous films. However, there are a few occasions in the franchise where Bond's body and/or touch encourage transtextual remembering. In *OHMSS*, Bond sits in his office after he resigns from MI6. This is the only film in which Bond is located in *his* office as his primary domain is the field (Fig. 2.2).

According to Marlisa Santos, memory comes into play as Bond begins cleaning out his desk. She writes:

> As he re-discovers various artifacts from past missions (Honey Ryder's knife from *Dr. No* [1962], the garrote-watch from *From Russia, With Love* [1963], the re-breather from *Thunderball* [1965]), the theme music from

Fig. 2.2   *On Her Majesty's Secret Service* (Eon Productions et al. 1969)

those films plays, to provide the viewer with a connection to the previous Bond chronology.[18] This was a deliberate reinforcement of the Bond character history to aid in the transition to a new actor, but the effect provides an unintended depth to this incarnation of Bond: a sense of the past, to link to his duty and obligation to the future. (2015, p. 104)

In this scene, memory is being invoked for a variety of purposes—such as transtextual connection, narrative clarity, and characterization—and is signaled through his touch and the material objects he fingers.

Another example of memory takes place in *For Your Eyes Only*, which opens with Bond walking through a cemetery. In the scene, Bond carries a bouquet of red roses and places them beside the gravestone for Tracy di Vicenzo—Bond's wife who was killed at the end of *OHMSS* but whose death was not overtly mentioned in the five films that followed (although it may have been implied when Bond confronts Blofeld in *Diamonds Are Forever*). This unexpected reference (in the chronology of the film franchise) plays a key role in defining the significance of the action sequence that follows. Bond is pit against a wheelchair-bound man who clearly resembles Blofeld (although due to legal reasons is never explicitly identified as such). This villain takes control of the helicopter in which Bond is travelling and intends to kill him. This thrusts a somber Bond into action who must climb out of the aircraft in order to get into the pilot's seat and bring the helicopter under his control. He then picks up the wheelchair-bound man and drops him into an industrial-scale chimney (presumably killing him). While these events make sense on their own, they take on greater significance when considered in relation to the 1960s Bond films in which Blofeld serves as Bond's arch-nemesis. Moreover, by connecting this action sequence to Bond's grieving at the cemetery, it frames his actions as vengeance for his late wife whom Blofeld is (partly) responsible for killing.

Memory is also invoked through iconography. As noted by James Chapman, the introduction of a new actor in the title role is usually accompanied by the intertextual referencing of established James Bond iconography (such as the tuxedo and martini) in order to create a sense of continuity across the episodic franchise (2000, p. 207). While *Casino Royale* includes this iconography, it also deviates from tradition by connecting Bond to the legacy of the Bond Girl. In the inaugural Bond film *Dr. No*, James Bond spies Bond Girl Honey Ryder exiting the sea wearing a white bikini with a dagger attached to her belt. This image "effectively positioned the first Bond Girl as an erotic object of the gaze" (Funnell 2011a, p. 467). In *Casino Royale*, this well-known Bond Girl iconography is referenced in relation to Bond and not his love interest Vesper Lynd:

> Bond is submerged in the ocean and enters the shot by dramatically lifting his head out of the water in slow motion, taking a notably deep breath... This scene presents the exposed muscular body of Bond as spectacular, passive, and feminized, positioning Craig in the role of Bond Girl as the visual spectacle of the Bond film. (Funnell 2011a, p. 467)

The depiction of Bond and the spectacularization of his body via Bond Girl iconography signal a shift in the generic and gendered conventions governing the franchise. Later, Bond's body is positioned as the object of the gaze, as it is longingly caressed by Solange Dimitrios and then Lynd. In the end, both women pay with their lives for their lustful touches of Bond.

The Craig-era Bond films continue to use memory differently given their more serial nature. *Casino Royale* is a prequel and provides the origin story of James Bond. *Quantum of Solace*, *Skyfall*, and *Spectre* serve as more traditional sequels given the continuation of the storyline across all four films. As a result, memory, and specifically the process of remembering via touch, plays a central role. This is most notable with Lynd. Although she dies in the arms of Bond at the end of *Casino Royale*, her presence can be felt throughout *Quantum of Solace*. This is one reason why the film does not have a Bond Girl proper since the characteristics of the Bond Girl have been divided between Lynd's memory (and Bond's continuing love for her) and Camille Montes (who serves as a good partner in action but never sleeps with him). The sexual interlude provided by British consulate contact Strawberry Fields, a classic Bond ingénue, proves to be a stern warning to Bond. After their haptic encounter, Fields is murdered by Dominic Greene's hench people and left in a death pose reminiscent of Jill Masterson in *Goldfinger*, she is found lying face down on a bed naked and covered in oil. Chastened by her death and still mourning the loss of Lynd and her betrayal, Bond parts ways with his female partner Montes rather than pursuing a romantic relationship with her, making *Quantum of Solace* the first film in the series in which Bond intentionally parts ways with his supposed Bond Girl. The memory of Lynd is embodied through an artefact, the Algerian love knot necklace she wears throughout most of *Casino Royale*. This was a present from her fiancé that she took off when she fell in love with Bond. After her death, Bond holds on to necklace and the memory of Lynd until he confronts her fiancé at the end of *Quantum of Solace*, revealing him to be a spy who uses service women to gain access to government secrets. After Bond interrogates the man off-screen and has him arrested, he drops the necklace in the snow as he walks away from the building, signaling that he is done with Lynd and is ready to move on. Rarely has there been an artefact that holds as much significance to Bond across more than one film.

In a similar way, *Spectre* intertextually references *Skyfall* through various artefacts that evoke memory. First, the film uses videotapes and/or video messages to encourage Bond (and the audience) to remember the two women in the Craig era whom Bond has loved the most: he is sent a video from the late Dench's M following her death in *Skyfall* and he discovers a tape containing the interrogation of Lynd from *Casino Royale* in Mr. White's secret room in Tangiers (Fig. 2.3).

Importantly, Bond watches the former and *not* the latter, demonstrating that while he still has (filial) love for M and will thus follow her final orders, he has moved on from Lynd and has no desire to hear from her beyond the grave (thus leaving him free to be with Dr. Madeleine Swann). Second, Bond's ongoing loyalty to M is signified through the Royal Dolton bulldog that once appeared on her desk and was bequeathed to him after her death at the end of *Skyfall*. This serves as a transtextual and

Fig. 2.3 *Spectre* (Eon Productions et al. 2015)

transcendental symbol of Bond's ongoing loyalty to Queen and Country as signified by M (see Chap. 8). Finally, the film includes images of characters from the previous Craig-era films. Images of Silva, Lynd, LeChiffre, and M appear (in that order) in the opening credit sequence, an approach that recalls the way in which *OHMSS* featured images of previous characters in the opening credits as a way to connect the first Lazenby film with those of the Connery era and root *OHMSS* in the Bond film tradition. These images are used in a different way in *Spectre* as Blofeld posts photos of these figures as well as one of Mr. White in the now derelict MI6 headquarters in order to trace for Bond and the audience his unseen involvement in the villainous schemes of the previous Craig-era films. While his claims are a bit of a stretch (and arguably the ramblings of a madman), the images offer a visual contrast between these past concerns, which cannot be changed, and present issues (such as the kidnapping of Swann), which Bond can affect with his saving touch.

The Calculative Body

Finally, James Bond possesses a calculative body that is defined by how he feels his way through missions. This is one way that the franchise embodies Bond's instincts. A good example occurs in *Moonraker* when Hugo

Drax invites Bond to hunt pheasant while staying at his country estate in California. Unbeknownst to Bond, or so the audience believes, an assassin is hiding in the trees ready to shoot him. While it initially appears as though Bond has missed the shot when the birds fly away, Bond has actually killed the sniper who falls out of the tree moments later. His instinct for survival coupled with a rapid calculation of distance enabled Bond to prevail, much to the surprise of Drax and the audience. It is often in staged encounters whether it takes the form of sporting activities such as shooting, horse riding, and golf, and/or when Bond is trapped in tight spots that his capacity to calculate and evaluate potential winning strategies is revealed.

While Bond appears omni-competent in the first four decades (or 20 films) of the franchise (with a few exceptions such as Domino Derval and Tracy di Vicenzo saving Bond in *Thunderball* and *OHMSS*, respectively), the Craig-era films feature the orphan origin story of Bond and show how he develops his calculative touch through trial and error. For example, at the beginning of *Casino Royale*, Bond and a colleague are tasked with detaining bomb-maker Mollaka in Madagascar. While the two are conducting surveillance at a cock-fighting match, Bond notices that his younger and less experienced partner is frequently touching his ear in order to hear his communication device. Although Bond quickly instructs the man to stop touching his ear, Mollaka has already noticed this action and flees the vicinity. This leads to a physically demanding parkour-inspired chase sequence. After this event, M describes Bond as a 'blunt instrument', and this descriptor certainly applies to his approach and tactics in Madagascar. Such is his determination to pursue Mollaka that he virtually destroys a foreign embassy and violates numerous diplomatic protocols in the process, creating an international incident.

Later in the film, Bond participates in a high-stakes poker game in order to bankrupt LeChiffre and turn him into an informant for MI6. Bond explains to Vesper Lynd that Texas Hold'em poker is a game of observation and physical control: it requires a player to carefully observe her/his opponents in order to discover their 'tell', their unconscious physical reaction to their hand. As a result, "the poker table in *Casino Royale* can be understood as an allegorical battlefield, an arena for the spectacle of masculinity whereby players attempt to defeat their enemies through exercisable physical control" (Funnell 2011a, p. 464). While playing against LeChiffre, Bond believes that he has uncovered his opponent's tell, which consists of LeChiffre touching his face when he bluffs. Bond, however, has been tricked by LeChiffre and is knocked out of the game as a result. Bond tries to rectify the situation by taking the 'blunt instrument' approach and resorting to violence; he picks up a steak knife and intends to kill LeChiffre. He is stopped, however, by CIA agent Felix Leiter who suggests a different course of action. Leiter stakes Bond who re-enters the poker game and eventually defeats LeChiffre. In the film, Bond learns an important lesson about how and when to use his body; that a soft touch can be just as, if not more, effective than brute force and that he can defeat an opponent by controlling, mobilizing, and directing his body in strategic ways.

This capacity to utilize a soft or forceful touch reveals itself again in *Skyfall*. While recovering in Turkey after an accidental shooting and mission meltdown, Bond displays remarkable composure by drinking a shot of alcohol while a scorpion crawls along his hand. He later traps the creature inside the glass and thus completes a drinking challenge for money. The power of his touch varies throughout the film from extracting bullet fragments from his own chest with a knife to constructing a bomb that destroys his childhood home in Scotland. While his body is visibly ageing and at times threatens to fail him,[19] his calculative touch prevails (to the extent of making vigorous love to femme fatale Severine in the shower of Silva's yacht) even when his adversary Silva appears to have outwitted him.

In/Out of Touch: Regulating James Bond and His Missions

A consideration of the haptic geographies of James Bond reveals the ways in which his body operates in a variety of environments and how his touch in particular conveys important messages about his identity and role in the films. Bond is presented with a fit body that serves as the heroic ideal as it is contrasted with the physiques of his opponents who are too weak or unnaturally/inhumanly strong by comparison. His body is sensual and his haptic encounters with women help to confirm his libidinal masculinity and establish his (hetero)normative superiority in the films. Bond's body is also technical as he demonstrates his mastery over various forms of technology and specifically cars, which are coded feminine in his films. In addition, Bond has a memorializing body that recalls key events in an episodic series and conveys powerful messages about the changing generic and gendered codes in the franchise. Finally, Bond possesses a calculative body that he can direct in strategic ways depending on the situation.

These haptic encounters draw attention to the representational and body politics governing the franchise.

Beyond corporeality, touch also plays a metaphoric role in the franchise. When Bond is sent on missions, he is required to 'keep in touch' with MI6. Bond is provided with a certain degree of autonomy to conduct his investigations and 'pump' his sources for information (as suggested by M in *Tomorrow Never Dies*). However, he is expected to reach out to MI6 if he requires assistance and to inform them when the mission has been completed. On numerous occasions, however, Bond puts off communicating with MI6 in order to have sex with his Bond Girl and this results in some awkward encounters with his boss and other dignitaries who are trying to express their gratitude for a job well done (e.g. Margaret Thatcher in *For Your Eyes Only*). For Bond, corporeal touch and specifically sex takes precedence over all other forms of communication, however apparently vital. It also provides the franchise with many opportunities to inject humor into the final scenes of the films such as Bond being caught *in flagrante delicto* with his Bond Girl Dr. Holly Goodhead while returning to earth from outer space in *Moonraker*. The films ends with one of the most memorable double entendres as Q says to M and his Soviet equivalent about Bond, "I think he's attempting re-entry."

Bond is also presented as being 'out of touch' (with mainstream/common/lowbrow culture) in the franchise. In the early films, this was one way to confer Bond's class status. For instance, in *Goldfinger*, Bond explains that "there are some things that just aren't done, such as drinking Dom Perignon '53 above the temperature of 38 degrees Fahrenheit. That's just as bad as listening to the Beatles without earmuffs!" Later he has dinner with the Bank of England chief and is accused by M of lecturing the senior banker on the merits of a particular type of brandy. There are many other examples of Bond noting his preference for particular highbrow/niche/non-mainstream drinks, food, clothing, watches, cars, and so forth. This emphasis on aspects of elite culture played a key role in connecting Bond to the gentlemanly tradition of heroism from which he has his roots. Bond's world is the casino, hotel, and restaurant, and not the café, disco, and pub. And in each of these elite environments, Bond knows how to occupy the space, and how and where to use his touch (see Chap. 7).

By the 1990s, however, Bond is presented as being out of touch in other ways. In *GoldenEye*, M describes Bond as being a "sexist, misogynistic dinosaur," signaling that Bond is out of touch with the changing gender politics of the 1990s. She also refers to him as "a relic of the Cold

War", and this helps to root him in the colonial/Cold War past rather than the modernizing present. In both cases, the franchise presents the impression that while the world around Bond might change, he remains relatively the same and in a time of crisis we need a hero who embodies traditional British values and practices to save us. But there are challenges along the way. In *The World Is Not Enough*, the promise of personal security by Bond is not enough to prevent a female associate of the villain Renard from committing suicide. Bond's sensual touch usually prevails but it appears a little less certain in terms of outcome. By the mid-2000s, Bond is presented as lacking touch or at least tact in *Casino Royale* and by *Skyfall* he has lost that touch completely. As a result, *Skyfall* functions as a redemption narrative in which Bond has to recover his bodily strength and (re)discover his mental fortitude in order to develop into the iconic superspy who is gifted in perpetuity with a 'Midas touch'. But in order to do that, others have to pay a heavy price and most notably M who dies in his family's chapel at Skyfall. Bond's comforting touch offers a little solace in her final few moments of life.

NOTES

1. While witnessing gypsy traditions in *From Russia with Love*, Bond claimed with conviction that he indeed '*J'aime les sensations fortes*' (1957b; 160).
2. For a detailed discussion, see Marks' *The Skin of Film* (2000).
3. For a detailed discussion, see Chapman (2000).
4. For a detailed discussion of the shift towards a more body-based heroic aesthetic in the Craig era, see Funnell (2011a).
5. For a detailed discussion, see Wood (2013).
6. For a detailed discussion, see Paterson's "Haptic Geographies" (2009).
7. See Rodaway (1994).
8. See Cooper et al. (2010).
9. Once an actor is considered to be too old (e.g. Roger Moore), he is replaced in the franchise by a younger actor who takes up the title role. Some would argue that Moore should have been replaced before his final outing as Bond in *A View to a Kill*.
10. In *Thunderball*, Volpe is accidentally killed by her allies while dancing with Bond.
11. For a detailed discussion of Romanova and Klebb, see Chap. 4.
12. *OHMSS* is an exception as Blofeld expresses sexual interest in Bond's fiancé Tracy di Vicenzo. He also seems to have a passing sexual interest in Tiffany Case in *Diamonds Are Forever*.

13. For a detailed discussion of the gendering of automobiles as well as trains and planes in the Bond films, see Chap. 7.
14. For a detailed discussion, see Stephanie Jones (2015b).
15. For a detailed discussion, see Berns (2015).
16. For a detailed discussion, see Funnell (2014).
17. For a detailed discussion of Onatopp's sexual threat to Bond, see Chaps. 4 and 7.
18. A similar approach is taken in the design of the opening title sequence, which features images from the previous Bond films in order to root *OHMSS* within the franchise.
19. For a detailed discussion, see Dodds (2014).

CHAPTER 3

The Anglo-American Connection

James Bond is a popular cultural icon of British identity. Working as a secret agent for the British organization MI6, Bond travels the world on missions and acts in the best interest of his country in order to safeguard their geopolitical interests.[1] While he can and does harbor doubts about these missions, he is nonetheless depicted as a loyal agent serving 'Queen and Country', as Domino Derval remarks in *Thunderball*. Although Bond operates as a solo agent and is not assigned a regular '00' partner, he often works opportunistically with those he encounters in the field, and more routinely with other non-British agents, collaborating frequently with American allies (Black 2005; Lawrence 2011; Moran 2011). These relationships, both opportunistic and planned, are crucial to mission success and have been seen by many scholars and fans as indicative of the changing contours of the post-1945 geopolitical world, and the Anglo-American 'special relationship'.

In the Eon/United Artists Bond films, these American characters usually work for the Central Intelligence Agency (CIA) and represent American geopolitical interests, such as furthering regional hegemony in strategic spaces such as the Arctic, Caribbean, East Asia, and even outer space. According to the historian Jeremy Black, "support for the United States [was] central to British policy during the cold war [and] is important to Bond's role" in the films (2005, p. 94). The depiction of Bond working with American allies not only helps to connect the common geopolitical interests of Britain with America vis-à-vis the challenge posed by China,

© The Editor(s) (if applicable) and The Author(s) 2017
L. Funnell, K. Dodds, *Geographies, Genders and Geopolitics of
James Bond*, DOI 10.1057/978-1-137-57024-6_3

Russia, and non-state entities such as SPECTRE, but it also serves as a way to attract American filmgoers to the films (Bennett and Woollacott 2003, p. 29). Even the choice to cast Sean Connery over David Niven for the role of Bond in *Dr. No* was judged a commercial necessity. Producer Albert R. Broccoli felt that Niven was 'too English' for the part and envisioned for Bond a more mid-Atlantic image with a tougher persona that would appeal to both British and American audiences.[2]

Not only did the films rely on the United States as a primary market, but the films themselves were strongly shaped by American creative personnel like Broccoli and screenwriter Richard Maibaum. Without United Artists underwriting the earliest Bond films, the franchise would never have developed in the manner that it did.[3] The Richard Maibaum papers held at the University of Iowa, where he studied in the 1930s, provide fascinating insights into how the Bond novels were translated into screenplays and the creative dialogue between those responsible for bringing Bond to the big screen (see Dodds 2005). Maibaum who had worked with Broccoli on *Hell Below Zero* (Robson 1954), was appointed the chief screenplay writer. After a wartime career working in the US Armed Forces' Combat Films Division, Maibaum and a co-worker Alan Ladd were responsible for a series of post-war productions including an espionage film *O.S.S.* (Pichel 1946) and *Paratrooper* (Young 1954). Ladd recommended him to the producers Cubby Broccoli and Irving Allen of Warwick Films in the mid-1950s. Maibaum's relationship with Broccoli extended to Harry Saltzman, when Eon Productions secured the film rights to Ian Fleming's novels. Maibaum was charged with turning the novels into films and as such he helped to transform locations, dialogue, and storylines sometimes in a dramatic fashion. As Adrian Turner notes, "Maibaum must be regarded as a key contributor to the Bond ethos and the Bond machine; its creation surely owes nearly as much to him as it does to Ian Fleming, or to Saltzman and Broccoli, or to Sean Connery and Ken Adam" (Turner 1998, p. 131).

What can be learned from the development of the screenplay relating to *Dr. No*, for example, is that it went through multiple iterations. Maibaum's drafts highlight how the original version featured a gang of Chinese-Afro-Caribbean assassins murdering the British operative Strangways, which the opening scenes of the film do retain. However, Maibaum and his co-writer Wolf Mankowitz proposed a further assassination—this time involving an American secret agent called Christopher on board the ship, *SS Orinoco*. The same gang murdered Christopher because he was trying to contact Strangeways and warn him that the ship was carrying explosives and bound for Crab Key. In the first version of the screenplay, Bond was sent to Jamaica to discover who killed both the British and American agents and was going to encounter Cuban agents working on the island. The Cuban connection was designed to highlight a fiendish plot to destroy the Panama Canal and thus weaken a major trading link for the United States and its allies. The second version made further changes to the basic geopolitical plotline and re-imagined Dr. No as being part of a Chinese criminal society and downplayed the Cuban connection. In an expanding second edition of the film treatment, he was described as a 'Red Chinese agent' who sought to convince Bond that he should join his organization because he wanted to provoke the United States to attack Cuba following the attack on the Panama Canal. This in turn, it was hoped, would prompt Soviet action against the United States and the ensuing conflict and chaos would present opportunities for China to exploit. By the third treatment, the role of Cuba disappeared and the focus was more explicitly on US-UK agents working together to prevent Dr. No from interfering with US rocket testing in Florida. The geopolitical link between Dr. No and 'Red China' was retained.

Maibaum recorded the creative tension between himself and the committee appointed to manage the screenplay development in his papers. The producers Broccoli and Saltzman, the production designer Adam, and the director Terence Young worked and re-worked the script with due attention given to special effects and set production. Maibaum's private papers reveal how frustrating this collective editorial process could be. As he recorded, "After I write and submit my first draft of the screenplay, revisions are discussed in committee…The writer is both the anvil and one of the sledges. He participates as a clanger in this nerve-wracking anvil chorus while simultaneously recording it. The wear and tear on the psyche is understandingly harrowing" (qtd. in Dodds 2005, p. 277). But this creative tension was important because by the time *Dr. No* was released to audiences in October 1962, the special relationship between Bond and Leiter was established and significantly the removal of the death of the American agent Christopher and references to the Panama Canal allowed Bond to dominate in the context of operating in the former British colony of Jamaica while acknowledging it was the geopolitical interests of the United States both in the Caribbean and even outer space that were also at stake.

This chapter considers the representation and geopolitical significance of Bond's American allies in order to better understand how Anglo-American geopolitical interests are refracted across the different eras of the film franchise. The intersection of nationality with gender, race, and class shapes the reading of American characters and informs the nature of their relationships with Bond. A number of recurring characters and character types appear across the franchise including Felix Leiter, a variety of American Bond Girls, and a handful of minor figures like J.W. Pepper and Jack Wade. But those intersections, however important, are not sufficient in their own right. Bond's repeated demonstration of what he can do, touch, and feel also matters to the 'special relationship'. His ability to connect is what makes the relationship special with his American allies—he can push the button at the right moment, seduce a key informant, and sense danger that others cannot. So while Bond may be the 'junior partner' operating in a Cold War geopolitical climate dominated by the United States, it is his personal intuition, touch, and movement that allows him to *connect* with people, objects, and sites/spaces, and thus emerge as a dominant/superior figure.

THE CONNERY ERA: ESTABLISHING THE ANGLO-AMERICAN CONNECTION

The Anglo-American connection was established in the Connery era through the pairing of Bond with a male CIA operative. Felix Leiter is the best-known American ally of Bond and a close friend who appears in 10 films across the franchise. Although Leiter is a recurring character that offers a sense of continuity across the episodic series, seven different actors have portrayed this figure. This casting practice is surprising given the fact that Bond's British support system—which consists of M, Moneypenny, and Q—is comprised of recurring characters *and* actors. And yet, Leiter is played by different actors in three key films in the Connery era that helped to establish the Bond film series: Jack Lord in *Dr. No*, Cec Linder in *Goldfinger*, and Rick Van Nutter in *Thunderball*.

As a character, Leiter occupies an important place in the Bond novels even if literary critics at the time were divided on his significance. Leiter is Bond's closest friend. For the British writer Kingsley Amis, Leiter was a 'non-entity' and a man who simply followed Bond's orders.[4] In comparison, James Chapman, writing some four decades later, notes that Bond is usually assisted by NATO allies in his adventures and most frequently by Leiter who appears in six novels. He writes more sympathetically about this relationship between the two men: "The professional and personal friendship between Bond and Leiter represents the 'special relationship', which has supposedly existed between Britain and the United States since the end of the Second World War, though, in a quaint reversal of the real balance of power, it is the American Leiter who is the subordinate partner to the British Bond" (2000, p. 39). The Bond novels deny the decline of British power as they "construct an imaginary arena in which Britain still occupies center-stage in world affairs" and their relationship with the United States is seen as something that is invited and strategic rather than desperate and unreflective (ibid. 39). Moreover, this 'special relationship' was coded through race and gender. According to Wendy Webster, this American connection

> had echoes of imperial identity [...] like relations between white settler communities and metropolis, as relations based around ties of common heritage, culture, ancestry, and descent. The version of the 'people's empire', which emphasized a racial community of Britons in Australia, Canada, and New Zealand was increasingly subsumed into a wider globalized identity that also encompassed America: the idea of English-speaking people. Indeed, a 'special relationship' foregrounded Britain and America, while the 'people's Empire' of a racial community of Britons became 'the rest'. (2005, pp. 16–17)

As embodied by Bond and Leiter, the 'special relationship' between Britain and America is contingent on their identities as white men who share a common ancestry and moral code.

In the Connery-era films, Leiter serves as the American connection that sanctions and supports Bond's insertion into global conflicts. Just like in the novels, Leiter's 'special relationship' with Bond is one that is founded on shared identities, culture, morals, and professions. Moreover, he continues to be presented as a supportive figure to Bond in the franchise. Leiter spends limited time on screen—an amount comparable to British supportive figures like M, Q, and Moneypenny—and offers Bond intelligence and at times tactical support when Bond ventures out alone to complete missions that impact Britain as well as the United States.

The Connery-era films set up the impression that the world needs Bond and that the American connection, while personal and convivial with regard to Leiter, is one that is engineered by Bond through his personal contacts, his professional instincts, and even his feel for danger. While

Bond and Leiter operate in environments where the scale of danger and threat can exceed the local and frequently the national/regional, their personal connection helps to disguise the obvious scale differences between their respective countries in terms of intelligence and military capacities. Operating in a discreet and intimate manner, the profession of spying, so the films suggest, invites an orientation and sensibility, which is both small scale and local while attentive to global geopolitical dynamics.

Leiter is first introduced in the inaugural *Dr. No* even though the character does not appear in the 1958 source novel. Prior to their meeting, the film signals a connection between MI6 and the CIA when M orders Bond to change his gun; Bond reluctantly surrenders his Beretta and exchanges it for a Walther PPK, the weapon of choice for the CIA. Bond grudgingly hands over an Italian-made gun that 'jams' repeatedly and is ordered to embrace a new automatic order. Bond makes a new connection with America (via a German gun manufacturer) through an object that will become part of his professional self. Even before he has met Leiter, his touch and feel have been re-engineered. Although Bond has various helpmates in the film like the black characters Quarrel and Puss Feller, Leiter serves as Bond's primary ally and represents American geopolitical interests in the mission. While their first encounter is initially tense, Leiter quickly develops a cooperative rather than competitive working relationship with Bond. The film further emphasizes this geopolitical and object-centered connection by its setting in the Caribbean—the geopolitical backyard of the United States but also a space where Britain's colonial presence remains detectable and where Bond can easily obtain a specialist Geiger counter, which reinforces his capacity to draw upon his own logistical-intelligence network. While films like *Goldfinger* and *You Only Live Twice* create the impression that Leiter is part of a much larger assemblage of money, technology, intelligence, and extra-territorial reach, this is mitigated by Bond's superior skill-set such as detailed knowledge of the international finance system (in *Goldfinger*) and him being multilingual (in *You Only Live Twice*). Thus, Bond's extra-territorial reach relies on an assemblage as well, but it is one rooted in an elite education, social networking, and professional autonomy that help him move, touch, and feel his way through missions.

From the outset of the franchise, Leiter has been presented as a mirror image to Bond. Leiter is briefly introduced at the airport in Jamaica. He can be seen standing on the second floor looking down upon the locals and waiting for Bond to arrive. A high-angle camera is positioned over Leiter's shoulder and presents his point of view as he watches the people below. As noted by Travis Wagner in his study of colonization in the Bond films, *Dr. No* relies on doubling in this scene and presents the impression that Leiter, like Bond, "can stand above non-normative bodies and gaze upon them in condemnation" (2015, p. 53). Wagner further contends that the binary relationship between the colonizer and colonized in the franchise is something that cannot be easily overturned. This is evident in a subsequent scene in which Bond follows Quarrel to a restaurant, deeming him to be suspicious. Here, he is formally introduced to Leiter who tells Bond that Quarrel works for him; the film positions the white American man as the boss of a black Caribbean man. Later on, the film again presents Bond and Leiter as mirror images when Bond instructs Quarrel to interrogate the unnamed Jamaican photographer played by Marguerite LeWars (Fig. 3.1).

While Bond condemns her verbally, he tells Quarrel to interrogate her physically by twisting her arm. According to Wagner, the scene centers around "a black male whose own otherness as a colonized body suggests that he can act out in a more physical and barbaric way" than the white man (2015, p. 54). Read another way, Quarrel uses a method of inter-rogation that Bond would have no hesitation in employing if searching for information (such as twisting Andrea Anders arm in *The Man with the*

Fig. 3.1 *Dr. No* (Eon Productions et al. 1962)

Golden Gun). While Leiter does not participate in the interrogation, he does not stop it either and offers silent approval of Quarrel's tactics. This draws attention to the privilege and power both men wield (over men and women of color) while operating overseas as representatives of their respective nation states.

Although Bond and Leiter are set up as peers in *Dr. No*, it is Bond and not Leiter who sees the mission through. It is Bond who shoots the devious scientist (Professor Dent) and uses his seduction of a British colonial secretary (Miss Taro) as a way of exposing the web of intrigue surrounding Dr. No. Even though Dr. No threatens to destroy American space rockets, it is Bond who sails out to Crab Key to defeat him with the aid of Quarrel rather than Leiter. While on the island, Bond single-handedly dismantles the entire operation by crawling through various watery spaces and tunnels in the complex, sabotaging the control panel, and drowning Dr. No. Leiter reappears at the end of the film after the conflict has been resolved and his scene on the Royal Navy motor launch was not part of the original screenplay. According to Chapman, the scene was added later to emphasize the fact that Bond has the capacity to sort out the crisis on his own (albeit aided and abetted by the extra-territorial reach of the Royal Navy; 2000, p. 78). Of course, as Chapman explains, "the Americans have rarely shown such deference to the remnants of British colonialism in the Caribbean [...] In the Bond films, as in the novels, the 'special relationship' was rather more equal than *realpolitik* would allow" (ibid. 78).

This position initially appears to be reversed in *Thunderball*, as the US Navy is the dominant military actor in tackling the fiendish underwater plans of Largo close to the city of Miami. But what makes the American intervention possible, however, is Bond's strategy of seduction, provocation, and alienation of those close to the evil genius, Largo. Using his touch and his skills in diving, swimming, and shooting, Bond establishes a series of personal connections, which prove instrumental in helping to locate a lost nuclear-armed British bomber plane. Moreover, it is Bond (and not his American contact Leiter) who later assists US Navy Seals during the underwater battle. So when Bond's logistical-intelligence reach appears dwarfed by US infrastructural power, his capacity to reach out and interact with a diverse set of characters is shown to matter to mission success. For example, the climax of the film features a solo Bond infiltrating Largo's ship, which is speeding away after being attacked by US Navy SEALS. Although Bond attempts to subdue Largo in the cockpit, the villain gets a hold of a gun but is impaled by a harpoon before he can pull the trigger. It was shot by Domino Derval, Largo's mistress, whose seduction by Bond proves to be the linchpin in his operation to recover the missing atomic bombs. It is only after the mission is complete that the US Navy picks up Bond and Derval.

American and Chinese relations also play a key role in shaping Bond films of the 1960s. At the time, China was considered a growing political threat and these concerns were far more pressing in the United States than in Britain. The foregrounding of this concern, according to Black, can be interpreted "as an aspect of the Americanization of the Bond films" (2005, p. 95). The Chinese play a sinister role in *Dr. No*, and the arch-villain tells Bond over dinner that his mother was Chinese. His hench people are all Chinese even if they are part of the transnational network SPECTRE. They are presented in a similar manner in *Goldfinger* and *Thunderball*, the next two Bond films in which Leiter appears, as a menacing presence that is not addressed in any detail. While the Chinese do not play a role in the novel *Goldfinger*, they feature in the film and are implicated in Operation Grand Slam, a plan to destabilize the US-led international financial system. The arch-villain, Auric Goldfinger supported by his Korean hench person Oddjob, is shown to be aligned with Mr. Ling, who is dressed in a Mao suit, a type of Chinese tunic suit frequently worn by Mao Zedong, the leader of China at the time. The Mao suit was a highly recognizable symbol of China and its "inward turn during the decades of the PRC" (Wu 2015, p. 192). Ling is an agent who specializes in nuclear fission and arms the bomb that is placed in the vault at Fort Knox in order to contaminate the gold supply of the United States and tank its economy.[6] Moreover, in *Thunderball*, although the Chinese do not play a strong role in Largo's plan to steal a NATO atomic bomb and detonate it in Miami, SPECTRE distributes Chinese drugs to the United States (in order to infiltrate American bodies) and the film continues to promote the theme of the "Oriental menace" with its own extra-territorial reach (Black 2005, p. 95).

In the Connery era, Leiter appears in Bond films that are set in the United States and/or include American geopolitical concerns directly. In both *Goldfinger* and *Thunderball*, Leiter's 'special relationship' with Bond helps to sanction and facilitate Bond's/Britain's inclusion in these conflicts. However, these films remain firmly about Bond, and Leiter is consistently presented as a secondary and supportive figure. In the end, it is the British agent who saves the day by touching and feeling his way through a series of challenging missions. And it is (white) British heterosexual masculinity that is celebrated in these films as Bond is able to go to places that Leiter would find socially inaccessible and even physically uncomfortable. Although Leiter, as a comparable agent to Bond, is presumably granted a similar 'license to kill', there is little to suggest that Leiter would be at ease seducing and killing if necessary regardless of class, gender, race, and nationality. In *Diamonds Are Forever*, Leiter's role is to organize surveillance and to orchestrate a helicopter attack on the arch-villain's base on an oil rig. Unlike Bond, he neither seduces any femme fatales nor does he touch, let alone attack, the arch-villain. As noted by Chapman, Bond is set up as a hero of the NATO alliance while Leiter functions as more of a 'yes' man who enables Bond even when the latter is dependent on US military objects and technology in order to save him and his accomplices (2000, p. 124). Significantly, *Thunderball* ends with Bond and Derval being rescued by a large sky-hook attached to a US naval plane. And as before, it is Bond's skillful touch that affects their rescue while Leiter sits on the sidelines.

THE MOORE ERA: CONCENTRATION AND DIFFERENTIATION OF AMERICAN ALLIES

The Moore era contains the largest concentration of American allies. They are featured in six of the seven Moore films with the exception being *For Your Eyes Only*, which depicts Bond working with Greek allies in the Eastern Mediterranean. American interests are still embodied by Leiter who is played by David Hedison in *Live and Let Die*. He serves as a figure of continuity as the franchise shifts from the Connery to Moore eras; although the actor playing Bond has changed, his friendship with Leiter and cooperative relationship with the CIA remains unaffected. This Anglo-American connection is reaffirmed through the narrative and visual conventions of the films. For example, *Live and Let Die* focuses on the drug trade in the United States run by a black criminal network controlled by Kananga who poses as an African American (Mr. Big). Not only are portions of the film set in New York and New Orleans, but the film taps into some of the conventions and aesthetics featured in American Blaxploitation films, which were popular at the time.[7] The film was heavily criticized by some commentators for its depiction of race and in particular of black American men (Metz 2004, p. 66)—a criticism that has been extended to the 1954 source novel—even though a black CIA agent, Harold Strutter, saves Bond from a near-death experience in the Harlem district of New York. Bond is shown to be out of place in urban America in a manner that is quite different to his experiences of being a white British man in the Caribbean.

In *Live and Let Die*, the United States is presented as being vulnerable and in a way that is far more embodied than earlier expressions of site-specific insecurity such as Fort Knox in *Goldfinger*. Black notes that the film focuses on "black power in cities and implied that a failure to control both black neighborhoods and small Caribbean islands could undermine America" (2005, p. 134). Institutional power is embodied through the white male subject and the CIA's Leiter remains a trustworthy ally to Bond. In comparison, the agent he assigns to work with Bond outside the United States, Rosie Carver, is a black woman played by Gloria Hendry. From the outset, Carver is identified as a mediocre agent; Bond teases her about her nervous disposition and early attempt to conceal her identity, and she is killed shortly after Bond discovers that she is a double agent working for the villain Mr. Big. The film uses race as a way to demarcate 'good' from 'bad' American characters and assess their professional competence. It presents the impression that while you can take white American figures at face value, all black American characters are suspect. Moreover, the film relies on antiquated racial stereotypes when presenting black characters[8] and this works to undermine their characterization and heroic potential in the film. For example, Bond is initially suspicious of Strutter, and grudg-ingly acknowledges that he was right to point out that a white agent chas-ing black suspects into Harlem was likely to attract attention. Strutter's understanding of the racial geographies of New York helps to bolster the perception of his professional competence only to have it undercut later it the film. Having explained to Bond the dangerous realities of living in an American city, he is murdered in New Orleans while watching an African American funeral. His skills in the field and cover story prove insufficient unlike Bond who is still able to navigate his way through different spaces and circumstances on account of his ability to reach out to, endure, and even seduce both allies and enemies during the mission.

During the Moore era, Bond Girls also represent American inter-ests in the franchise and unlike Bond's relationship with Leiter and other American men, he enters into a series of sexual relationships with these women. Bond's touch proves crucial to his pairing with Dr. Holly Goodhead who works undercover for the CIA in *Moonraker*, and who struggles to be taken seriously by Bond. As with Rosie Carver, Bond doubts Goodhead's professional credentials even though she is introduced as both a doctor and an astronaut. Bond never treats male CIA agents like Leiter in such a brazen and disrespectful manner. Bond is also paired with other American allies who are not government agents: he works with jewelry thief Octopussy in *Octopussy* and geologist Stacy Sutton in *A View to a Kill*. The CIA continues to have a strong presence in these films in terms of providing infrastructural and surveillance based support. For instance, Agent Chuck Lee, a Chinese American, is featured in *A View to a Kill* but his presence is ultimately unthreatening to Bond and his physical and sexual abilities. Moreover, when an American Bond Girl agent is featured in the film, Leiter is absent (Funnell 2008, p. 69) and thus there is no competition between male and female CIA agents for Bond's exclusive attentions.[9]

Gender plays a key role in the relationship between Bond and his American allies. Bond maintains both a cooperative and friendly relationship with Leiter; he never competes with Leiter for attention or access to resources. The same cannot be said for the Bond Girls who appear in the Moore era. Their relationships are defined by competition, a struggle for power and control over a situation, and aspects of patriarchy. Whether she is a professional agent or academically/professionally qualified, Bond always tries to one-up her while simultaneously seducing her. In these cases, what Bond brings to the 'special relationship' is an ability to make physical and sexual connections with allies and enemies. For Bond, the Cold War is an embodied and intimate experience—an opportunity to make trans-racial and trans-national sexual alliances that oftentimes involve American women.

In *Moonraker*, a film that taps into popular interest about space technology and the extraordinary commercial success of *Star Wars* (Lucas 1977), Bond's superior touch is given full flight. As Black notes, "space was a crucial site of superpower rivalry in the late 1950s and 1960s, an arms race in which the United States, not Britain, represented the West" (2005, p. 94). In the film, Bond is sent to investigate the disappearance of an American space shuttle that was on loan to Britain, which vanished in space and caused the destruction of the British transporter airplane somewhere in Alaska. He is paired up with CIA agent and trained astronaut Goodhead and the two work in concert to thwart a plan involving the transmission of a deadly virus from outer space. The film connects Bond, who represents Britain, with the substantial technological-scientific-academic legacy of the United States, which is associated with Goodhead and the space shuttles. Although Bond and Goodhead are set up as equal partners, there are moments in the film where each agent tries to one-up the other in order to establish their superiority as an agent (and by extension alliance with the stronger superpower). In addition to undercutting her accomplishments, Bond takes great pleasure in telling her that he knows she is an undercover CIA agent. He prolongs this revelation by first toying with all of the CIA gadgets in her hotel room: a pen filled with poison, a diary that shoots a dart, a flame-throwing perfume bottle, and a radio transmitter hidden in a purse. Using his intuition and touch, Bond demonstrates that Goodhead's feeble attempt to disguise herself or distract Bond with these feminine gadgets will not suffice. This technology is clearly gendered and the film uses sexism as a way to position Bond (and his touch) over Goodhead (and her knowledge) as the superior agent, and, by extension Britain, as the key player in the race to space in the 1970s. Interestingly, in the film Bond is shown to travel on the Anglo-French supersonic jet, Concorde, to Brazil and whilst in Brazil there is a scene in which an advertisement billboard for British Airways lingers on the screen, as if to suggest that Britain is a popular and widespread technological superpower, with substantial extra-territorial reach.

This mode of belittlement requires sexualization and marginalization in order to re-calibrate the Anglo-American connection in favor of Bond and Britain. It is also evident in the costuming of the American Bond Girls who appear in revealing dresses, bathing suits, and lingerie—unlike Bond's American male allies who are fully clothed and never appear shirtless.[10] It is only Bond who appears shirtless with the exception of a few strongman hench people like Red Grant and Necros. This persistent representation diminishes the Bond Girl's capacity for heroism (and being recognized as such by Bond and others) in the films. The arch-villain kidnaps virtually every Bond Girl in the Moore era at some point. Moreover, the romantic relationship between Bond and his American Bond Girls also predicts these dynamics, as the series has long relied on traditional gender roles particularly when it comes to taming and domesticating women.[11] There are exceptions such as the bodyguard turned ally May Day in *A View to a Kill*, but her obvious sexual and physical dominance over Bond is 'managed' by her eventual self-sacrifice to save him from being blown up by a bomb. It is Bond, rather than May Day, who eventually kills arch-adversary Zorin in San Francisco thanks to his ability to stop Zorin from fleeing in his airship.

In the Moore era, the Bond films focus more intently on the relationship between Bond and his Bond Girl. These films signify a response to the second wave feminist movement and feature the "putting-back-into-place of women" (Bennett and Woollacott 2003, p. 28). A consideration of the intersection of gender with nationality helps to uncover the geopolitical significance of such representations. For example, Octopussy is an American businesswoman who uses her circus as a front to transport stolen jewels. She shares a lot in common with Tiffany Case from *Diamonds Are Forever* in that she is tricked and betrayed by her business partners and needs Bond to step in to rescue her and other American women who are placed in danger by the villain.

As noted by Black, Bond represents "reasonable order," is presented in the "role of lawman," and is described by Octopussy as "a man of principle" (2005, p. 98). The foregrounding of Bond's integrity influences our reading of these American Bond Girls who are seduced by Bond's touch away from their criminal lifestyles. Not only does his romance with Octopussy (as well as Case) function as a tipping point in the plot as it aligns her with his mission, but it also helps to connect the ethics (in addition to interests) of Britain and the United States—an ethics that ultimately is reassuring on the point of the rightfulness of the two countries. Notwithstanding the help of Octopussy, it is Bond who disarms the nuclear bomb (after stealing a car and trespassing), which the circus has unwittingly transported to a US base in West Berlin. As before, Bond's American ally gets kidnapped and Bond's mission shifts from being overtly geopolitical (i.e. preventing a nuclear bomb from exploding in the divided city of Berlin) to rescuing an accomplice and lover.

The partnership of Bond with an American Bond Girl in the Moore era reframes the 'special' Anglo-American relationship that was previously advanced by Bond's friendship with Leiter. The British male and American female partnership featured in *Moonraker, Octopussy*, and *A View to a Kill* parallel the connection between Prime Minister Margaret Thatcher and President Ronald Reagan. Although the gender dynamics in the Bond films are reversed, the Reagan-Thatcher partnership (1981–88) was often characterized as a close working relationship involving two individuals deeply committed to 'winning' the Cold War and embracing a form of neo-liberal economic thinking, which was to radically restructure the global economy. And yet, in Bond's world, gender plays a key role in tipping the balance of power between Britain and the United States to the former's advantage. Bond offers up an 'omni-competence' that not only safeguards him from the schemes of diabolical villains but also "serve[s] to both shore up traditional notions about Britain and to support notions of an effective new

Britain" (Black 2005, p. 98)—a new Britain that is untroubled by the grim realities of the 1970s, a decade characterized by industrial strikes, economic decline, and urban disorder. Margaret Thatcher, interestingly, assumed office several weeks prior to the UK premiere of *Moonraker* in June 1979.

Black contends that the films present the impression that the "British imperial mission and gentlemanly tradition were still valid, because, thanks to their character and temperament, the British still had something to teach" (2005, p. 100). While Octopussy claims that she and Bond are 'two of a kind', she (like Case) is, on the one hand, presented as being less capable and competent due to her skewed moral compass that requires a sexual recalibration from Bond, and is, on the other hand, in need of Bond's touch in order free them from kidnapping by the adversary and his hench people. So it is not just a question of character and temperament since Bond's body and abilities also are crucial to this sense of mission and his connection to American allies.

The American Bond Girl, who has taken her freedom and independence too far, gets realigned within a traditional gendered order and the United States who she represents is encouraged to seek out the support of the United Kingdom in order to safeguard their geopolitical interests. As a result, the kidnapping and capture of American Bond Girls in these films is highly significant. American men may be killed in action but they are never captured and imprisoned in the same way as American women in the Bond films. Bond's rescue of American women is critical in consolidating his (and by extension Britain's) superior position over them. It is Bond who rescues American women from captivity, echoing earlier stories in American cultural history about white women being captured by Native Americans in frontier environments (Colley 2002, p. 13). While James Bond appears far removed from 'Indian country', Bond acts a male protector to these American women, helping them traverse the complex Cold War geopolitical frontier spaces of the Caribbean, Latin America, and Asia.

Beyond Leiter and the American Bond Girls, there are a handful of other American allies that appear in this era. The most notable is J.W. Pepper played by Clifton James, a sheriff from Louisiana who appears in *Live and Let Die* as well as *The Man with the Golden Gun*. Pepper is depicted in a highly stereotypical way. He is presented as a 'redneck' or 'hillbilly', terms used to describe a rural poor white person from the southern United States who often holds and loudly professes conservative and bigoted opinions. Humor is created through the interactions of Bond with Pepper during action sequences and particularly through the contrasting of nationality and class. Bond is presented as being upper/upper-middle class, refined, and competent while Pepper is depicted as being working class, crude, and incompetent. The presence of Pepper particularly in *The Man with the Golden Gun* can also be associated with a touching or even intimate geopolitics. The film is based in Thailand and advances the impression that Pepper like America is 'out of place' in the Vietnam era. His clothing and mannerisms including brief interactions with his wife are deliberately foregrounded to emphasize this sense of cultural and physical dislocation. He is heavily sweating and appears uncomfortable about his close proximity to the locals. In comparison, Bond is shown to be an expert in martial arts and adept at fighting in a karate school as well as proficient in driving motorized canoes and navigating the streets and waterways of Bangkok. The ease he experiences while making his way through Thailand naturalizes his access, and that of Britain, to Southeast Asia. Interestingly, this mode of contrast is reserved for scenes with Pepper; Leiter is never presented in a derogatory or unflattering way in his films. But when taken together, these men are neither kidnapped nor imprisoned in the Moore era (see the discussion later in the chapter), a fate that is reserved for an American woman, Andrea Anders, who is the kept woman of the villain. Like other American women in the Moore era, she is marginalized by the villain and domesticated by Bond (and thus made useful to him) through his seduction of her.

DALTON ERA: AMERICAN-FOCUSED AND AMERICAN-CENTRIC

Although there are only two films in the Dalton era, Leiter appears in both of them. He is played by John Terry in *The Living Daylights* and David Hedison in *License to Kill*. The first Dalton film has only the briefest of references to Leiter as he, along with his female colleagues, rescue Bond from the Moroccan police in Tangiers after Bond is implicated in the assassination of a Soviet general. While Leiter offers some relevant intelligence regarding arms dealing, their relationship is a fleeting one and reveals minimal personal warmth. In contrast, *License to Kill* contains the strongest American presence as a portion of the film takes place in Miami and Bond is accompanied on screen with additional American allies like Pam Bouvier and Sharkey. In addition, the film features Hedison reprising the role of Leiter. This is the first time that an actor has played the role in more than one Bond film. This (re)casting draws attention to the fact that *Live and Let Die* is a source novel for both the films *Live and Let Die* and *License to Kill;* the torture of Leiter via shark, which takes place near the end of the novel, is featured at the beginning of *License to Kill* and inspires Bond's personal quest for revenge that is at the heart of the film's narrative (see below). This (re)casting also creates a strong narrative connection between these two Bond films released 16 years apart in different eras, which are both set in the United States while tracing narcotic-related connections with the Caribbean and Latin America. In *License to Kill*, however, the stakes are even higher as the drug trade also involves Chinese investors and the franchise reframes Chinese involvement from participating in nuclear plots to destroy America in the Connery era to being investors in a drug trade aimed at America and the American market in the Dalton era.

License to Kill also offers the most in-depth characterization of Leiter with the exception of the Craig-era films. The first half the narrative centers on Leiter's friendship with Bond who serves as the best man in his wedding (Fig. 3.2).

Prior to the ceremony, the two embark on an impromptu mission to capture a drug lord. Although the mission is serious, the two men have fun working together and their brotherly bond is foregrounded in the

Fig. 3.2 *License to Kill* (Eon Productions et al. 1989)

scenes. This friendship also becomes the driving motivation for Bond in the film. After Della is killed and the drug lord harms Leiter, Bond seeks revenge. He defies orders from M and escapes the custody of MI6 in order to avenge his friend. This personal narrative serves as a way to explain Bond's interference and Britain's stake in halting a Latin American drug trade that was on the face of it a problem for the US government and specific cities such as Los Angeles and Miami. Isthmus City was designed to suggest Panama and villain Frank Sanchez resembled General Manuel Antonio Noriega (Black 2005, p. 151). Since Britain did not have a stake in Panama or America's subsequent invasion in 1989, Bond's insertion into the struggle has to be framed as a personal mission of revenge in order to align the interests of the US and UK rather than something set against a broader Cold War geopolitical canvas and the US-led 'war on drugs'.

The film suggests that if there is a 'special relationship' between the two countries then first and foremost it has to manifest itself through the loyalty and even affection its male representatives feel for one another in the 'field' and beyond.[12] By having Bond preside as the best man at Leiter's wedding, the film idealizes the Anglo-American connection by demonstrating that the geopolitical and the personal intersect with one another. The homosocial relationship between the two men is overturned after Della's death. In the hypermasculine world south of the US border in Latin America, Sanchez's lover Lupe Lamora and CIA agent Pam Bouvier act as interim allies of Bond as they fight for his affections. Bond's touch becomes critical to managing his Hispanic and American female allies; while Bond seduces both women he grudgingly acknowledges Bouvier's proficiency as a pilot and undercover agent.

The film also uses parallelism when depicting Leiter and intertextually references *On Her Majesty's Secret Service* (*OHMSS*), the only Bond film starring George Lazenby as the title hero. The connection between Leiter in *License to Kill* and Bond in *OHMSS* is striking: both men go after a dangerous villain, believe that they have neutralized the threat, get married, and then witness the death of their bride at the hand of the villain and his hench person.[13] Both films relay the same impression that marriage is not sustainable for a secret agent; it divides the agent's loyalty between his job and family, rendering him unable and/or unwilling to do whatever it takes to complete the mission at hand.[14] In the case of *OHMSS*, however, Leiter is nowhere to be seen suggesting that he needs Bond, but Bond can endure without Leiter's support and friendship.

The 'special relationship' is an intensely homosocial one where hetero-sexual women on the one hand and homosexual men and women on the other have to be put in their places.[15] Bond only makes sexual connections with women and at times even falls in love. While *License to Kill* references the events in *OHMSS* through a conversation between Della, Leiter, and Bond after Della suggests to Bond that he should marry, Bond quickly exits the conversation. It is Leiter who explains to Della that Bond was previously married and that it ended in disaster (even though he was not in attendance at Bond's wedding). This level of intertextual referencing is rare but noteworthy. Until *License to Kill*, Leiter's marital status was never addressed in the franchise and Bond's short-lived marriage was only referenced during a conversation in *The Spy Who Loved Me* as well as the pre-credit sequence in *For Your Eyes Only* in which Bond visits his late wife's grave. As a result, the conversation between Bond and Leiter draws an even further connection between the two men across various Bond texts and sounds a warning about the professional vulnerabilities posed by marriage. This is depicted in *License to Kill* as Leiter is kidnapped and tortured immediately after his wedding, and spends the remainder of the film recovering (off-screen) from his injuries.

The American Bond Girl also plays a central role in *License to Kill*. After Leiter is hurt, Bouvier works with and under Bond. Unlike Bond's coop-erative and collaborative relationship with Leiter, he is more competitive with and hostile towards Bouvier. He underestimates her abilities, takes credit for her work (after she saves him from the bar fight), and treats her poorly even though he is aware of her growing affection for him. In addi-tion, Bond not only puts her down verbally but he also physically assaults and restrains her and his use of violent force has sexual undertones. The scene takes place in a hotel bedroom. Bond leads Bouvier in by the arm, throws her on the bed, and reaches up her skirt in order to disarm her; in the process he reveals her underwear. He then smacks her and holds her down as he questions her. A high-angle camera captures the image of Bond hovering over a terrified Bouvier and the film conveys problematic messages about gender, violence, and power (Funnell 2015a, p. 89). Even though Bouvier is one of Bond's strongest American allies, her heroism is undercut by Bond and his dismissive treatment of her. Bond reserves this type of interaction for his female American allies, as he has never spoken down to or assaulted Leiter or any other male American ally.

The film emphasizes the role that gender plays in defining and disciplin-ing Bond's relationship with American allies. Even though the film deals heavily in Latina/o stereotypes, Bouvier is treated worse than Sanchez's lover (Lupe Lamora) who is positioned through her role in the narrative as more vulnerable, needy, and deserving of Bond's protection. Tellingly, there is a moment in the film when Lamora declares her love for Bond to Bouvier, who responds with an obvious sense of contempt for her transparent neediness. But even though Bouvier despises that neediness, Bond repeatedly refuses to treat her with the same respect that he would accord Leiter. The Anglo-American connection remains thoroughly patriarchal and if anything the Latin American setting of the film—described by Bond as 'a man's world'—allows for the gender and racial disciplining of non-white and female characters, including white American women, in order to reaffirm the supremacy of Bond and through him the comparative strength of Britain geopolitically.

Brosnan Era: Bond Girl Take Over

Although Leiter was an important recurring figure in the Connery, Moore, and Dalton eras, the character does not appear in the Brosnan films. He is replaced by an older CIA veteran Jack Wade. His age, gender, and Cold War field experience is significant because it coincides with a moment in the series when Bond is clearly thought of as antediluvian by a new female and older boss, M. Wade is featured in *GoldenEye* and *Tomorrow Never Dies* and appears to take up the role as Bond's American male counterpart. The recurring casting of Joe Don Baker in the role works to firmly establish the character as Bond's CIA contact albeit one without the intimacy that Bond enjoyed with Leiter in the Dalton era.

The presence of Wade in these films is significant. As noted by Chapman, *GoldenEye* straddles the Cold War by opening with Bond destroying a Soviet chemical weapon research center. The remainder of the film takes place after the dissolution of the Soviet Union and features Bond traveling to St. Petersburg in Russia as opposed to Leningrad in the Soviet Union. Chapman argues that the relocation and reframing of Bond in a post-Cold War context is nuanced. The film presents the impression that while the Communist regime has fallen, there still remains a threat from Russia and a new distribution of intelligence and military power (2000, p. 253). This can be taken a step further as it represents an even greater threat, as the reassuring presence of M's opposite number General Gogol has disappeared.[16] *The Living Daylights* already introduced viewers to this more fluid view of a declining Soviet Union where Gogol is now working for the

Foreign Service and no longer heads up the KGB. Thus, Bond must also be a figure that straddles the Cold War and post-Cold War eras in order to protect Britain from these lingering threats and uncertain networks of power and influence.

In *GoldenEye*, M's description of Bond as a "dinosaur" and "relic" shape the impression that the world around Bond has changed, particularly in terms of gender and international politics, while Bond remains somewhat rooted in the past (Chapman 2000, pp. 252, 256). But it also raises the possibility that his old methods such as seducing women, relying on his intuition, and knowing when to use his touch to good effect may be outdated. Is Bond ill equipped to cope with a new geopolitical and gender order? This becomes a site of struggle between Bond and his new boss, as well as the various women with whom he interacts. In this changing climate, Bond finds support in the field by way of an old Cold War CIA handler (himself a well-connected 'dinosaur') who helps Bond navigate his way through these fluid and confusing times. Black notes that Bond (with his old-school ways) "is vindicated throughout the film" as he "thwarts the GoldenEye conspiracy, he kills the three leading villains, and he wins Natalya's heart, as well as her body" (2005, p. 164). In these fluid times, moreover, Bond strikes up an unlikely sounding strategic alliance with a former KGB agent and now Russian mafia boss Valentin Zukovsky who is the main business competitor with the man (codename Janus) he is trying to track down. It is revealed that the two men know each other, and Bond actually shot Zukovsky on a Cold War-era mission. Both Zukovsky and Wade stand as stark reminders to Bond that you cannot always choose your allies, especially when the geopolitical compass is being re-calibrated. But if you need to trust someone then it would appear safer to trust men who understand your profession.

In the remaining Brosnan films, however, it is the Bond Girl who embodies American geopolitical interests. Bond works with Dr. Christmas Jones in *The World Is Not Enough* and Agent Jinx Johnson in *Die Another Day*. The films cast as Bond Girls a notable Hollywood star (Halle Berry) and an actress (Denise Richards) who found notoriety (if not acclaim) in *Starship Troopers* (Verhoeven 1997) and both were already associated with the action genre to some degree. Interestingly, neither character works for the CIA: Jones is a scientist employed by the International Decommissioning Agency (IDA) while Johnson is an agent for the National Security Agency (NSA). However, both women work for agencies addressing global challenges, namely nuclear decommissioning in the former Soviet Union and

North Korean militarism. This shift away from the pairing of Bond with a CIA field agent particularly in *Die Another Day* can be attributed to the release of the film after 9/11 as the United States began to focus more on national security (i.e. looking inward) rather than international interests/ threats (i.e. looking outward). Following 9/11, the CIA came under fire for not doing enough to stop the terror attacks and this perception might have influenced the decision to focus on the NSA (Zegart 2008, p. 3). Moreover, both the IDA and the NSA focus more on signals intelligence gathering than field-based work. This becomes one way to contrast Bond and his (Cold War) field-based instincts with American female allies who are involved in gathering a different kind of intelligence (in a post–9/11 context). It also provides an opportunity for Bond and his touch-oriented methods to endure and, like *GoldenEye* and *Tomorrow Never Dies*, harkens back to the tried and tested Cold War days. One illustration of this is the value Bond places on a global network of personal contacts he has built up over the years, however trivial, such as hotel staff recognizing him in Hong Kong and his ability to sense danger when a female hotel employee suddenly turns up at his room for an unscheduled massage. She turns out to be working for a Chinese spy and Bond feels her out both physically and intuitively before blowing her cover (much like he did to Dr. Goodhead in *Moonraker*).

Die Another Day features one of the strongest American Bond Girls. Johnson is a highly competent agent who is comparable to Bond in all aspects of the job. This is significant given the poor treatment of black characters in the franchise like Rosie Carver. And yet, the representation of Johnson shares much in common with Carver in *Live and Let Die*. Both women sleep with Bond early on in their respective films and their sexual encounters require little seduction on the part of Bond. If anything Carver actually expresses a strong desire not to fall into that sexual pattern of behavior but then changes her mind after being scared by voodoo. Johnson never expresses any such reluctance but this is signaled as sexual confidence rather than weakness as in the case of Carver. In addition, Charles Burnetts notes the names of the two characters reflect upon one another:

Parallels between Jinx and Carver are signaled furthermore by questions levelled at Jinx by Bond with regards to her name and its connotations of 'bad luck', echoing the anxieties featured in *Live and Let Die* particularly in regards to the treatment of Voodoo culture and the film's mystification of black identity. If Bond's distrust of women is officially uninfluenced by race, the playful foregrounding of luck and the supernatural in these comments seems marked again by the possibility of unnatural, demonic powers at play when Bond encounters a black woman. (2015, p. 67)

Although Johnson is positioned as Bond's true love and partner in the film, her standing in the narrative is challenged by the foregrounding of Bond's romantic and professional relationships with two white British women: Miranda Frost and Moneypenny. Both women offer Bond support in the field (although Frost is a double agent) and are featured in steamy sex scenes (one imagined and one material) with him as well. Burnetts argues that these sexual encounters help to return the film to "a topos of white hetero-normativity" (2015, p. 67) and work to reduce the competence and strength of Johnson as an ally.

In the Brosnan era, the CIA is presented as being male, masculine, heterosexual, and white, as well as being field based while MI6 enjoys a female head and a black deputy in the form of Charles Robinson. However, Bond's American allies from other agencies have greater diversity in terms of gender and race, and are more intelligence based. Spy work in the Brosnan era is coded or defined particularly through gender: while men are field-based agents, women do signals intelligence gathering. This taps into broader gendered conventions in the Brosnan era in which M, Bond's boss, is not only presented as a woman but is also characterized repeatedly as a bureaucrat or "bean counter." The films present a clear contrast between M's strategic calculation of risk and Bond's instinct-driven field work. In the end, Bond's hands-on approach always brings about the best results. This leads to the perception that intelligence gathering, which is coded as feminine, is not as effective as taking action, which is coded as masculine.

And when M does enter the field in films such as *The World Is Not Enough*, she is captured and Bond is forced to rescue her from captivity. So while these films foreground geopolitical and gender re-ordering, the reality is that for Bond's female allies (and now boss) the nature of the Anglo-American connection remains largely intact. If the women appear too powerful, resourceful, and capable they then are literally put in their place. They either fall victim to the arch-villain who captures them and/or require Bond to rescue/seduce them so that they can be better acquainted with the true order of things, namely Bond as protector-figure and field agent.

CRAIG ERA: RE-VISIONING AMERICAN IDENTITIES

The Craig-era films constitute a rebooting of the Bond franchise and much like Bond, Leiter is given his own origin story. He is re-introduced and re-imagined in the franchise, and *Casino Royale* features the pair first meeting at the casino and depicts the start of their working relationship. After Bond loses his money at the poker game, he picks up a steak knife with the intention of killing LeChiffre. He is stopped by Leiter who tells him that he/the CIA/America wants to bankroll Bond so that the British agent can defeat (rather than kill) LeChiffre. Leiter shows a faith in Bond that is not shared by Vesper Lynd, his British love interest and UK official bank roller in the film. It is this trust, based initially upon strategic risk assessment, which Bond and Leiter share, that has defined their 'special relationship' throughout the series. A fellow field agent (like Leiter) is shown to appreciate better the real-time realities of fieldwork rather than office-based civil servants (like Lynd) working with conventional indicators of risk management. And unlike Bond's female American allies, the two men even have time to talk contemporary geopolitics without having to negotiate the usual sexual politics associated with American women. They can share a beer rather than a bed.

The 'special relationship' between Leiter and Bond continues into *Quantum of Solace*. Leiter goes out of his way to offer Bond a 'heads up' so that he can evade CIA capture while enjoying a convivial drink in a bar. He is eventually promoted for aiding Bond and getting the mission done. Originally, Leiter was supposed to play a much larger role in the narrative but his part was diminished during a succession of rewrites.[17] In *Skyfall*, Leiter does not appear nor does any other American ally and/or agent. This is consistent with the more British focus of the film in which a restored Bond emerges as the super British spy.[18] With no outside assistance, Bond is forced to rely on his own wits with some support from a younger female field agent and younger male Q. An aging M does not survive the final encounter with the archenemy Raoul Silva, and a noticeably middle-aged spy and his new male handler Gareth Mallory are shown to be the ones with the necessary experience and wherewithal to endure. This is carried over into *Spectre*, in which Bond undertakes a solo mission sanctioned by the late Dench's M while under the surveillance of C, the head of the Joint Intelligence Service, who is intent on closing down the '00' section. Bond receives covert tactical support from Moneypenny and Q even after Mallory reluctantly instructs them not to help (while still covering for his secret agent). In the end, it is Bond *and* Mallory who each dispatch of one of the film's villains in intercutting sequences—Bond removes the external security threat (Blofeld, the head of SPECTRE) while Mallory removes the internal one (C, a secret agent working for SPECTRE)—thus restoring order while justifying the existence of MI6 and the ongoing need for the touch-based approaches of secret agents in the current era of digital surveillance.

In the Craig era, there are no American Bond Girls or female ally agents. The films share a lot in common with the Connery era given its representation of British and American geopolitical interests via the heterosexual male body. Only this time, Leiter is played by a black actor, Jeffrey Wright. The change in race certainly has significance. Given the supportive role Leiter plays to Bond, he appears to be aligned with the other black sidekicks featured in Hollywood films. The biracial 'buddy narrative' was frequently used in Hollywood action films of the 1980s and 1990s. It featured the pairing of a white hero with a black buddy who played a supportive role (e.g. the *Lethal Weapon* series [Donner 1987, 1989, 1992, 1998]). These films presented biracial homosocial relationships that did not necessarily challenge the prevailing social order of white primacy through the figure of the lone and unattached male protector figure (Guerrero 1993, p. 239). In *Casino Royale*, Leiter is arguably positioned as a "black buddy" to Bond and never steals his spotlight. While Bond is beaten, battered, and bruised, Leiter is not physically harmed. While Bond finds a way to rise up against adversity—he is poisoned and dies in *Casino Royale* but is revived and returns to the poker table looking refreshed—Leiter never appears to be in mortal danger. While Bond is featured at the heart of the narrative and stars in numerous high-octane action sequences, Leiter remains on the periphery of the narrative and the film's action. He lends money discreetly. He advises discreetly. He reinforces discreetly. He never throws a punch in anger or shoots a weapon. The film stays true to the typical biracial buddy narrative whereby the white protagonist is the primary hero and the black buddy offers him support, much of it vital but 'support' nonetheless. One of the striking aspects of this contemporary relationship is that Bond never discusses his sexual conquests. By way of contrast, in the Connery era, Leiter is complicit with Bond's sexual strategies, and even asks about how Bond managed to persuade Pussy Galore to help them in *Goldfinger*.

This change in race extends beyond Leiter to Moneypenny who is played by black actor Naomie Harris. This is a significant development as

Moneypenny is the most recurring character and longest running ally of Bond in the series. Although Moneypenny has long flirted with Bond, she also aids him in navigating the office space and politics of MI6 by warning him, for instance, about his boss' mood. According to Kristen Shaw, Moneypenny "effectively replaces Leiter as the 'black helper' in *Skyfall...* [but] is presented as a threat to Bond as she competes with him for heroic status" (2015, p. 73). One reason for this can be attributed to nationality. On the one hand, Leiter circulates in the same networks as Bond but never competes with him on the same field. His is presented as a positive and supportive figure that assists Bond and never challenges his sexual prowess. As noted earlier, Leiter is never shown to be the subject of sexual desire (even when he marries Della in *License to Kill*). On the other hand, Moneypenny performs beside Bond in action and attempts to occupy the same field. This renders her a competitive and threatening character and one that is challenged throughout the film after a disastrous mission in Istanbul (Shaw 2015, p. 73).

Gender also plays a role in their differing representations. *Skyfall* presents the impression that male agents belong in the field over female ones because they are older, more experienced, and have greater proficiency (Dodds 2014, p. 220). Moreover, while male agents like Bond and Leiter trust their guts and each other, female agents like Moneypenny follow the rules and orders, which can lead to catastrophic consequences. Unlike Leiter who believes that Bond can defeat LeChiffre in the poker tournament, Moneypenny is unsure if Bond can defeat the man he is fighting on the train; she caves to M who commands her to "take the shot" and accidently shoots Bond who tumbles into the river below. While Leiter is promoted for putting his career on the line for Bond, Moneypenny is demoted to a desk job for following orders and 'killing' 007 who was presumed by M to be dead. Moreover, Moneypenny is not given the chance to prove herself to Bond or the audience at large. She disappears for large portions of the film and is not present in the climax when Bond defeats Silva. Overall, Moneypenny is characterized and scrutinized in ways that Leiter (let alone any other British agent) never has been. While Bond has never mocked Leiter—teasing yes, but mocking no—he shows obvious disdain and condescension towards Moneypenny and almost revels in her shortcomings.

In the Craig era, neither Leiter nor Moneypenny are presented as being equals to Bond in terms of screen time or narrative significance. Their difference in character treatment can be attributed to their gender. While

Leiter is given a positive character trajectory and is promoted for his trust in Bond, Moneypenny is punished for following M's order and is demoted for not trusting in Bond enough. Although the Craig-era films are revisionist particularly in terms of race, they re-inscribe the gendered conventions of the Bond franchise in which men navigate the field and women are relegated to the role of intelligence officers.

THE ANGLO-AMERICAN CONNECTION

The intersection of nationality with gender, race, and class strongly informs the nature of Bond's temporary and long-term alliances. The 'special relationship' between Britain and the United States is reflected through the collaboration of Bond with American allies. In the first four decades, this American connection is facilitated through an array of recurring male characters like Leiter, Wade, and Pepper. On the one hand, Bond develops co-operative relationships with Leiter and Wade based on the shared geopolitical interests of their agencies and nations (be they real or imagined). Bond views each man as his equal given their common social locations (as white, upper/upper-middle class, men) and professions (as field agents), which leads to mutual respect. However, Bond remains the primary hero of the films while Leiter and Wade serve more as 'yes' men who sanction and support Bond's missions. On the other hand, Bond is pit against Pepper who is positioned differently in the narrative due to his lower class and culture (as a "redneck"), as well as his profession as a parish sheriff (rather than jet-setting spy). As a result, Pepper lacks the qualities that would render him an adept ally and equal to Bond—namely, social grace, knowledge in the field, cultural competency, and access to resources—and is thus presented as a figure of ridicule in the series.

Beginning in the Moore era, Bond is paired onscreen with various American women with whom he develops both professional and romantic relationships. Although many of these Bond Girls are also secret agents (like Goodhead, Bouvier, and Johnson), they are not treated as equals by Bond in their respective films. Their relationship with him is inherently competitive as they challenge his dominance in 'the field' and even the bedroom (which arguably falls within the purview of Bond's 'fieldwork'). The Moore-era films in particular reiterate the problematic notion that in order to pull a woman up in society, you have to push a man down and thus women need to remain inferior in order for men to maintain their social standing. Moreover, these relationships are defined by traditional gender roles and this is clearly conveyed through Bond's touch. While Bond never physically interacts with his male American allies beyond a customary handshake, he has both sexual and physical encounters with American women that help to establish and confirm his masculinity and (narrative and embodied) dominance.

The shift from male to female American allies is accompanied by a shift in the representation of the 'special relationship' between Britain and the United States. By presenting Bond's dominance over the American Bond Girl, the films work to reframe geopolitical relations in an embodied realm whereby Britain is presented as the key superpower and the United States is portrayed in a supportive and somewhat dependent role. Moreover, Bond demonstrates his superpower using haptics in other key ways: it is Bond who pushes the button in order to destroy the dangerous object (e.g. *For Your Eyes Only*), makes the final dramatic escape from near certain danger (e.g. *The Spy Who Loved Me*), and breaks into foreign/guarded places and spaces with ease (e.g. *Octopussy*). The haptic geographies of Bond remind us of how his body and the bodies of others are caught up in a 'special relationship' that is embodied, albeit unequally.

In the Craig era, the relationship between Bond and his American allies is being re-framed once again. The re-imagining of Leiter as a black man influences the power dynamics between the two characters and their respective nations. This is signaled quite powerfully through touch. When Leiter first approaches Bond in *Casino Royale* on the stairs, he grabs Bond's arm and pulls him in close. The film features a close-up shot of Leiter's hand positioned on Bond's forearm just above the steak knife Bond intends to use to kill LeChiffre. Bond appears notably surprised that Leiter is challenging his actions/intentions/resolve via touch.

Through dialogue, however, the film works to recode this relationship via the biracial buddy narrative. Leiter introduces himself to Bond as "your brother from Langley." The use of the term "brother" is significant here. The term was often employed during the civil rights movement of the 1960s to express the unity formed between black men based on their shared experience of oppression and racial strife (Alexander 2013, p. 368). Moreover, as Bryant Keith Alexander notes, "the status of being a 'brother' often invokes a culturally specific performative criterion of a Black masculine ideal" (2013, p. 368). This exchange between Leiter and Bond can be interpreted in a few ways. First, it demonstrates that Leiter perceives Bond as being his equal in the field. He not only physically stops Bond from making a bad decision, but he explains his intrusion by using language that works to connect the two men and their shared field-based objectives. Second, the use of the term works to 'Other' Leiter in a franchise that has long centered on white masculinity. He follows up this self-descriptor with the statement that he is less proficient in poker ("I'm bleeding chips") and requires Bond's help in order to trap LeChiffre ("You have a better chance, I'll stake you"). Through this exchange, Leiter effectively positions himself as a helpmate/enabler of Bond.

The conversation between Bond and Leiter is whispered for the most part and the two men stand extremely close to one another and less than a foot apart at times (Fig. 3.3).

Their conversation is captured in close-up and medium close-up shots, which are usually reserved for more intimate exchanges (such as courting or kissing) that denote a sense of familiarity or a desire for it. When Leiter moves into Bond's space, Bond does not cede the territory or challenge the invasion. Instead Bond stands close to Leiter as he accepts his terms for an alliance. The two men show a sense of trust, transparency, and even intimacy that Bond lacks with his other supposed (female) allies like Lynd and Moneypenny (relying more on Q especially in *Spectre*). Thus, in the Craig era, Leiter possesses some of the qualities traditionally associated

Fig. 3.3   *Casino Royale* (Eon Productions et al. 2006)

with the American Bond Girl and perhaps helps to prepare the viewers for the absence of this character in *Skyfall* and *Spectre*.[19]As the film series demonstrates, the Anglo-American connection is something that can be resurrected as and when needed, but as of late (with *Skyfall* and *Spectre*) it has been put on ice.

NOTES

1. For a detailed discussion, see Dodds (2003).
2. For a detailed discussion, see Funnell (2011a).
3. For a detailed discussion, see Balio's *United Artists* (1978).
4. For a detailed discussion, see Amis (1965).
5. Dr. No is of Chinese and German descent. He is played by Joseph Wiseman who is presented in 'yellowface'; a racist form of cinematic representation. For a longer reflection on this practice, see Park's *Yellow Future* (2010).
6. In the novel, Goldfinger intended to rob Fort Knox. This aspect of the plot was widely criticized given the magnitude of such a feat. Chapman notes that the film redresses this issue by adjusting Goldfinger's plan and, in the process, creating a more exciting finale in which Bond has to disarm a bomb (Chapman 2000, p. 101).
7. The film also taps into the popularity of *Dirty Harry* (Siegel 1971) and its sequels by having Bond discard his Walther PPK for a Smith and Wesson .44 Magnum, the same long-barreled handgun used by Clint Eastwood's Harry Callaghan (Chapman 2000, pp. 154–55).
8. For a detailed discussion of the representation of black women in the Bond films, see Burnetts (2015), Shaw (2015), and Wagner (2015).
9. Rosie Carver is a double agent whose primary allegiance is with the villain. As a result, Leiter appears in the film in order to embody a more loyal and reassuring image of American allegiance.
10. For a discussion of Bond Girl costuming, see Funnell (2008) and Severson (2015).
11. For a detailed discussion of female domestication in the franchise, see Funnell (2011b).
12. This affection is clearly relayed in the novels. In *Live and Let Die*, for example, Fleming writes: "Bond's heart was full. He looked out of the window. 'Tell him to get well quickly,' he said abruptly. 'Tell him I miss him.'" (1954, p. 177).
13. Moreover, in both films Bond leaves the service: he resigns in *OHMSS* and is suspended in *License to Kill*.
14. For a discussion of marriage in the Bond franchise, see Nepa (2015).

15. For a detailed discussion, see Black (2005).
16. For a detailed discussion of General Gogol, see Chap. 4.
17. See Broccoli (2008).
18. For a detailed reading of Bond's restorative narrative in *Skyfall*, see Dodds (2014).
19. There is certainly a precedent for this reading. As Funnell notes, *Casino Royale* features character hybridity and Craig's Bond is presented through some of the imaging conventions of the Bond Girl such as emerging from the sea in a bathing costume. See Funnell (2011a).

CHAPTER 4

Shaken, Not Stirred: Shifting Representations of the Soviet Union and Russia

As an agent of MI6, James Bond is sent on important missions in order to safeguard the national security of Britain and its closest allies. In spite of various international conflicts and shifting geopolitical relations over the past 53 years, the Bond films remain focused on the consistent influence (both real and fictional) of the Soviet Union and later Russia in shaping international relations and facilitating global terrorism. While the Soviet Union does not play a meaningful role in the first film, *Dr. No*, Cold War tension strongly frames the narrative arc as Bond discovers that the evil genius, Dr. No, and SPECTRE, a nationally unaffiliated terrorist organization, are hell-bent on stoking antipathies between the United States and the Soviet Union. By interfering with the missile/rocket testing programs, Dr. No hopes to bring these superpowers to the brink of war. Even though the villain is dismissive of geopolitical divisions such as the 'East' and 'West', viewing them as merely points on a compass, he and his SPECTRE-funded operation at Crab Key depend on those very cartographies of the Cold War to enable their pursuit of chaos and extortion.[1]

The Bond films from *From Russia with Love* onwards depict Britain's complicated and shifting relationship with the Soviet Union through Bond's interactions with various characters over the course of the series, and at least 15 Bond films feature Soviet/Russian characters and locations (Lawless 2014, p. 82). These relations vary greatly from deadly exchanges and betrayals to professional appraisals and love affairs. Other films like *Live and Let Die* do not feature Soviet figures directly but include references

© The Editor(s) (if applicable) and The Author(s) 2017
L. Funnell, K. Dodds, *Geographies, Genders and Geopolitics of
James Bond*, DOI 10.1057/978-1-137-57024-6_4

through dialogue such as the comment by Sherriff Pepper of the Louisiana State Police that, "We got a swamp of black Russians driving boats to beat the band down here." His throwaway remark to Bond is not challenged but reveals how the register of race is being mapped onto the ideology of communism and judged as being incompatible with American life. Additionally, Bond encounters Soviet/Russian objects such as secret communication machines, tanks, planes, and secret plans that also convey geopolitical meaning, such as the chase scene in *GoldenEye* in which Bond commandeers a Russian tank and drives it around the streets of St. Petersburg, crashing into vehicles and structures that obstruct his path (see later in the chapter).

In helping audiences account for and audit Bond's personal dealings with the Soviet Union and later Russia, the film franchise utilizes binary pairs to depict and differentiate good and bad Soviet/Russian characters. In a binary system, two terms are not simply defined (as individuals) but they are defined through difference (via their relationship). According to Joan Scott, "meaning is made through implicit or explicit contrast" and is based on the assumption "that a positive definition rests on the negation or repression of something represented as antithetical to it" (1990, p. 137). As a result, fixed oppositions are in fact interdependent as they derive meaning through contrast (1990, p. 137). Binary terms, according to Jacques Derrida, are positioned in a hierarchy in which one term is viewed as dominant and primary while the other is viewed as weaker, secondary, and/or derivative (qtd. in Scott 1990, p. 137). Moreover, as Elizabeth Gross notes, "the primary or dominant term derives its privilege from the curtailment or suppression of its opposite" (1986, p. 73).

In his structural analysis of the Bond novels, Umberto Eco argues that Ian Fleming utilized a series of binary pairs to shape character relations. These include Bond and M, Bond and the Villain, the Villain and the Woman, and Bond and the Woman (1979, p. 164). In a similar way, the Bond films also rely on binary oppositions when depicting Soviet/Russian characters and relations in various films utilizing gender, sexual orientation, age, occupation, and nationality/national loyalties to contrast. These binary oppositions are shaped and sometimes sharpened by how these encounters and relationships unfold in the field. But these depictions of the Soviet Union and its spying and military personnel are capable of being 'hardened' and/or 'softened' depending on the prevailing geopolitical context. For example, the office of the head of the Soviet spying machine (M's opposite number) is usually presented in darkened conditions with the Red Square of Moscow as a backdrop in sharp contrast to M's office that appears brighter, more intimate, and convivial. In *The Spy Who Loved Me*, however, General Gogol, head of the KGB, is depicted in a far more sympathetic fashion as he shows compassion towards his own agents and even exudes warmth towards Bond and M when they work together for a common cause. It is also the first time in the series that M and Gogol are in a room together to discuss a common mission and this sympathetic rendering of Gogol continues throughout the series and most notably in *Octopussy* when he is pitted against more hardline Soviet senior army officers such as General Orlov.

This chapter examines three binary oppositions that help to shape and trace the shifting geopolitical position of the Soviet Union and Russia in the Bond franchise: the Bond Girl and the Bad Girl, Bond and Soviet female agents, and Older and Younger Soviet Generals/Agents. These personal encounters and relationships are crucial to the franchise because the material-military power of the Soviet Union in the Cold War era of Bond is rarely the subject of sustained exposure or reflection. In *You Only Live Twice*, Soviet representatives are shown to be discussing global space matters with British and US colleagues inside a telecommunications 'golf-ball' structure, and the scene serves more to emphasize the British as 'honest brokers' rather than remind viewers that the other parties are the real space powers. For all its Cold War origins, the Soviet Union in the 1960s and 1970s was eclipsed by the transnational operations of SPECTRE, and Bond is not shown as operating in Russian territory until *A View to a Kill*.

BOND GIRL AND THE BAD GIRL

Over the course of the franchise, Bond interacts with both 'good' and 'bad' women whose position in the narrative is determined by their national affiliation, loyalty to Bond, and support of his mission. Moreover, their characterization is dependent on the nature/depth of the romantic relationship they develop with Bond. A woman is considered a Bond Girl if she loves and supports Bond, and a Bad Girl if she aligns with the villain over Bond and works against Britain. While Bond encounters some 16 Russian/Soviet female characters in the franchise, only a small number qualify as Bond Girls and Bad Girls, and most often these women are depicted in diegetic contrast. In comparison, the franchise features more than double the number of Soviet/Russian men and Katerina Lawless has investigated in detail their representation, examining, for instance, their proficiency in English, use of the Russian language, and how they are positioned in the narrative as representativeness of Russia/Soviet Union (Lawless 2014). We supplement this useful analytical work with a specific focus on how gender and geopolitics intersect to shape the relationship between the Soviet/Russian Bond Girl and the Bad Girl.

From Russia with Love

As the second film in the series, *From Russia with Love* solidifies the generic formula of the franchise while establishing the geopolitical context of the early Bond films. Although the film is set during the Cold War, it presents SPECTRE rather than SMERSH (a Soviet counterintelligence agency) as the instigator of tension between the West and the East. This artistic/screenplay decision was taken in consultation with Ian Fleming as his novel placed far greater emphasis on the continued involvement of SMERSH (Fleming 2015, p. 109). In September 1955, Fleming travelled to Istanbul and his visit coincided with a General Assembly of Interpol meeting (confirming Turkey's status as a NATO/Western ally) and an outbreak of Greek-Turkish inter-communal violence (Fleming 2015, p. 109). As a result, the city is depicted as being on the (literal) border of the Cold War as well as on the edge of Europe and Asia. Bond's arrival in Istanbul and his subsequent car ride from the city's airport to the offices of Station T in the midst of the Grand Bazaar is punctuated by a matter-of-fact revelation by Bond's driver that the Cold War is a game, with its peculiar rules regarding surveillance and the role of Eastern European agents supporting their Soviet masters. As the driver informs Bond, it is the 'turn' of Bulgarian agents to trail their car and that he is not going to escape their monitoring gaze.

Having established that the Cold War in Istanbul has banal and mundane qualities, the geopolitics of the narrative are complicated by the return of SPECTRE. In many early Bond films, SPECTRE tries to pit the United States against the Soviet Union, and Britain intervenes as an intermediary to diffuse the possibility of further conflict. The role of this third party was to allow the prevailing geopolitics of the Cold War to be re-calibrated and to provide opportunity for Bond to work in between the gaps of the US-UK-Soviet relationship through his personal interactions in a range of formal and informal sites and spaces. This is stated explicitly in *From Russia with Love* as well as *You Only Live Twice*. The former opens with a chess match between a Canadian player (Adams) and Kronsteen, an Eastern European grandmaster who produces a stunning victory over his Western opponent. While chess becomes more bound up with Cold War tensions in the midst of the 1972 World Chess Championship, it still conveys geopolitical friction in the 1963 film. As it turns out, Kronsteen is actually a senior secret operative for SPECTRE who devises a plot to steal a Soviet decoder device (with the intention of selling it back to them) using a female lure to distract Bond and leave him vulnerable to mortal attack; his death is framed as vengeance for his killing of Dr. No (in the previous film).[2] Kronsteen is not only vilified for his plan but also for masquerading as an Eastern/Soviet loyalist and this castigation of national traitors is continued throughout the film.

The success of Kronsteen's plot hinges on two Soviet women—Tatiana Romanova and Rosa Klebb —who are contrasted in the narrative via age, nationalism, gender expression, beauty, and sexual orientation. While the film idealizes the former for her willingness to work with Bond, it demonizes the latter for targeting him and challenging his libidinal masculinity, which represents the strength and potency of Britain and the West. Bond's first contact and (jocular) encounter with Romanova is through her picture, which he gazes at while discussing his assignment and the romantic appeal of Istanbul and the Bosporus with Moneypenny in her office back in London. This one-sided interplay, however awkward, is important in offering up a sympathetic and appealing vision of Romanova, and importantly positions her as an attractive character who is fundamentally unthreatening to Bond and Britain. With apparent insouciance, Bond takes his pen and writes 'From Russia with Love' on the photograph of Romanova given to him by M.[3] If Bond is entering a 'trap' in Istanbul regarding access to the decoder then Romanova is to be understood as someone who is unknowingly drawn into this conflict and subsequently motivated by her growing love for Bond.

As the Bond Girl in the film, Romanova is defined by her striking beauty and sexual appeal to Bond, and this is the primary reason why she is selected to be a pawn. Although she is positioned as Bond's love interest, Romanova remains a loyal and unthreatening subject of the Soviet Union, as she believes that she is acting on the behest of her country. In other words, her theft of the decoder and defection to the West is depicted as a mission objective and not her personal desire. She is unaware of the SPECTRE plot and follows the orders of her female superior, Klebb, who she believes is still a colonel in SMERSH. Klebb, however, is now aligned with SPECTRE, ranking number 3 in their organization and works as their chief operations officer. She selects Romanova for the role and oversees the operation.

Romanova and Klebb differ in terms of their age and this factors into their working relationship. Romanova is young, presumably in her twenties, and her age (along with her beauty) renders her a suitable love interest for Bond. It also lends support for reading her character as naïve since age is often associated with knowledge and experience in the Bond franchise while youth is linked to inexperience and errors in judgment (Dodds 2015, p. 220). In comparison, Klebb is much older—Lotte Lenya was in her mid-sixties when the film was shot—and her age, which is emphasized by her short hair, renders her unsuitable as a love interest (Funnell 2011b, p. 203). As a point of comparison, Judi Dench was 61 when she was cast as M and her characterization as a matriarch with maternal overtones certainly strengthens across the Brosnan and Craig eras.[4] Although Klebb is not presented with maternal qualities, her age (in addition to her military rank of a colonel in SMERSH) arguably increases her authority over Romanova as it taps into the broader conception of Mother Russia, a national personification and matrifocal characterization (Rancour-Laferriere 1995, p. 138) that works to imbue Klebb with national authority over Romanova who is positioned as an obedient child. This is made strikingly clear when Klebb conducts an interview with Romanova in order to determine whether she is suitable for the mission bequeathed to her, and asks her about her past love life.

The two characters are also contrasted in terms of gender expression. On the one hand, Romanova is presented with a more traditionally and aesthetically feminine image, which positions her as an object of desire for Bond. In addition to wearing costumes that draw attention to her figure— such as a formfitting blue turtleneck and a transparent white blouse—she is also depicted in various stages of undress. Bond first sees Romanova in person through a periscope that has been hidden in the floor of a building. From this low angle, Bond can only view her from the waist, and later the shoulders, down and this renders her bare legs the focal point.[5] Later, Bond spies Romanova again only this time through the window of his hotel room. For a brief moment, Bond (and by extension the audience) gets a glimpse of Romanova, naked, climbing into bed. When Bond enters the room, her body is covered in a sheet but her black choker necklace tied into a bow conveys the impression that she is a gift (sent by Klebb) for Bond to unwrap. Later in the film, when the pair is travelling from Turkey by train, Bond provides Romanova with various flowing nightgowns that not only emphasize her cleavage due to their stylization but also reaffirm her positioning in the narrative as an object of desire now possessed by Bond and travelling under the cover story of being a Mrs. Somerset, a name that emphasizes her apparent transformation into a recently married 'British' woman returning from her honeymoon. On the other hand, and remaining faithful to Fleming's source novel, Klebb is presented with a more masculine image that confirms her authoritative and unattractive position in the narrative. When masquerading as a SMERSH colonel, she wears an olive green military uniform replete with a jacket, shirt, and tie—a uniform that is worn by other male Soviet generals like Gorgel, Orlov, and Pushkin throughout the franchise (see later in the chapter). However, she maintains this style of dress while working at SPECTRE, appearing in olive and neutral colored suits and coats with high collars that are straight cut and obscure her frame. Even when she dresses up as part of the housekeeping staff in the final scene of the film, she is not sexualized or fetishized in a 'French maid costume'; instead, she wears a bulky uniform and a grey wig that emphasize her age rather than sexual desirability in order to be overlooked by Bond, thus rendering him vulnerable for attack. The venom-laced blade hidden in her shoe, which she used earlier to deadly effect, symbolizes her devious nature. She is cruel, manipulative, and vindictive with personal qualities that she shares with the male SPECTRE assassin Red Grant who is redeemed, in part, by his apparent conviviality with Bond in the earliest stages of their encounters on the Orient Express. Grant appears to have the capacity to be charming and enacts a series of private-school mannerisms (e.g. calling Bond "old man") with which Bond is likely familiar. By comparison, Bond never has a conversation with Klebb in the film and thus her backstory remains unknown; this renders her one of the most villainous and unpredictable figures in the film if not the franchise at large.

The intersection of geopolitics, gender, and sexual orientation conveys powerful messages about each woman. As noted by Thomas Barrett, "Russian women were often coded as dangerous for their non-normative sexuality. They either used their feminine allures for political ends such as the image of Catherine the Great with her enormous sexual appetites… Or they 'perverted' their femininity to become 'manly' fighters, such as the lesbian coded Women's Battalion of Death" (2015, p. 42). The film emphasizes Romanova's heterosexuality and desirability through her sexual encounters with Bond and past history of male lovers. She is set up as a female lure and successfully initiates a sexual relationship with Bond.

However, as Barrett notes, "If she is a femme fatale, she is an unintentional one, which diffuses most of the power that comes with that trope" (2015, p. 45). Throughout the film, Romanova is more ingénue than femme fatale, finding herself in a position where she is so in love with Bond that she clearly relishes playing her role as Mrs. Somerset as opposed to performing her professional duties as an employee of the Soviet Embassy in Istanbul. She even has to be carried to a waiting car by Bond, in the midst of their escape from the Orient Express, because she is incapable of standing after being drugged by Grant, a gesture that not only conveys romance between the pair but also her positioning as a damsel in distress in need of his repeated saving.

In comparison, the film presents Klebb as a predatory lesbian suitor who challenges Bond for the affections of the Bond Girl and in that sense remains faithful to Fleming's unflattering descriptions of her as a character. Klebb's homosexuality is suggested during her initial meeting with Romanova in her office. After commending Romanova for her excellent record, she instructs her to take off her jacket and turn around, commenting "Hmm, you are a fine looking girl." After telling her to sit down, she inquires about Romanova's sexual history and chastises Romanova for protesting about being asked "intimate questions." Klebb then hands a picture (of Bond) to Romanova as she leans on the desk and places her hand on Romanova's leg, which clearly makes the young woman uncomfortable. After threatening Romanova with death if she shares information about her new mission, Klebb stands behind the seated woman and caresses her shoulders and face with her hand (Fig. 4.1).

While sexual harassment abounds in the early Bond films, Klebb's advances are deemed inappropriate due to the politics of representation in the franchise at the time. Bond's touch, by comparison, is not only shown to be surer but also welcomed by the women he encounters, such as the two unnamed Gypsies he meets midway through the film in addition to Romanova.[6]

Rooted in the British lover literary tradition, the Bond films differentiate Bond's heteronormative heroic identity from the deviant attitudes and behaviors of his adversaries (Black 2005, pp. 96–97). In the early Bond films, homosexuality was considered a form of sexual deviance and linked with notions of criminality and moral impropriety (see Chap. 2). As a result, Klebb is depicted as a "middle-aged sexual deviant" (Funnell 2011b, p. 203) who attempts to deny Bond and his phallic masculinity—which according to Black is emblematic of the maleness of the British

Fig. 4.1   *From Russia with Love* (Eon Productions et al. 1963)

Secret Service (and public anxieties at the time of homosexual double agents who fled to the Soviet Union in the 1950s such as Guy Burgess)—his "tipping point", and final reward (2005, pp. 107–09). Klebb's challenge to Bond is arguably evident in the final scene when Romanova has to choose between her lesbian suitor and her male lover. Importantly, this encounter does not appear in the source novel as Bond faces off against Klebb alone. But in the film, it is Romanova who eventually shoots and kills Klebb, and her choice results in the (re)establishment of heteronormative order.

This shooting sequence can be read in a few ways. On the one hand, Romanova sides with Bond who represents Britain and the West. She confirms the power of Bond's libidinal masculinity and the attractiveness of capitalism over communism while at the same time being positioned as a commodity herself in a captivity narrative. As Barrett argues "By escorting Romanova to the West, Bond enacts a contemporary conversion fantasy that makes Soviet women ripe for Western consumption" (2015, p. 41). Somewhere along the line of the Orient Express, Romanova becomes Mrs. Somerset and her sexual-geopolitical loyalties shift decisively. And it is sex on the train with Bond that transforms her "from an enemy to an émigré, a Soviet to a Westerner, and a communist to a consumer" (Barrett 2015, p. 41). While Bond first sleeps with her in his hotel room, it is unclear how far Romanova is prepared to go to fulfill her mission. As the audience later discovers, that moment of intimacy was being secretly recorded and there was no reason to believe, from Bond's point of view, that it was anything other than a 'trap'. On the other hand, Romanova sides with Bond, a man who is a loyal servant of his country, rather than a fellow Soviet woman who is a traitor. Moreover, she herself remains a patriot as she is tricked by SPECTRE into defecting, which is not something she initially desired.[7] As noted by Christine Bold, "the equation never fails: beauty, heterosexuality, and patriotism go together" and are set against "ugliness, sexual 'deviance' and criminality" (2003, p. 174). In both cases, it is a Soviet woman who saves Bond from a SPECTRE operative and traitor in the climax and chooses travel with Bond to the West.[8] Her conversion is confirmed emphatically in the Italian city of Venice and Bond is able to toss the earlier recording of their first sexual encounter in Istanbul into the Grand Canal. It no longer matters because the young Soviet agent has turned towards Bond but not necessarily Britain and this distinction becomes easier when she witnesses Klebb's attempt to kill Bond in Venice while disguised as a maid. Although Klebb beckons to Romanova not to alert Bond to her presence, Klebb's death is not stopped nor mourned by Romanova; in *From Russia with Love*, national traitors are cast as villains who must die while loyal subjects like Bond and Romanova are rewarded for their patriotism.

GoldenEye

This mode of representation is employed 32 years later in *GoldenEye* to help reframe Britain's relationship with a post-Cold War Russia. The year 1991 saw the dissolution of the Soviet Union and the subsequent formation of more than a dozen post-Soviet republics. This event effectively ended the formal cartographies of the Cold War (which was a consistent focus of the Bond franchise) and ushered in a new era of geopolitical exchange between Russia and Western nations. As the first film to appear after the fall of the Iron Curtain, *GoldenEye* explores Britain's new geopolitical relationship with Russia and provides Bond with unprecedented access to the formerly insulated nation. It also brings Bond into contact with fellow spy 006, Alec Trevelyan, who turns out to be a double agent, further reminding Bond and audiences that a newly created Russia in 1991 does not result in a world free from (Russian) intrigue and danger. If anything, Bond's initial encounter with 006 in a Soviet-era chemical weapons factory illustrates some of the apparent dangers of the collapse of the Soviet Union, an entity armed with multiple sites of weapons of mass destruction storage and deployment.

Much like *From Russia with Love*, Britain's (new) relationship with Russia is traced through Bond's encounters with two Russian women: Bond Girl Natalya Simonova and Bad Girl Xenia Onatopp. Although Russia remains feminized through the female subject, the film adapts the character types in key ways to facilitate a new reading of the post-Cold War nation. Unlike Romanova, Simonova is not initially presented as a pawn but rather as a target of violence. She narrowly escapes the massacre at the secret weapon research facility in Siberia undertaken by General Ourmenov, the commander of Russia's Space Division, and hench person Onatopp; both figures are traitors to Russia and work for the Janus criminal syndicate. Although Simonova becomes a person of interest to both the British and Russia governments and requires constant saving from Bond, she plays an active role in the film. She is one of the most vocal and demanding Bond Girls and yells at Bond quite a bit. They first meet while strapped into the stolen Eurocopter Tiger, which is being targeted by missiles. She screams until Bond wakes up and it is her voice that propels him into action. A similar situation takes place on the train after the pair is trapped in one of the cars. As she begins hacking into the computer, she looks at Bond sternly and yells "But don't stand there! Get us out of here!" Bond complies and facilitates their escape, and the pair continue their 'brains and brawn' partnership until the end of the film. Unlike Romanova, it is clear that Simonova has a professional competence and skill set that is critical to aiding and abetting Bond. Her encounter with Bond is happenstance and not something engineered by senior Russian agents or a global terrorist organization.

Although Simonova is presented as an assertive and educated modern Russian woman, she is still objectified in the film and thus indicative of how the ending of Cold War geopolitics did not erode some of its gendered qualities. She is captured on more than one occasion and becomes an object of struggle between two British agents: Alec Trevelyan (formerly 006) and James Bond (007). This is reflected in mirrored sequences depicting their first kisses. After kidnapping Simonova, Trevelyan tells her "You know, James and I shared everything...You may even learn to like me." He forces a kiss on her and after squirming to break free she slaps him. A similar scene takes place on the beach in Cuba with Bond pulling in Simonova for a kiss. While she initially resists, she eventually gives in and the film cuts to an image of the two in bed.[9] As the film progresses, Simonova becomes defined in relation to two British men and her affections help to confirm the phallic masculinity of Bond (and thus Britain) over Trevelyan (a British traitor operating in Russia) and decisively shape her willingness to help Bond stop the Janus syndicate from committing global terrorism. While the film does not offer a vision akin to a new era of Anglo-Russian co-operation, as imagined by *The Spy Who Loved Me* (see later in the chapter), it suggests that co-operation is possible again, especially once Bond has initiated a sexual accord. So while Bond can lament to the Russian Defense Minister, "What, no small-talk? No chit-chat? That's the trouble with the world today. No one takes the time to do a really sinister interrogation anymore. It's a lost art," some things remain stubbornly similar. With the right kind of "girl," Bond's Cold War sexual repertoire can still yield useful results.

Unlike Klebb, Onatopp does not have a professional or personal relationship with Simonova; her attack on the weapons facility and subsequent targeting of Simonova is impersonal. The two women are also much closer in age (as Famke Janssen is only five years older than Izabella Scorupco) and there is no chain of command granting one woman authority over the other. Instead, Onatopp is initially set up as a potential love interest for Bond and her introduction shares much in common with other Bond Girls like Tracy di Vicenzo in *On Her Majesty's Secret Service* (*OHMSS*) who Bond first encounters while driving in coastal Portugal. Similarly, Bond initially meets Onatopp on the road and the two engage in a flirtatious chase in the South of France before Bond tracks her down at the casino. Dressed in a cleavage-enhancing black gown, she plays baccarat until she is defeated by Bond. Although Bond orders her a drink, she leaves with another naval officer (an Admiral in the Canadian Navy) and exits the courtship ritual before she can be fully transformed into his love interest. Prior to her departure, she takes pleasure in telling Commander Bond that he is out-ranked by her love interest after earlier accusing Bond of being a traffic warden when he notices that her Ferrari is equipped with fake number plates. The encounter is all the more jarring because in the midst of the car chase, Bond finds time to seduce a British colleague (Caroline) who was supposed to be monitoring his performance as a field agent. Unlike Caroline, Onatopp is neither charmed nor seduced by Bond.

Initially, Onatopp appears to be aesthetically feminine and seems to fill the role of the femme fatale (in a literal sense) as she asphyxiates men between her legs;[10] she is presented as a sadist who gains sexual pleasure by inflicting pain on the men she subordinates and kills. While some might consider her to be a dominatrix, Onatopp is actually engaging in a masquerade of femininity by wearing her womanliness as a mask to hide her possession of masculinity (Doane 1991, p. 25) in order to appear disarming or at least less alarming to men. As noted by Barrett in his discussion of the characterization of Russia women, "defects such as hyper-intelligence and martial prowess are intertwined with their suppressed emotions, which render them more masculine and less womanly" (Barrett 2015, pp. 43–44). Through her attacking style, Onatopp challenges the professional and sexual dominance of (Western) men and in the final sequence she even insists to Bond that "the pleasure will be mine." When Simonova tries to intervene, Onatopp tells her to "wait her turn" before pushing her down and knocking her unconscious. Given the sexual pleasure Onatopp experiences when fighting, her comment takes on sexual connotations and positions her not as a love interest to Bond but as a sexual threat to the Bond Girl. Bond confirms his status as libidinal hero by killing Onatopp via suffocation, and this is one of the few times that Bond has killed a woman in a film.[11] This is a significant moment in the franchise for a British agent who tries to either restrain/save women from their death and/or is caught up in the killing of women by others.

Much like *From Russia with Love*, the villains in *GoldenEye* are traitors to the nation state and loyal to a non-state actor, the Janus syndicate. On the one hand, British traitor Trevelyan is given significant background treatment. He reveals to Bond that "his parents were Lienz Cossacks who had supported Hitler and whom the British had turned over for slaughter by Stalin" (Black 2005, p. 162). Although his parents survived, his father killed his mother before committing suicide out of shame and guilt. This left Trevelyan an orphan (like Bond) who was recruited by MI6 and began plotting his revenge. This revelation takes place in the Graveyard of Fallen Monuments in Moscow, a dumping site for the statues of Soviet leaders who have fallen from grace. As noted by Brink Lindsey, here "the soaring ambitions and ruthless power of the Soviet era have been reduced to kitsch…[but] the cruel gazes of the fallen leaders still cast a pall—still chill the soul with their inhuman, all-too-human arrogance. The past, though dead, still haunts" (2002, p. 2). This setting is significant as it symbolizes Trevelyan's desire to destroy Bond and the treacherous Britain he represents, something to which later villains and other former British agents such as Raoul Silva in *Skyfall* draw attention. This scene also works to humanize Trevelyan through the parallels drawn between him and Bond as both men are orphans who became secret agents.

Trevelyan works closely with Onatopp who operates as his hench person. However, she is not provided with a detailed backstory and her motivation to betray her country and work for a Russian crime syndicate are unknown. Basic information about her character is only provided during an intelligence briefing. Unlike May Day in *A View to a Kill,* she is not given an opportunity to tell her own story and this works to dehumanize her in the film. Similar to Klebb, this renders her a more dangerous figure whose intentions are unknown and whose future actions cannot be predicted. Moreover, the information relayed to Bond emphasizes her killing techniques rather than offering any insights into her personal background. Male contract killers such as Emilo Locque in *For Your Eyes Only* are given a professional backstory. We know, for example, he was a Belgian enforcer in the criminal underground. Beginning with her character, the Brosnan-era films explore the rise of global terrorism enacted by individuals and organizations rather than nation states. This is a significant shift from the Dalton-era films like *The Living Daylights,* which explores the role that an identifiable Soviet Union has played in facilitating conflict in Afghanistan, and later the role of countries such as China in the international drugs trade in *License to Kill.* In the Brosnan era, it is Russia and specifically its border regions that are depicted as the breeding ground for global terrorism as seen in the opening sequence at the arms bazaar in *Tomorrow Never Dies* and the pipeline dispute in *The World Is Not Enough.*

Importantly, it is through the (physical and sexual) excess of the Russian woman (in addition to the organization SPECTRE) that global terrorism is embodied and emboldened. This renders Bond's seduction of the Russian Bond Girl (who can be known and wooed to help the West) and killing of the Russian Bad Girl (who is unknown, untamed, and threatening) crucial to his mission to safeguard British and Western geopolitical interests. Bond's sexual professionalism matters in a context where, in the Brosnan era, there was far less physical fighting with his opponents compared to the Connery and Moore eras.

BOND AND THE SOVIET FEMALE AGENT

While the Cold War and its demise are the focus of the Connery and Brosnan eras respectively, with Britain positioned as an intermediary diffusing global conflict, Bond films of the Moore era focus more directly on the uneasy relationship between British and Soviet intelligence agencies—MI6 and the KGB. These films explore the physical challenges, professional constraints, and sexual limits of collaboration as the agencies work with and against each other to ensure their geopolitical interests while avoiding military conflict. This complicated relationship is best depicted in *The Spy Who Loved Me*, a film that features Bond, for the first time, working alongside a Soviet agent, Anya Amasova. This partnership is assigned rather than being accidental or situational and the two agents are tasked with working together to overcome a mutual threat, Karl Stromberg. As part of his fiendish plan, Stromberg commissions the theft of nuclear submarines belonging to the American and Soviet navies so that he can attack Moscow and New York; he intends to start a nuclear war that will destroy the world so that he can build a new civilization under water. The submarines are hidden in a super-tanker, which appears to have spent its entire existence in the realm of international waters.

From the outset of the film, MI6 and the KGB are presented as parallel agencies. This is effectively established through the mirroring of their agency heads, M and General Gogol.[12] Not only are both men similarly introduced as they contact their best agents (using red phones) for the mission, but they actually describe the other as their equal. M refers to Gogol as his "opposite number in the KGB" and Gogol speaks often about a new era of "Anglo-Russian cooperation." When the two men are featured in the same scene while inside a British operating center located inside an Egyptian pyramid, such as during Q's briefing, they sit parallel to each other and are balanced within the frame; in other words, neither man is featured in the shot or in the foreground to suggest their importance. After leaving the debriefing, each man demonstrates respect for the other by offering the opportunity for his counterpart to walk first by politely stating "after you." And at the end of the film, both men seem to be shocked upon discovering their agents having sex in the pod, each calling out his agent's name in astonishment. While the film goes to great lengths to set up parallels between M and Gogol, there is no Soviet quartermaster or counterpoint to Q. Interestingly, it is Q who leads the intelligence briefing and provides the gadgets for the mission, and the briefing is hosted in a country where Britain has had a long-standing imperial presence. Given the location of Egypt, the lack of an American presence in the briefing room is also significant in light of the US's humiliation of Britain in the midst of the Suez Crisis in 1956. Moreover, there is also no Soviet technology used in the film and both Gogol and Amasova defer to Q's knowledge, skill, and experience. The positioning of Q and his technological inventions such as the underwater capabilities of the Lotus sports car in the narrative suggests that, even in the face of collaboration, MI6 is superior to the KGB, and this anticipates Bond's eventual emergence as a superior hero over Amasova.

In the beginning of the film, Bond and Amasova are introduced as comparable agents. After Gogol states that he will be contacting his best agent, the film cuts to a shot of a man in bed with a female lover. The film leads the audience to believe that *he* is the best agent as the camera focuses on him first and the woman expresses her desire to spend more time with him. Yet, when Gogol contacts his agent, it is Amasova and not her male lover who responds. Bond has a similar introduction with M stating that he will contact his "best man." The film cuts to a shot of Bond sleeping with a woman and then leaving upon receiving the message. The woman begs him to stay as she is a double agent setting a trap to have him killed. Bond leaves no doubt that he is the best/better 'man' for the job by promptly leaving the chalet and brushing off his dangerous lover before easily outmaneuvering Soviet assassins on skis. Unlike Amasova who is emotionally invested in her lover, Bond lacks attachment ("Britain needs me") and this renders him more proficient and focused at his job. It is this (stereotypically feminine) emotionality that causes Amasova to shift between being a good character, ally, and Bond Girl who collaborates with Bond, and being a bad character, opponent, and Bad Girl who wants to kill him. Unlike *From Russia with Love* and *GoldenEye*, the contrasting of good and bad Soviet women takes place within a single character based on her emotional status, which is not dependent on her sexual intimacy with Bond. When she threatens to kill Bond in Sardinia, they have already become lovers but Amasova's loyalty to the Soviet Union and the mission itself prevents her from killing Bond there and then.

The film continues to present Bond and Amasova as comparable agents. When the pair meets, they are both dressed in their military uniforms and set up as professional representatives of their respective nations. When they run into each other at the bar in Cairo, they seem to be well informed about their counterpart as each agent orders the other person's drink of choice and relays key pieces of biographical information. While Amasova hits a nerve when she mentions Bond's dead wife, Bond later strikes a blow when it is revealed that he (unknowingly) killed her lover during the opening ski sequence. Given these parallels, Bond and Amasova compete against each other to prove which agent (and by extension agency) is superior. For example, when they chase Jaws through an Egyptian architectural site, each agent wants to take the lead and go first, and their conflict offers an explicit contrast to the consideration given by their bosses. Each agent, however, saves the life of the other during the confrontation with Jaws but their collaboration is presented more as a directive rather than a personal desire. During the intelligence briefing that follows, both agents offer information in succession but it is Amasova who corrects Bond when he makes a rare mistake about the geographical location of Stromberg's laboratory in the Mediterranean. And later when Bond drives his Lotus Esprit into the water, it is Amasova who pushes the button to transform it into a submarine. While Bond seems to have a more intuitive relationship with technology (as evidenced by him driving away from Q before he can be given instructions about the car), Amasova is better prepared (as she has read the blueprints for the car even before Bond knew of its existence—reflecting contemporaneous anxieties that the Soviets were more than capable of getting their hands on British and American secrets regarding science and technology) and her approach, at least initially, seems to be more effective. For instance, she uses a cigarette equipped with powder to incapacitate Bond to steal the secret microfiche while the pair is having an apparent moment of intimacy on an Egyptian dhow. As noted by Fernando Berns, *The Spy Who Loved Me* "centers on the idea that Bond has finally met his match with his new counterpart, who was marketed as a 'female Bond'" (2015, p. 120).

Although they are initially set up as equals, the competency of Amasova as an agent is undermined by her explicit sexualization and unwillingness to forgive Bond for a professional hit on her lover (rather than, say, her husband). This is signaled through her codename, Agent XXX, which while echoing that of Agent 007 also contains an "extra sexualized and almost pornographic connotation" (Jones 2015b, p. 209). The overt sexualization of action-oriented women has historically worked to undermine their heroic achievements in their films (Funnell 2014, p. 173; Brown 2015, p. 227). In the first half of *The Spy Who Loved Me*, Amasova is explicitly sexualized in order to emphasize her positioning as a seductress, a role frequently employed by Soviet women in Western popular culture.[13] When she first meets Bond at the bar, she is wearing a navy blue gown with a plunging neckline, low-cut back, and a high slit up to her mid-thigh. Although her body is mostly covered, the gown draws attention to her frame and specifically her sex characteristics like breasts and legs. Wearing such a costume while attempting to one-up Bond subsequently diminishes the impact of her challenge and impedes her mobility, such during their encounter with Jaws at the pyramids. When Jaws drops the secret microfiche on the ground, Amasova takes her eyes off of him as she bends down in her figure hugging dress to retrieve the object. As her attentiveness drops, Jaws is able to quickly move her arm away from the object and uses her loss of balance to his advantage.

Amasova's image changes after she sleeps with Bond. As she begins to fall for him, she shifts from being a Soviet seductress with a dangerous femininity capable of seducing Bond towards an alluring form of Communism, into a Bond Girl who has been domesticated by Bond and rendered safe through her alignment with Britain/West/Capitalism. When the two agents, posing as a married couple in Sardinia, make their first contact with Stromberg, Amasova wears a white pantsuit and a brown shirt that covers her body and obscures her frame. She is contrasted in the scene with Stromberg's personal assistant Naomi who wears a transparent white beach robe over a brown string bikini that emphasizes her figure. The contrasting costuming (in the same color palette) signifies the different (and competing) roles of these women (i.e. girlfriend/wife vs. seductress) and visualizes the internal changes that Amasova has undergone (Fig. 4.2).

She is now expected to be the demure Mrs. Sterling and Bond tells her when they get to Stromberg's laboratory not "to be a bother to Naomi."

Fig 4.2 *The Spy Who Loved Me* (Eon Productions et al. 1977)

Amasova, however, reverts back to her original image after Bond confesses to killing her lover. Vowing to murder Bond after their mission is complete, Amasova shifts from being an ally to a dangerous threat and her change of heart is signaled via costuming. For instance, when she first enters the submarine with Bond, she is wearing a blue military uniform and insists that she should not be given any special treatment on the ship. The captain suggests that she use his personal shower as the crew is not used to working alongside a woman. When an officer comes in to speak with the captain, there is a shot of Amasova in the background bathing, her naked body clearly visible through the frosted glass. This scene is superfluous and does not advance the plot in any way. Instead, it has been included to re-emphasize the sexual appeal of the now-single Amasova and the threat she poses to Bond as she is no longer Mrs. Sterling. Later, when Stromberg captures Amasova, she is dressed in a revealing outfit that consists of a red halter bikini top crossed in the front to enhance her cleavage and a matching pair of pants.[14] This outfit draws attention to her body and positions her as a captive object of desire and struggle between two white men (much like Simonova). Captured by Stromberg, she is (literally) stripped of her agency and positioned as a damsel in distress. She previously needed to be rescued by Bond after a near-death experience on a train with Jaws while travelling through Italy.

More importantly, after Amasova sleeps with Bond she is moved to the periphery of the narrative arc. She does not meet Stromberg with Bond during their initial contact as she is stuck playing Bond's wife and has to interact with Naomi. She is not involved in the fight sequence on the submarine as she is kidnapped by Stromberg and disappears for the entire assault on the vessel; all of the credit goes to Bond who facilitates the release of the ship's crew and launches an Anglo-American attack on Stromberg's men. In addition, the captive crew of the Soviet submarine is nowhere to be seen and their release is not depicted in the film. Moreover, Amasova does not help Bond kill Stromberg as she is tied up in a different room. She does not fight Jaws, the primary hench person of the villain, or participate in his defeat. And even as she is being rescued by Bond, she screams in fear for Bond to help her get into the pod—this from an agent who claims to be self-sufficient through her description of survival training on the Egyptian dhow. With the proficiency of Amasova being undercut by her sexualized image, sentimental attachment to men, and removal from the action narrative, Bond emerges as a solo hero in the film and

MI6 is cast as the superior intelligence agency—the KGB needs MI6 and not the other way around. This comparison is clearly gendered through the elevation of Britain (coded masculine) over the Soviet Union (coded feminine) and relies on patriarchal protection logic that justifies the treatment and marginalization of the Soviet woman and by extension that of the USSR.

The Spy Who Loved Me sets the tone for the uneasy relationship between Britain and the Soviet Union in the Moore and Dalton eras. Interestingly, Bond is not paired with another female Soviet agent in subsequent films apart from a brief moment in *A View to a Kill*. Instead, he competes against male Soviet agents and collaborates more directly with the head of the KGB.[15] During this time, General Gogol is presented as more virile leader. In *Moonraker*, for instance, he interacts with a younger blond woman who is lying in his bed. And in *For Your Eyes Only*, he kisses the hand of a blond secretary who sits on his desk. Moreover, Gogol's successor in *The Living Daylights*, General Pushkin has a blond mistress who he meets at a hotel. Since these scenes have limited impact on the plot, they serve as a method by which the film draws a parallel between the KGB leader and Bond rather than M—as M does not develop a romantic relationship with any woman including his secretary Miss Moneypenny—and the Soviet woman is defined solely in terms of her sexuality as she is relegated to the position of lover/mistress.

OLDER AND YOUNGER SOVIET GENERALS/AGENTS (OR SOVIET DOVES AND HAWKS)

In the Bond franchise, while Soviet/Russian women are analogous with the interests of the state, men are depicted as the leaders and protectors of that state. As Colleen Tremonte and Linda Racioppi argue:

> Men are the main agents of the state and the international system of states; women, as some feminist scholarship has argued, are positioned as subordinate helpmeets and often embodied as symbols of the 'nation' [...] National identities, such as Britishness, therefore, have been constructed within the context of a binary gender/political order; they are differentiated for men and women and reflect direct gender roles. Historically, men protect and defend the nation-state, if necessary sacrificing their own lives; women serve the nation through reproducing and socializing its children and supporting militarized men who may be way from home. (2009, p. 187)

Spanning the Moore to Dalton eras, six consecutive Bond films—from *The Spy Who Loved Me* to *The Living Daylights*—explore British and Soviet relations. Not only do they surmise Soviet interests, but they also present conflict within the Soviet military-industrial complex as to the proper direction of the nation state. This is done primarily through the contrasting of older Soviet generals, who are presented as "doves" and try to resolve international conflict through diplomacy and limited military spying engagements, with their younger counterparts who are depicted as "hawks" and advocate for an aggressive foreign policy through the direct use of military power. According to Jeremy Black, "the idea of Soviet 'hawks' and 'doves' was indeed popular in Western discussion at this point" (2005, p. 92). This is reflected in three sequential films *Octopussy*, *A View to a Kill*, and *The Living Daylights*. While the older generals (Gogol and Pushkin) support détente, demilitarization, and increasing trade with the West, the younger generals (Orlov and Koskov) and agents (Zorin and Necros) aspire to return the Soviet Union to its previous glory; they 'go rogue' by moving forward with unsanctioned and illegal plans that will spark military conflict with the West in order to expand the Soviet empire and its geopolitical interests in Europe, Africa, and Asia. In *The Living Daylights*, for example, this leads to geopolitical brazenness as British agents are assassinated while on a training mission in the British overseas territory of Gibraltar. British soldiers guarding the military base are shot as well. While violence might have afflicted British interests in places such as colonial Jamaica, this was the first time British territory is shown to be attacked directly in the Bond films.

Octopussy

Octopussy provides a glimpse into the command structure of the Soviet government. Early in the film, a meeting of Soviet officials takes place presumably at the Kremlin. Eleven men are seated around a half-circle table while discussing the security of the Soviet Union. This room is filled with Soviet iconography. There is a large map of the world on the back wall that highlights the Soviet Union in red and its allies in pink. While the map is an established visual trope in Bond films since *Dr. No*, this particular map is unusual as it depicts the world through a Soviet rather than British operational context. On the left wall of the meeting room is the state emblem for the Union of Soviet Socialist Republics and on the right wall is a large portrait of Vladimir Lenin, a Russian communist revolutionary who formed the Soviet Union in 1922. On the floor in front of the table is the iconic hammer and sickle symbol, which is featured on the national flag. General Gogol is seated near the center of the table beside a minister and his olive green uniform is adorned with many medals. Speaking authoritatively, he discusses the importance of disarmament to the future of the Soviet Union.

He is contrasted in the scene by General Orlov, whose is slouching in his seat as a way to show his contempt toward Gogol's suggestions. When he stands to speak, a large map tracks down from the ceiling and he loudly suggests a military strategy to invade Western Europe that will result in "total victory in 5 days!" He is far more aggressive and abrasive in his pitch, and as he moves to the middle of the room he is challenged by Gogol who describes him as being "paranoid" and having a "thirst for conquest." The two men continue to argue until a minister rejects Orlov's plan. The film presents a power struggle between two Soviet generals, which arguably reflects broader ideological conflicts taking place within the then Soviet Union. Through the vectors of age and direct experience of dealing with UK counterparts, the wisdom and experience of Gogol (who functions as an ally to Bond/Britain) is depicted as far more welcoming than the impetuous and insolent Orlov (who is an enemy to the West and shows little respect for authority and international diplomacy).

Although Orlov is overruled, he puts into motion his plan to destroy the US Air Force base in West Germany using an American bomb. Since the attack cannot be traced to the USSR and will be viewed as an accident, it will lead to European disarmament and increase the effectiveness of a Soviet attack. His plan appears to reflect the 1983 "war scare" that "brought U.S. and Soviet political relations near to the point of violent conflict" (Cimbala 2001, p. 23).[16] In addition, Orlov's partnership with an Afghan Prince, Kamal Khan, also touches on the Soviet–Afghan War (1979–89), which pit Soviet-led Afghan forces against insurgents who were funded primarily by the United States. Although this conflict plays a central role in the narrative of *The Living Daylights* (see later in the chapter), this partnership would have been deemed suspicious at the time. By defusing the bomb and killing Khan, Bond helps to safeguard American interests in this conflict.

Importantly, it is Gogol and not Bond who is present for Orlov's death. After launching an investigation into Orlov's activities at the Kremlin, Gogol discovers that Orlov has stolen jewels to fund his plan. Gogol is particularly concerned about the loss of the Romanov Star, one of the pre-revolutionary Russian Crown Jewels, which he refers to as a national treasure. Orlov is willing to sell off relics of the past in order to attain new glory for the future. After Gogol recovers most of the jewels, he heads to the border of East Germany and watches as Orlov runs past the guard to jump onto a train. Shot in the back, Orlov tries to pull himself forward along the tracks. Gogol walks slowly up to him and calls him a "common thief" and "disgrace to the uniform." With his dying breath, Orlov states "Yes, but tomorrow I shall be a hero of the Soviet Union." Although Gogol is aware of an impending plot, he cannot take action and has to rely on Bond to neutralize the threat to all of them. It is Bond who disarms the bomb inside a US Air Force base in West Berlin, and unlike *Goldfinger* there is no helping hand from an American agent. If anything, American service personnel were trying to prevent Bond from doing his job because they were unaware of what was happening. At the end of the film, Gogol is in M's office at MI6 and comments that his country will never admit that the incident happened, a move that will not only save face but stop tensions from escalating. He also asks if Bond will return the Romanov Star and demonstrates his willingness to work diplomatically with, rather than tactically against, the West. And through the actions of Bond and the personal diplomacy of M, Britain continues to play an important role as intermediary and peacekeeper during the Cold War.

A View to a Kill

The following film, *A View to a Kill*, also centers on the conflict between Gogol and a rogue Soviet agent whose plans threaten the diplomatic relationship between the Soviet Union and the West. Max Zorin is a KGB agent who has become a key player in the oil and tech industries in the United States in particular. As the film progresses, it is revealed that Zorin was born out of a genetic experiment conducted on pregnant women in German concentration camps during World War II. While the goal was to increase fetal intelligence, few women carried their babies to term and those born turned out to be psychopaths, an unforeseen side effect of the drugs. Zorin was one such child and was relocated to Russia after the war; he was raised by the scientist who was tasked with developing steroids for Russian athletes.[17] Years later Zorin joined the KGB and entered into the United States as a 'sleeper agent'.

The film presents the relationship between Zorin and his superior Gogol as being tense. Using KGB resources, Zorin discovers the true identity of

James Bond and orders him to be killed without approval. As a long-term ally of Bond, Gogol is notably upset and chastises Zorin for putting other KGB operations at risk. When Zorin expresses his desire to the leave the KGB, another agent begins to berate him by calling him a "biological experiment" and a "psychological freak." Gogol then reminds Zorin that no one leaves the KGB. When Zorin ignores this warning, Gogol sends two KGB agents to spy on him, collect evidence, and then kill him. When his agents fail, Gogol relies on Bond (again) to kill his rogue agent and in the process thwart the plan to flood Silicon Valley and destroy a large part of California. By doing so, Bond ensures continued peace and diplomacy between the Soviet Union and the United States and, as before, saves the latter from disaster.

Much like *Octopussy*, the film ends with Gogol in M's office. This time he bestows the Order of Lenin on Bond and comments that Bond is the first British man to earn it rather than, say, an American counterpart. According to John Clarke, those eligible for "the highest decoration of the USSR are military personnel, civilians (including foreigners), cities and public and commercial organizations who have rendered conspicuous service to the USSR" (2001, p. 191). This recognition gives credit to Bond (and Britain) for once again neutralizing the threat of a young rogue Soviet agent on the United States. Moreover, it brings to a fitting end the collaborative relationship between Bond and Gogol in the Moore era. Both men have demonstrated repeatedly that there is value in cooperation and détente, even when others and especially Soviet generals and agents are intent on pressing home a military advantage.

The Living Daylights

Although *The Living Daylights* is the first film of the Dalton era, it shares much in common with *Octopussy* and seems to expand on a few key elements in significant ways. Both films center on the conflict between an older soviet general and his younger counterpart. Much like Gogol, General Pushkin is steady and unwavering in his support for the détente. He wants to maintain peace and work towards establishing stronger ties with the West. He is also willing to listen to reason (something that Bond reminds M about while discussing a possible British hit on him) and serves as an ally to Bond; Bond disobeys M's order to assassinate Pushkin in Tangiers precisely because he believes that he and by extension Britain can do "business" with the Soviet general. Pushkin is contrasted in the narrative with the more volatile General Koskov who, like Orlov, disagrees with the establishment's position and wants to instigate a war with the West. He revives the *Smiert Spionem* or "death to spies" operation targeting British and American agents, which was develop during Stalin's time and deactivated many years ago.[18] He also defects to the West in order to profit from the Soviet–Afghan War. Unlike Orlov, however, Koskov does not die and is taken into custody by Pushkin to answer for his treason.

The Living Daylights was released four years before the dissolution of the Soviet Union in 1991. The majority of the film's narrative takes place in Czechoslovakia and Afghanistan, two countries that border the USSR. On the one hand, Czechoslovakia was part of the Soviet Eastern European Bloc/Warsaw Pact and served as one of the USSR's most faithful allies in Europe. In 1968, the Soviet Union even sent troops into Czechoslovakia to support their Communist Party and curb the reformist 'Prague Spring'. However, it was only after Mikhail Gorbachev came into power and refused to use military force in Europe that the Bloc collapsed (Kramer 2010, p. 35). This led to the subsequent dissolution of Czechoslovakia in 1992. In the film, this Soviet satellite serves as the site for Koskov's defection via a cross-border pipeline, as Bond would not be able to travel in and out of the USSR and facilitate safe passage. Czechoslovakia's proximity to non-NATO Austria is mentioned twice as the film deals explicitly with border regions. Koskov's innovative route out of the country is shown to be a wise one as Bond's car is searched by Czech border security guards. Later Bond and his Bond Girl, Kara Milovy, are able to escape pursuers at the Czech border by literally sliding into Austria while seated in Milovy's emptied cello box.

On the other hand, the latter half of the film takes place in Afghanistan during the Soviet–Afghan war, which lasted from 1979 to 1989. On the request of the leaders in Afghanistan, Soviet troops were deployed to fight against Mujahedeen rebels, an opposition group funded by the United States. The film is set at the height of the war. Bond and Milovy are briefly held captive at a Soviet airbase in Afghanistan before they escape. In the process they free Kamran Shah, an Oxford educated man who turns out to be the leader of the local Mujahedeen. Together, they destroy a shipment of opium that would provide monies to supply the Soviets with arms and then blow up a bridge that helps Shah win a battle against the Soviets. The film presents the impression that Bond/Britain has intervened during a crucial time in the war and facilitated a few large victories, and that an Oxford-educated man proves his worth to Britain by acting as a strategic ally to Bond. In so doing, the film hints at a time when Britain and Russia were involved in their own 'Great Game' for strategic influence in South and Central Asia during the nineteenth century.

The Living Daylights offers a British perspective on the geopolitical status of the Soviet Union and its allies in the years leading up to the dissolution of the USSR. While criticizing Soviet intervention in Afghanistan, the film does not necessarily blame the USSR or its leader Pushkin. Instead, it places the blame on rogue agents who are facilitating this conflict for their own selfish profit. The film not only identifies Koskov as a traitor, but also his partner Brad Whitaker, an American arms dealer who is profiting from the conflict as well as their hench person Necros, who is a KGB assassin. Although he lacks a military rank,[19] Whitaker dresses like a general, collects weapons and war memorabilia, and recreates battles through the use of miniature toy sets. Whitaker is contrasted with Pushkin when the latter cancels a weapons shipment. Standing in Whitaker's "pantheon of great commanders," which consists of life-sized figurines of leaders like Napoleon and Hitler, Pushkin comments that these men were "butchers" while Whitaker retorts that they were "surgeons...[that] cut away society's dead flesh." His hench person Necros serves as one of these "butchers" when he kills various British agents during the *Smiert Spionem* operations. The film presents the impression that a rogue Soviet General, an American arms dealer, and a KGB agent are responsible for prolonging the war in Afghanistan while increasing the tension between the Soviet Union and the West purely for personal profit as opposed to any wider geopolitical objectives such as strategic domination of South and Central Asia.

The final scene takes place in London and the film presents the image of a new (and idealized) era of cooperation that is facilitated by Britain. After Milovy finishes her cello performance, she meets with M who brings her to see Gogol who is now working for the Foreign Service rather than KGB. M facilitates the conversation and reveals that Gogol will provide her with a visa so that she can "come and go" as she pleases—a reward for assisting with the mission. When Kamran Shah arrives with two of his soldiers (adorned with crisscrossing bullet sashes), it is M who introduces him to Gogol and the two exchange pleasantries. When Shah inquires about the whereabouts of Bond, the camera captures all six figures in the same shot—a Mujahedeen leader, two Afghan fighters, a Czechoslovakian defector, the head of MI6, and the former head of the KGB—interacting politely at the symphony, a space of refinement and high culture (Fig. 4.3).

Fig. 4.3 *The Living Daylights* (Eon Productions et al. 1987)

Depicting a new era of geopolitical relations, *The Living Days* presents Britain as facilitating a new peaceful alliance through the figures of Bond and M—one where London is positioned as a site for such transnational cultural and diplomatic encounters.

CONCLUSION

Much like the novels, the Bond films rely on binary oppositions to depict Soviet/Russian characters and shifting geopolitical positions particularly in relation to Britain. Yet, in spite of this binary system, the films released during the Cold War present Soviet characters moving through traditional national boundaries from the East (and particularly the Soviet Bloc) to the West. For instance, the conversion fantasy of Tatiana Romanova in *From Russia with Love* takes place on a train travelling westward and the film uses an onscreen map to depict her journey from NATO-supporting Turkey through the former Yugoslavia, a Soviet ally, to her eventual arrival in NATO-supporting Italy and the city of Venice. In *Octopussy*, General Orlov is killed while running to catch a train travelling from East to West Germany but this is something that he singularly fails to achieve. He is shot in the back in order to prevent him from (illegally) crossing over the border. And in *The Living Daylights*, General Koskov travels in a westerly direction through a gas pipeline linking Czechoslovakia to Austria. These border crossings present the West as a (redemptive) sanctuary that is difficult for the Soviet subject to access, unless he or she is invited to do so. There are exceptions, of course, and liminal countries like Austria, Turkey, and Istanbul, and cities such as Vienna serve as places where it is possible for British subjects to be injured and killed by Soviet and or Bulgarian assassins.

In the Brosnan-era films set after the Cold War, it is the border crossings by individuals that are presented as threatening rather than heroic. This is best depicted in the opening sequence in *Tomorrow Never Dies* at the terrorist bazaar on the unruly border of Russia. The rise of global terrorism is reflected in Charles Robinson's description of the situation: "It's like a terrorist supermarket. Chinese Long March Scud, Panther AS-565 attack helicopter, a pair of Russian mortars, and the crates look like American rifles. Chilean mines. German explosives. Fun for the whole family." While both a British and a Russian general are overseeing this mission, the film frames the rise of global terrorism in relation to Russia extremists and a Russian inability to keep their weapons 'locked up' within secure national limits. Leaky borders allow dangerous men, weapons, and ideas to proliferate. This sentiment, which is relayed in both *GoldenEye* and *The World Is Not Enough*, is one reason why Bond reaches out to former Cold War contacts like CIA agent Jack Wade and KGB agent turned gangster Valentin Zukovsky since he knows where they stand ideologically, and also understands that their insights into how and where the old Soviet Union and the new Russia really works will be invaluable.

In the Craig era, the threat of global terrorism moves beyond Russia and extends into Britain in ways with which MI6 is struggling to come to grips. But the cartographies of global terrorism bear no resemblance to those late Cold War-era mappings. M describes the situation in *Skyfall* during a government inquiry and it contrasts sharply with the one her male predecessors had to face:

I'm frightened because our enemies are no longer known to us. They do not exist on a map. They're not nations, they're individuals. And look around you. Who do you fear? Can you see a face, a uniform, a flag? No! Our world is not more transparent now, it's more opaque. It's in the shadows. That's where we must do battle.

While M in *Skyfall* complains that she is battling with an opaque geopolitical world, Mallory, the new M in *Spectre*, is working in a global environment that is arguably too transparent and visible as facilitated by the rise of Nine Eyes. By depicting the meeting in Japan, the film implies that the traditional allies such as the UK, USA, Australia, Canada, and New Zealand are now joined by others (although South Africa is shown to be vetoing its establishment) in a new consortium designed to operationalize global surveillance. It appears that SPECTRE might have been behind the monies required to establish this new network but the exact genesis of Nine Eyes appears obscure.

Although geopolitical relations have changed since the fall of the Iron Curtain, Russia is still viewed by the West as an adversary especially in light of their recent military activities including the war in Ukraine and snap-drill military exercises in places like the Arctic (which was touched on in *A View to a Kill*). In light of this, Russia will continue to factor into the geopolitical landscape of the Bond films in the foreseeable future and what remains clear in the most recent film *Spectre* is that Russia is not part of the Nine Eyes surveillance consortium. It remains out in the cold, geopolitically.

NOTES

1. See Chap. 3 for details.
2. Importantly, the novel *Dr. No* was published a year after *From Russia with Love*. As a result, the SMERSH plot in the latter was designed to damage "the enemy *apparat*" (1957b, p. 38) to bolster their reputation. Eventually, the council arbitrarily decides on the English Secret Service and specifically James Bond as their target (ibid. pp. 43–44).
3. The symbolic act of M handing over Romanova's picture manifested in literal terms as she is 'given' to Bond as part of a SPECTRE plot masked as a Soviet mission.
4. For a detailed discussion, see Boyce (2015), Holliday (2015), Kunze (2015), and Parks (2015).
5. Much like the photograph, the depiction of Romanova in fragments essentializes her body and increases her sexual appeal to Bond (and the audience who shares his gaze). It also works to dehumanize her as Bond's spoken words (similar to the writing he inscribes in the photograph) rather than her own provide the context through which the audience sees and interprets her character.
6. Compared to the novel, the film version of *From Russia with Love* does not recreate one particular scene in which Klebb attempts to seduce Romanova in her apartment by dressing up in lingerie. According to Romanova, "She looked like the oldest and ugliest whore in the world" (Fleming 1957b, p. 116).

7. A similar situation takes place in *The Living Daylights* when Kara Milovy becomes a pawn in a Soviet defection plan.

8. A comparable situation occurs in *Thunderball* as Domino Derval saves Bond by killing Largo. The film also lays out the choice between good and evil, heterosexuality and deviant sexuality, Bond and the villain, and Britain and SPECTRE.

9. This is a problematic trope that appears throughout the Bond franchise. There are numerous examples in which Bond physically and forcibly sways a woman to consent to sex. Pussy Galore in *Goldfinger* is the best example.

10. A precursor to Onatopp was introduced in *The Living Daylights*. Bond asks Moneypenny to provide him with a list of female Soviet assassins so that he can identify the sniper at the concert hall is Czechoslovakia. While Bond is conversing with Q, the final two on the list are shown: Ula Yarkov who strangles her victims with her hands or thighs and Natasha Zappa who specializes in child impersonation and uses an explosive teddy bear. In both cases, these Soviet assassins use unconventional methods to get close to their targets and kill them. However, Moneypenny does not mention whether either woman gains sexual pleasure when killing, an element added to enhance the perversity of Onatopp, rendering her more evil.

11. For a detailed discussion, see Funnell (2011b).

12. In *From Russia with Love*, Walter Gotell was cast in the role of Morzeny, a hench person who worked for SPECTRE. This is not the first time an actor who initially played a villain was recast as a protagonist in the franchise. Maud Adams first portrayed Andrea Anders in *The Man with the Golden Gun* before she was featured as a Bond Girl in *Octopussy*. In addition, Joe Don Baker initially played villain Brad Whitaker in *The Living Daylights* before serving as Bond's CIA contact Jack Wade in *GoldenEye* and *Tomorrow Never Dies*.

13. In *A View to A Kill*, Soviet agent Pola Ivanova (Fiona Fullerton) is also set up as a seductress. After Bond catches her spying on Max Zorin, the two reminisce while taking a bath at a Japanese spa. She mentions a previous mission where her objective was to seduce him. After the two have sex, Ivanova leaves with what she believes is her original audio recording only to discover that Bond had switched the tape. She is embarrassed in front of General Gogol and this scene reveals Bond to (still) be superior to the female Soviet agent.

14. Stromberg is not the first villain to dress a kidnapped Bond Girl in a revealing outfit. A similar situation occurs in *Diamonds Are Forever* and *The Man with the Golden Gun* with Bond Girls Tiffany Case and Mary Goodnight being displayed in similar ways.

15. This shift might be due, in part, to the sickness of Bernard Lee, who played M from 1962–1979. During the transition to Robert Brown, who took over the role from 1983–1989, a government minister and bureaucrat takes on a leadership role in MI6.
16. For a detailed discussion of the events leading up to the "war scare" see Cimbala (2001).
17. This plot might be in response to the exceptional performance of East Germany and the Soviet Union in the 1984 Winter Olympics where they won 24 and 25 medals respectively, almost double than any Western country.
18. This policy is outlined in the Bond novel *From Russia with Love* (Black 2005, p. 150).
19. Pushkin calls out Whitaker when he tries to cover a lie stating "As one solider to another, you have my word of honor." Pushkin responds "Spare me your military pretensions. What army did you serve in? You were expelled from West Point for cheating. Then a short stint at a mercenary in the Belgian Congo. Later you worked with various criminals to help finance your first arms deals."

CHAPTER 5

The Asian City: Modern/Vertical vs. Pre-modern/Horizontal Spaces

Asia and Asians plays an important role in the Bond films. In his account of *Thrilling Cities*, Ian Fleming selected Hong Kong, Macau, and Tokyo as his three 'thrilling' Asian cities. Writing initially for *The Sunday Times* newspaper in London, Fleming told his readers that

> All my life I have been invited in adventure and abroad, I have enjoyed the *frisson* of leaving the wide, well-lit streets and venturing up back alleys in search of the hidden, authentic pulse of towns. It was perhaps this habit that turned me into a writer of thrillers and, by the time I had the two journeys that produced these essays, I had certainly got into the way of looking at people and places and things through a thriller-writer's eye. (1963, p. ix)

Armed with this perspective, Fleming's journeys were facilitated, for the first time, by the De Havilland Comet, the world's first commercial jet airliner. As his plane lands in Beirut, Fleming tells his readers "the hatch clanged open and the first sticky fingers of the East reached in" (1963, p. 4). Along the way to Hong Kong, Fleming complains about the state of the toilets in Bahrain international airport and casually tells the reader that "India has always depressed me" (1963, p. 7) although he is at pains to justify his summary a few sentences later.

Things look up when Fleming lands in Hong Kong after some 26 hours of flying. Readers are offered a description of the view over Hong Kong harbor and told that Fleming has had the pleasure of a soothing massage. Hong Kong is described as a sensual city and Fleming relishes "the streets

© The Editor(s) (if applicable) and The Author(s) 2017
L. Funnell, K. Dodds, *Geographies, Genders and Geopolitics of James Bond*, DOI 10.1057/978-1-137-57024-6_5

of Hong Kong [because they] are the most enchanting night streets I have ever trod" (1963, p. 16). Compared to London, the Asian city more generally is awash with color and smell, and filled with intriguing food and people. In the film, *You Only Live Twice*, a post-coital Bond asks his Chinese lover "Why do Chinese girls taste different from all other girls?" Ling answers, "You think we better, huh?" Bond responds with "No, just different". But this evocation of difference was certainly something with which Fleming's *Thrilling Cities* and the Bond films based in Asian filming locations are preoccupied. Not only does Bond transverse the Asian continent stretching from Istanbul and Beirut in Southwest Asia/Middle East to what was called in Fleming's time the Far East and in particular Japan and later Korea, but he also works with foreign agencies and local fixers and helpers who aid him on his missions. Although 'Asia' is frequently mistaken for 'East Asia' in the North American popular and critical imagination—a generalization that overlooks the range and diversity of Asian nations, identities, and cultures—the Bond franchise does not present Asia in monolithic terms and instead depicts a fundamental contrast of East Asia with South, Southeast, and Southwest Asia.

This is particularly evident in the visual representation of Asian cities, which convey different impressions about the relationship between Britain and these specific Asian regions/nations. On the one hand, East Asian cities like Tokyo, Hong Kong, and Shanghai are depicted as highly developed, modernized, and cosmopolitan spaces, which are defined vertically—via high-rise buildings and underground lairs—and through the use of reflective surfaces that emphasize the cityscape. On the other hand, South, Southeast, and Southwest Asian cities like Bangkok, Udaipur, Istanbul, and Ho Chi Minh City are presented as being lesser developed, pre-modern, and unsophisticated; they are defined horizontally and primarily on the street level, more chaotic in feel, and through more natural materials and lighting.

EAST ASIAN MODERNITY IN THE CONNERY ERA

Although China maintains a nefarious presence in the Connery-era films *Dr. No* and *Goldfinger*, Bond does not travel to East Asia and Chinese geopolitical interests are represented primarily through the figures of Dr. No and Goldfinger's hench people, respectively. It is not until *You Only Live Twice* that Bond travels to Japan, after earlier location filming in Hong Kong, to uncover Blofeld's theft of an American spacecraft, which he will use against the USSR in order to start a war. Bond is sent to Tokyo to investigate (after faking his death in the opening scene in Hong Kong Harbor) and spends the duration of the film there.[1] He works in concert with Tiger Tanaka, head of the Japanese Secret Service, and two of his female agents, Aki and Kissy Suzuki, and collectively they undermine the plot of the villain. Bond's presence is explained by the listening and tracking station facilities in Hong Kong, and a set-piece involving British, American, and Soviet representatives provides a rationale and justification for Bond's role and Britain's place in East Asia.

Tokyo is initially introduced at night through the use of billboards and neon signs. The scene opens with two shots of signs, one in Japanese and the other in English, welcoming the viewer to Tokyo. The film then cuts to an extreme long shot of the center of the city with large buildings covered in neon signs as the head- and backlights of the cars below flow by. The film cuts again to various close-up shots of these electric billboards, which advertise Japanese companies like Toshiba, as a sweeping Japanese-infused Bond score plays with the sound of car horns in the background. As noted by Miya Elise Mizuta, "electric lighting is a universal feature of modernity" that materializes in different ways depending on the culture (2015, p. 109). Unlike Europe, where technical advances in lighting developed across a century, Japan experienced a rapid electrification that inundated the streets with artificial light (Mizuta 2015, pp. 109–110). By the 1950s, neon advertising towers emerged on the Tokyo skyline and "became the new cultural monuments of postwar Japan, making Tokyo's nightscape instantly recognizable" (Mizuta 2015, p. 112). In *You Only Live Twice*, the modern Tokyo cityscape is illuminated by electric signs that emphasize the city's postwar economic and technological growth. It is a very different entrée to the city then offered save for Istanbul in *From Russia with Love*. In the latter, Bond is driven slowly and carefully through the streets after arriving from the airport via a Pan Am flight in the daylight. The lingering shots of Istanbul are ones that concentrate on the Hagia Sophia Mosque and the Grand Bazaar as if suggesting that Bond is travelling back in time rather than about to embrace the avant-garde in Tokyo.

In *You Only Live Twice*, Bond can first be seen walking the streets of Tokyo at night. Captured in medium shot, the images relay the height of the surrounding buildings as Bond travels along the sidewalk. At one point, the film presents Bond's point of view as he watches a woman climb into a rickshaw as a cyclist passes on the busy street lined with illuminated signs hanging from the buildings. After rendezvousing with his contact,

Aki, at a sumo wrestling match, he is driven to meet Dikko Henderson in a Toyota 2000GT sports scar. The scene features various shots of Bond, taken from the left side and back, questioning Aki as she drives him through the city, with the buildings clearly discernable in the background. This mode of representation is repeated when Aki provides Bond with a quick escape from the Osato Chemical Engineering building the same night. Thus, Bond's initial movements through the city are largely facilitated by Japanese technology (in the form of an iconic Japanese car brand) and the film presents Tokyo in much the same way that Fleming does in *Thrilling Cities* as a "wide-open city" with an established network of roads and highways (1963, p. 64).

In addition to depicting the cityscape, *You Only Live Twice* presents the interior of one high-rise building. When Bond first approaches the Osato building by car, the lower levels are captured in a low angle shot that tilts upward to emphasize both the height and importance of the building. Inside, the building features a modern design style that is characterized by an emphasis on horizontal and vertical lines, neutral colors, large and unadorned windows, natural materials (such as unpainted wood, metals, and leather), and use of reflective surfaces (like steel, chrome, and glass).[2] For example, the office of Mr. Osata, located on the top of the building, features floor to ceiling windows, light-colored hardwood flooring, modern black leather furniture with chrome legs, a glass table, and a stainless steel chair railing across a large portion of the room.[3] (Fig. 5.1).

Mixed in are some elements of traditional Japanese architecture like shojis (door or room dividers comprised of lattice wood frames covered with translucent paper) as well as Asian artwork and statues. This works to root the modern design in a Japanese context.

The verticalism of the city is further emphasized through the depiction of subterranean architecture but in a way that works very differently than the subterranean Istanbul in *From Russia with Love*, for example. When Kerim Bey takes Bond on a boat ride, through the flooded underground chambers of the Basilica Cistern (Yerebatan Sarnici), he tells the British agent of its ancient Roman provenance. By way of contrast, the headquarters of the Japanese Secret Service in *You Only Live Twice* are located underneath an old subway station and Bond first enters the office of Tiger Tanaka by sliding down a (metal) floor trap and landing on a leather chair that looks like it has been transplanted from SPECTRE headquarters in Paris (*Thunderball*). Tanaka's office is similarly designed in the modern style with concrete floors, stone walls, a metal door, light brown leather

Fig. 5.1 *You Only Live Twice* (Eon Productions et al. 1967)

furniture, a glass table, and two monitors housed in stacked copper balls rotating on the wall, with a few traditional Japanese decorations mixed in. Tanaka takes Bond on a tour of the facility, which includes a ride on his private underground train (as it is unsafe for him to travel through the streets, something that M in London apparently does not have to worry about). When Tanaka comments "I imagine that your Mr. M in London has a similar arrangement" Bond replies with "Oh yes, but of course" even though the series presents the contrary with M travelling by car often in the Brosnan- and Craig-era films, with accompanying armed protection. If this is a lie than it is one told in an attempt to save face at the sign of Japanese technological advancements. The Tokyo underground and later highway system, as represented in the film, offer additional spaces for the mobility and effectiveness of the Japanese Secret Service whether it is through the subway or the operation of a helicopter especially designed to remove a suspect car via a powerful drag magnet.[4] This leads Aki to ask Bond, "How's that for Japanese efficiency?"

The film contrasts the vertical spaces of the city with the horizontal expansiveness of private estates (i.e. the office vs. the home). Bond visits the homes of intelligence officer Dikko Henderson and Tiger Tanaka, both of which are traditionally styled and sit on an expanse of land with manicured gardens and water features. Given the high cost of living and the limited space available in the city, these guarded estates on the edge of town reflect the class privilege of the trans-national wealthy elite. Moreover, they help to connect the modern city and its technological advancements with traditional values (such as the patriarchal discourse forwarded during the infamous bathhouse scene) and this opens up space for the phallocentric Bond to insert himself (literally and sexually) into Japanese culture. And his success seems to be foreshadowed by the bevy of Japanese women who are attracted to him over Tanaka, who attributes Bond's appeal to his hairy body. In spite of the technical superiority of Tokyo and Tanaka, it is Bond's touch that uncovers Blofeld's lair by piloting an auto-gyro helicopter (assembled on site by Q but tellingly described as a 'toy' by Tanaka)[5] and facilitates its destruction by leading a group of Japanese ninja. His touch proves vital as do his keen senses because it is Bond (rather the intelligence division of the Japanese Secret Service) who deciphers a surveillance photograph of a suspect ship and cargo. The film conveys the impression that Japanese technology, however impressive and expansive, is not enough to ensure national security especially when confronted by an evil genius with truly global ambitions.

Vertical and Horizontal Contrasts in the Moore Era

In the Moore era, East Asian cities are visually contrasted with those from South and Southeast Asia. This is most evident in *The Man with the Golden Gun*, which features Bond travelling from Macau to Hong Kong in East Asia before heading to Bangkok. Much like *You Only Live Twice*, the film introduces Macau (once called the 'Monte Carlo of the Orient') at night through use of a close-up shot of an electric sign with the words "Casino de Macau" in white lettering and red Chinese characters set against a blue background. The camera pans out to a shot of a busy street on which Bond (in contrast to Tokyo) is being transported by a rickshaw. He travels on a side street before arriving at a family-run store, which provides cover for the workshop of Lazar, a gunsmith who manufactures gold bullets and other specialty weapons; his craftsmanship is of such high quality that both Q and the MI6 ballistics expert Colthorpe recognize his work during the briefing in the previous scene.

His workshop, much like the headquarters of the Japanese Secret Service, is located underground although it is far smaller in size. While it is not decorated in a modern style, it is a raw and functional space without décor but one that contains various metal tools, materials, and even a shooting range. This underground workshop affords Lazar a discrete location for his 'booming' business and a place for Bond to safely interrogate the gunsmith about his supply and demand patterns to his global network of assassins.

In pursuit of the gold bullets and the man who pulls the trigger, Bond travels to Hong Kong by ferry during the day. While on the ship, Bond (as well as the audience) is provided with descriptions of the harbor, the positioning of Hong Kong and Kowloon in relation to the boat, and information about the RMS *Queen Elizabeth* shipwreck, which resulted after a mysterious fire in 1972. This voice-over narration from the ship's captain is paired with various shots of the many ships travelling through the water. These scenes, which are superfluous to the narrative, help to establish Hong Kong as a global center of trade (and commerce) while signaling its geopolitical and royal relationship to Britain as a colony. In spite of this scene, Bond's arrival in Hong Kong is signaled by a close-up shot of a sign for the Hong Kong Macau Hydrofoil company. Although a Bond Girl driving a British MG convertible picks him up (much like in *You Only Live Twice* but only this time it is a British not Japanese car), there are relatively few shots of the pair driving and the film cuts to Bond arriving at the Peninsula Hotel (the same hotel he returns to in *Die Another Day*). Moreover, the film does not contain shots (in the daylight) that emphasize the scale of the buildings.

The city is defined in more detail at night as Bond stakes out the Bottoms Up Club.[6] Bond can be seen standing beside the window display of a storefront underneath the sign for the Golden Dragon Company. The film cuts to a close-up of the electric sign for the club and then back to a close-up shot of Bond before showing his point of view of the street lined with electric signs that are also strung across the roadway. These lights are linked with Asian technological advancement as Bond adjusts his tie while looking into a SONY television monitor that provides his reflection. The film cuts between Bond's image on screen presented in a blueish hue with medium close-up shots of his face watching the monitor from a low angle that captures a blue electric billboard over his left shoulder (on the right of the screen). The film emphasizes Asian modernity through the diegetic connection between the Chinese electric signs and the electronics of a Japanese company.

The city is best defined in the scene that follows as Bond is arrested by Hong Kong Police's Lieutenant Hip and transported to headquarters. He is first taken by car and the scene includes aerial shots of the vehicle as it moves through the streets of Hong Kong. Bond is seated in the back with Hip and through the rear and side window the tall buildings and electric lined streets fly by. He is then escorted by boat and the scene includes various shots of the iconic Hong Kong nightscape taken from the water. Seated in the stern with Hip, Bond views the city through a doorway leading to the bow. The scene also features various shots of the boat moving away from the nightscape as Bond is being taken towards the New Territories; his questioning the direction of travel of the police motor boat emphasizes his familiarity with Hong Kong. In addition, the film highlights the colonial roots of the city by including a shot taken from the water with the RMS *Queen Elizabeth* in the right half of the frame and the illuminated city on the left. As a British colony, Hong Kong became a key port city for managing trade with China in the nineteenth and twentieth centuries (Petty 2015, p. 167). Its role as a financial and cultural gateway is emphasized in the cityscape through the erection of towering structures that stand as monuments to this economic growth. According to Ackbar Abbas, Hong Kong serves as an extreme example of cosmopolitanism as the city has historically been suspended between the political and economic tensions of the West and the East. He writes, "Hong Kong, culturally speaking, was caught in the double bind of divided loyalties. It was politically ambivalent about both Britain and China; ambivalent about what language, English or Chinese, it would master; and confident only about capital" (2000, p. 777). Although MI6 has located its base outside of the city and on the partially submerged ship, this is described as a being a choice (in order to avoid spying from China) rather than a reflection of a fractured relationship with Hong Kong. And this connection is relayed visually through the depiction of the illuminated cityscape and the British ship, as well as through the partnership of Bond with Hip.

Cities in East Asia are depicted differently than those in South and Southeast Asia. In *The Man with the Golden Gun*, Bond travels to Bangkok Thailand to make contact with Hai Fat, a wealthy Thai businessman he suspects is connected to Francisco Scaramanga. While he spends the majority of the time operating within the expansive estates of both men, he does travel into town and the film offers two different images that suggest less/limited economic development. First, after Bond escapes from Hai Fat's compound, he travels towards the city on a long tail boat (possibly along the Chao Phraya River). The waterway becomes increasingly congested with tour boats, houseboats, and small boats transporting goods like fruit and building supplies. As Bond weaves his way through this traffic, he passes various low-level buildings—only one to two stories high—with metal roofs and wooden docks/ladders. This scene forwards the impression that Bangkok is far less developed and cosmopolitan than Macau and Hong Kong, and not populated with a dense ferry network that crisscrosses Hong Kong harbor let alone the sleek-looking hydrofoil service to Macau. Bond has to do his own navigating through the riverine geographies of Bangkok.

Bond ventures out into the city the next day. Unlike Macau and Hong Kong, the streets of Bangkok are not shown at night nor is the city introduced with an electric sign. Instead, when Bond follows Scaramanga by car through the downtown core, the city appears far less modern and majestic. The multilane streets have fewer cars and almost no painted lines while the sidewalks are lined with mobile vendors rather than permanent storefronts. The buildings are not only spread out but they also extend more horizontally than vertically (and range from one to six stories). As a result, the aboveground power lines often stand out as the highest structures along stretches of the road. Moreover, there is significant 'green-space' as most streets are lined with trees, shrubs, and grass. Overall, the downtown lacks the urban density and development of Macau and Hong Kong. The lack of cosmopolitanism is further emphasized through the pairing of Bond with J.W. Pepper, an ignorant Louisiana sheriff who was previously featured in *Live and Let Die*. While his recasting is clearly an attempt to create comedy and parody, his offensive comments demonstrate a lack of worldliness that contrasts greatly with the cosmopolitan Bond. As a result, Bond spends most of his time travelling through Bangkok (horizontally) by boat and automobile rather than walking the streets and digging deeper into the city (as it has limited vertical development above or belowground). As if to compensate for that apparent lack of verticality, Bangkok's busy streets are used to stage a chase involving two American AMC cars as Bond with Pepper in tow attempts to pursue Scaramanga and his hench person. The lack of modernity renders it a less visually stimulating place for the narrative to unfold and the climax takes place on Scaramanga's private island somewhere in the South China Sea rather than in the city center of Bangkok.

In *Octopussy*, Udaipur, India is depicted in a similar way to Bangkok only this time there is no diegetic contrast with an East Asian/Chinese city. India is introduced through a lingering shot of Taj Mahal in Agra, which is simply there for its iconic/touristic significance to global audiences, as it is located hundreds of miles away from Udaipur. Instead, Bond travels to Udaipur early in the film and spends the majority of his screen time there in the hunt for an exiled Afghan prince Kamal Khan. The film presents a visual contrast between the spaces claimed by foreigners and those predominantly occupied by local dwellers. From the palatial mountain estate of Khan to the luxurious Hotel Shiv Niwas Palace where Bond and predominantly white visitors stay,[7] these images recall Britain's colonial history of India (from 1858 to 1947) and the division of wealth between the rich, white foreigners and the poorer locals. These buildings are the most developed in the city: they are slightly taller structures (between two to five stories) designed in the Mughal architectural style that expand horizontally and are well fortified (via metal bars, walls, and guards). Moreover, they sit on the highest points of land and tower over the rest of the city, which reflects their wealth and strategic importance.

In contrast, urban density defines the rest of the city, as it is comprised of low-story buildings that are either attached or stand in very close proximity. Bond is transported through the city along the dirt roads on a tut-tut driven by his contact Vijay while being chased by armed thugs. The streets are densely populated with pedestrians with only a few other vehicles passing by. Instead, the locals use other modes of transportation from walking and cycling to riding camels and elephants. This conveys the impression that the city of Udaipur and the province of Rajasthan are far less industrialized and developed than other Asian cities and regions, and the lack of street lines to organize the traffic gives the place a chaotic feel. The streets are also lined with mobile vendors rather than permanent glass storefronts and the urban architecture lacks complexity as most buildings are made from stone and other natural materials and adorned with colorful textiles. At one point, Bond jumps out of the tut-tut and escapes into the crowd while interacting directly with the locals. As he makes his way through a street festival (getting 'lei-d' in the process), Bond passes a variety of male performers including a sword swallower, flame spitter, flame juggler, fire walker, and a man who sleeps on a bed of nails. While parodying the filmic character Indiana Jones in *Raiders of the Lost Ark* (Spielberg 1981), this scene conveys a sense of everyday exoticism (more akin to the gypsy life that Bond witnesses outside Istanbul rather than the kind exoticism Bond encounters in night clubs in Hong Kong and Beirut) and heightens the danger of the attacks on Bond who has to defeat his opponents while mastering the elements from the local space. Bond establishes his colonial authority when he makes claims over these aspects of the Indian city. For instance, he throws a man onto the bed of nails and steals a torch that is being juggled. He takes a sword out of a man's mouth to attack an opponent and then kicks a cooking plate to set the firewalker's path ablaze. Although Bond is polite in his appropriation—as he returns the sword and thanks the man for it—he demonstrates colonial authority in his exploitation of local elements for his own purpose. This conveys the subtle geographies of the Bond franchise as the hero makes claims on spaces and resources he (socially, culturally, politically) values less and the very act of saying thank you works to naturalize his demeanor and what he is able to touch in his self-defense. As with Bangkok, Bond has been forced to improvise with his hands and/or take what he can find to ensure his survival.

The scene ends with Bond jumping back into the tut-tut and escaping through a secret passage hidden by a large poster of a dragon. From there, Bond is taken to Q's laboratory, which is hidden behind a stone wall. Architecturally, this space is traditionally styled with elaborate archways and detailed floral mosaics. The space is both large and airy, which is typical of the Mughal style, and (horizontally) expansive as the camera follows Bond as he moves from the front to the back room. The furnishings within this space, however, contrast with the traditional design. The rooms are filled with wooden desks, workbenches, metal frames, and various electronic devices, as the space is a covert British research facility specializing in producing spy gadgetry. On the one hand, this scene emphasizes the British appropriation of local space and ongoing post-colonial authority in India. Local staff members are employed at the British facility so one might conclude that the Indian government has given prior approval in the same way that the Egyptian authorities permitted the secret station inside a pyramid-like structure outside Cairo in *The Spy Who Loved Me*. By way of contrast, the Turkish station in Istanbul is run by a local man who Bond has an affectionate and effective professional partnership with and that is operated by his extensive family members. On the other hand, the traditional architecture helps to enhance the impression that Britain is technologically advanced whereas India and Turkey, by comparison, lack modern development. This representational mode is indicative of what Edward Said terms Orientalism whereby "the Orient" is contrasted unfavorably with "the Occident." While the West envisions itself as developed, flexible, and superior, the East (from North Africa to Asia) has largely been viewed in binary opposition as less developed, static, and inferior (1994, pp. 1–4). Said writes,

> Orientalism can be discussed and analyzed as the corporate institution for dealing with the Orient—dealing with it by making statements about it, authorizing views of it, describing it, by teaching it, settling it, ruling over it: in short, Orientalism as a Western style for dominating, restructuring, and having authority over the Orient (1994, p. 3).

This patronizing perception is relayed in the Bond franchise, most forcibly, through the representation of South Asian cities like Udaipur in *Octopussy* as well as Southeast Asian cities like Bangkok in *The Man with the Golden Gun*. Not only are they contrasted with Britain but also Chinese and Japanese cities that appear more modern, cosmopolitan, and technically advanced. This technical and modern divide is elaborated more fully in the Brosnan era.

THE TECHNICAL/MODERN DIVIDE IN THE BROSNAN ERA

In the Brosnan era, the contrasting depiction of East and South/Southeast Asian cities conveys important messages about shifting geopolitical relations in the 1990s and early 2000s. For example, in *Tomorrow Never Dies*, Bond travels to Vietnam to investigate the disappearance of a British frigate, the HMS Devonshire, in the South China Sea. The relationship with this maritime space is very different to *The Man with the Golden Gun* where it appears that the Chinese authorities are complicit with Scaramanga's secret base. Twenty-five years later, Bond teams up with Wai Lin, a spy for the Chinese People's External Security Force, to take down Elliot Carver, a British media mogul who plans to provoke a global war in order to bolster his (American) conglomerate. After the pair is captured by Carver, they are transported by helicopter to his headquarters in Ho Chi Minh City, the largest city in Vietnam. This film provides a number of aerial shots of the city that emphasize the height and scale of Carver's skyscraper, which towers over the lower-lying buildings below. The skyscraper is adorned with a large poster of Carver's face, which the camera zooms in on as the chopper moves closer to the building (Fig. 5.2).

Fig. 5.2 *Tomorrow Never Dies* (Eon Productions et al. 1997)

This establishing shot is significant in a number of respects. On the one hand, it offers a visual representation of the power Carver yields and the kind of personality cult he encourages amongst his organization. While Bond comments that the building reflects Carver's "edifice complex," the structure also relays the impression that Carver is far more technologically advanced, as this building also serves as his communication station.

On the other hand, it offers a profound comment on post-Cold War geopolitical relations. The Vietnam War (1955–75) was an international conflict that pit South Vietnam and its allies France and the United States, supported by Australia and other anti-communist countries, against North Vietnam and its allies, supported by China[8] and the USSR. Notably, the UK government under Harold Wilson refused to commit British troops to Vietnam. The conflict, which lasted two decades, came to an end after the United States withdrew its troops and Saigon (the former name for Ho Chi Minh City) came under the control of the North Vietnamese Army. In the United States, support for the war dwindled in the 1960s as many Americans viewed the invasion as a "mistake" and even "immoral."[9] Moreover, the conduct of American soldiers in Vietnam—who participated in various acts from psychological warfare[10] to war crimes—has left a lasting mark on the international reputation of the United States, which is hinted at by the touristic presence of Sheriff Pepper and his wife in *The Man with the Golden Gun*.

In *Tomorrow Never Dies*, Ho Chi Minh City becomes the nexus for a new global conflict. This is signified through the erection of Carver's towering skyscraper, the internal design of which emphasizes Western occupation and appropriation in much the same way that MI6 repurposed a building in Udaipur for Q's workshop in *Octopussy*.[11] In Carver's office, the walls are painted dark grey and red, and half of the room (near the doorway) is filled with Asian art from gold and wooden statues to stone wall plaques and paintings; the positioning of the art suggests that it has either been smuggled in to decorate the office or is being set aside (and packed away) to open up space in the room for the communication station. The other half of the office contains Carver's desk in front of three large screens onto which Carver's newspaper stories are projected. This is his primary workspace and becomes the focal point of the scene as Carver composes the obituaries of Bond and Lin. It is here that Carver uses war terminology when describing his plan for global media domination. He says to Bond, "You see we are both men of action but your era and Miss Lin's are passing. Words are the new weapons, satellites are the new artillery." When Bond asks Carver if he sees himself as "the new supreme allied commander," Carver responds in the affirmative stating that "Caesar had his legions. Napoleon had his armies. I have my divisions: TV, news, magazines. And by midnight tonight, I will have reached and influenced more people in the history of this planet save God himself." It is in the heart of Ho Chi Minh City that Carver oversees his plot to instigate a(nother) war between China and the United States, who were on opposites sides during the Vietnam War.

The film offers a contrast between Carver's skyscraper, which is defined vertically and in relation to technology, with the rest of the city, which is experienced horizontally and appears less developed. This is established through the escape of Bond and Lin from Carver's custody. After fighting and shooting their way out of the office and onto the balcony, Bond and Lin quickly descend from the building by using the outside banner to repel down, tearing a line through the center of Carver's portrait in the process. The skyscraper is so tall that this repelling only gets them halfway down; the pair has to crash through a window and uses the elevator to complete their descent. They then board a motorcycle and drive the vehicle (while handcuffed) through the streets of Ho Chi Minh City. As they flee from their pursuers, Bond and Lin drive along paved roads (filled mostly with bicycles) and alleyways as they pass by low-story buildings and mobile food vendors. Not only do they use their local surroundings to create barriers—unlocking water barrels and evading a crate of fireworks, which are hit and destroy their pursuers—but they also drive on the rooftops of various apartments creating a path of destruction as they evade a helicopter shooting at them. At one point, they drive through a local business and crash through the ceiling of an apartment, startling a couple making love. When the pair finally returns to the street, they make their way through a crowd in order to evade a tilted helicopter that is using its propeller as a blade to destroy anything in its path. Using a (horizontal) skidding maneuver, they are able to attach an anchor to the helicopter and jump into a well before it explodes. While the chase sequence is dynamic, as it takes place on a number of low levels from the street to the rooftop and interiors of low-story buildings, it is also highly destructive as the city, in addition to Bond and Lin, is being attacked. This destruction is inflicted by the motorized vehicles—a motorcycle, helicopter, and SUVs—driven by foreign agents through the streets of Ho Chi Minh City.[12] This conveys troubling messages about subtle geographies in the Bond franchise in which foreign agents (Britain and China) can not only erect vertical monuments reflective of their power but they can also horizontally invade and destroy the public and privates spaces in the Southeast Asian city. Buildings and people appear disposable and as Bond notes in *The Spy Who Loved Me*, 'Egyptian builders' were clearly inferior to their European counterparts; a similar impression of Vietnamese architecture is relayed through this scene.

Additionally, the film emphasizes the lack of modern development in Ho Chi Minh City through the depiction of Lin's apartment. Following the chase sequence, she returns to her pad (which doubles as a bicycle shop) located off of a busy street. The dimly lit space is cluttered with repair parts (located on shelves and hanging from the rafters) and contains few decorations. Hidden within this workshop is a secret Chinese communications post and arsenal that emerges from the desk and walls with the push of a button: this includes two computer consoles, a wall with a dozen monitors and various control panels, and two rotating displays filled with handheld, automatic, and explosive weapons. The metal cases and control panels contrast greatly with the wood and natural materials that make up the apartment. Moreover, the fluorescent lights emitted by the monitors and display cases offer a visual contrast with the warm yellow light cast from the room's fixtures. As Bond fingers the various devices, he comments that he "has always been a fan of Chinese technology" and the film is the first since *You Only Live Twice* to depict another foreign agency with a similar range of Q-like and technologically advanced gadgetry. Taken together, this scene offers a visual contrast between Chinese modernity via electronics, metalwork, and florescent lighting, and the premodern status of Ho Chi Minh City as defined through bicycles (which are human powered rather than electrically operated), natural materials, and basic lighting.

The emphasis on Chinese modernity is carried over in the opening scenes of *Die Another Day* when Bond, after escaping the custody of MI6, swims to the Hong Kong yacht club. The scene opens with the iconic view of the Hong Kong (Island) nightscape from the Tsim Sha Tsui waterfront of Kowloon. However, the film contains a geographical error, as the Royal Hong Kong Yacht Club referenced in the sign is actually located on the north end of Hong Kong Island (and thus the cityscape of Kowloon should be visible in the background).[13] This oversight draws even more attention to the depiction of the Hong Kong nightscape (relayed here digitally as Brosnan shot the scene in front of a bluescreen), which has developed substantially since its last depiction in *The Man with the Golden Gun*. The nightscape is filled with more towering skyscrapers adorned with lights that reflect on Victoria Harbor. While emphasizing the modernity and cosmopolitanism of Hong Kong in material and spatial terms, the shots of the city's iconic nightscape contain geopolitical significance as Hong Kong serves as Bond's first point of contact after he 'goes rogue'. He returns to a familiar ground in the hope of reestablishing contact with previous connections and is greeted as a familiar guest by the hotel staff.

In 1997, Hong Kong was handed over from British to Chinese rule. While *Tomorrow Never Dies* presents the renegotiation of Anglo-Chinese relations through the collaboration of Bond and Lin on a common mission, *Die Another Day* depicts Bond's first trip to post-1997 Hong Kong.[14] Much like Bond who finds himself on the outs with MI6, Hong Kong is renegotiating its social and cultural identity as a special administrative region of China. The cityscape plays a role in this. As noted by Margaret Maile Petty

> As a former colonial harbor city without a clear or unifying cultural foundation and defiant, even mercenary, undercurrents driving its development, local identity is drawn from that upon which Hong Kong was built—trade, that is to say, the fluid traffic of goods and money between traders, merchants and developers and the harbor that sheltered them. Thus, its towers

are not just houses of commerce and international banking, but also symbols of continued survival and independence. (2015, p. 167)

The image of the Hong Kong nightscape helps to link the endurance of a city responding to significant shifts in its geopolitical terrain through decolonization with the plight of Bond, who finds himself disavowed by MI6 but who is nonetheless eager to trade in secrets. Given their shared colonial roots, the endurance of Hong Kong serves as a metaphor for the challenges Bond will face and overcome in the narrative, as the shimmering lights serve as a beacon of hope for him and Britain. Ultimately, mission success for Bond begins in Hong Kong even though it started with his torture by North Korean agents and ended in rural South Korea.

TECHNO-ORIENTALISM IN *SKYFALL*

In the Craig era, Chinese modernity is no longer presented in positive terms, as the Chinese city becomes a perilous space for Bond and Chinese technology is depicted as a threat to the communication information systems and infrastructure of Britain. This shift in representation is informed by Techno-Orientalism, a concept that has largely been discussed in relation to (the Western gaze of) Japanese culture and expands on Said's theory of Orientalism (see earlier in the chapter). According to Toshiya Ueon

the Orient exists in so far as the West needs it, because it brings the project of the West into focus [...] If the Orient was invented by the West, then the Techno-Orient also was invented by the world of information capitalism. In "Techno-Orientalism," Japan not only is located geographically, but also is projected chronologically. Jean Baudrillard once called Japan a satellite in orbit. Now Japan has been located in the future of technology. (2003, par. 12–14)

Kevin Robins and David Morley relay similar sentiments in their book *Spaces of Identity* when they discuss the association between Japan and high-technology (or the technologies of the future) via "screens, networks, cybernetics, robots, artificial intelligence, [and] simulation" (1995, p. 168). This technological progress, which transcends and displaces Western modernity, has had a destabilizing effect as the West has to come to terms with its "technological emasculation" (ibid. p. 168).

In *Skyfall*, Techno-Orientalism is projected onto China (and not Japan) and the film relays Western anxieties about cyberwarfare and cyberterrorism. In the new millennium, the People's Liberation Army (PLA) of

China has engaged in "integrated network electronic warfare" (*wangdian yitizhan*), which centers on "information confrontation" (*xinxi duikang*; Inkster 2015, p. 42). As Timothy L. Thomas explains

> China's cyber tools enable it to work toward attaining a strategic advantage or *shi*. Cyber, or computer-related, tools can deceive, influence, attack, defend, and conduct reconnaissance activities anonymously from strategic distances. They perform activities over the Internet as forces do on the ground but from distances and surreptitious postures that actual forces cannot achieve [...] Cyber tools help uncover vulnerabilities in the digital files of other nation-states, vulnerabilities that could be manipulated in times of crises. (2012, p. 410)

Between 2006 and 2007, the governments of Britain, Germany, and New Zealand separately accused China of cyber attacks and in 2012 the United States made similar claims of an attack on the RSA security system used in the Pentagon (Inkster 2015, p. 43). Moreover, in 2013, the IT security company Mandiant based in the United States "released a report detailing the activities of Shanghai-based PLA Unit 61398 as being responsible for conducting cyber attacks on the United States and other English-speaking countries dating back to 2006" (ibid, p. 43). While the Chinese government has denied any wrongdoing, these claims draw attention to the increasing technological threat of China to the structure and security of Western information and technological infrastructures.

The threat of Chinese modernity in *Skyfall* is relayed through the depiction of the city. Following a conversation between Bond and Q about cyberwarfare that ends with Bond stating the words "brave new world," the film cuts to an aerial shot of Shanghai at night with its nightscape illuminated by florescent lights thereby linking cyberterrorism with the electric city. After the words Shanghai appear on screen, the film cuts to three additional aerial shots of the city that feature closer-up shots of various illuminated skyscrapers, some of which were actually filmed in the city of London. The fourth shot tracks towards one tall building with a rooftop pool and zooms in towards the water. It then cuts to an interior shot with the camera tracking left as it follows Bond swimming in the water that glows electric blue. In the background, the illuminated buildings of the nightscape are visible through the glass that encapsulates the complex. This scene establishes three elements that define Shanghai in the film: tall buildings illuminated with fluorescent lights and signs, transparent and reflective surfaces, and electric blue lights on technology. These aspects are evident in the following scene that depicts Bond sitting at the hotel bar. The illuminated nightscape is visible through the floor to ceiling windows and reflected on the shiny black counter that functions like a mirror. The windows of the building just over his right shoulder emit an electric blue light that from a distance looks like computer coding—an image that recalls the representation of digital infrastructure (albeit green) in *The Matrix* (The Wachowskis 1999). This link between electric blue lights and digital technology is evident when Bond receives a call on his smartphone, which emits the same bright blue light.

The film connects this digital technology to the city through the blue lighting, which is used on both the skyscrapers and the cell phone. Moreover, the previous scene featuring Bond in the electric-blue pool not only creates the impression that cyberspace is fluid but also symbolizes the way in which Britain is enveloped and relies on its digital infrastructure. And just as the injured Bond sits heaving on the side of the pool after his exercise, Britain also has vulnerabilities that can (and will) be exploited however fit for purpose it might think its people and infrastructure are.

The film continues to depict Shanghai through these more than representational architectures. This is evident in the following scene in which Bond tails an assassin named Patrice from the airport to a building. The materiality of the city and its infrastructure is deliberately foregrounded, as the film cuts between medium close-up shots of Bond in his car and a variety of images of the city. The first is an extreme long aerial shot of the highway system, which is comprised of various interwoven roads that are perched on top of multilane city streets below. While the car lights on the upper roads glow yellow, the streets underneath that move through the heart of the city glow an electric blue. The film contains various point-of-view shots from the vantage point of Bond and/or the roof of his car that depict his transit through the city center past soaring and illuminated skyscrapers. Although the scene takes place at night, the light from the buildings is so bright that the sky appears to be a hazy dark blue. When Bond arrives at his destination, the film emphasizes the scale of the building (which is framed by skyscrapers on both sides) by cutting to a low angle shot that pans downwards from the top of the building to the ground below and captures Patrice stepping out of the cab. Through this scene, the city is defined by the scale of its buildings and electrified infrastructure, which serves as a metaphor for its development in the area of digital technology.

When Bond follows Patrice into the skyscraper, he is initially in an inferior position as the structural elements do not work in his favor. Not only is the exterior made up of glass, but the escalator, elevator, and some interior walls are as well, making it difficult for Bond to stealthily approach his target. Although the lobby is dimly lit, the technology in the space glows electric blue from the elevator buttons to the escalator track to the computer consoles embedded in the walls. This light reflects on the glass and foreshadows its ability to provide camouflage. At the last second, Bond manages to grab onto the base of the elevator before it ascends to the top and a high-angle shot captures Bond struggling to hold on as the ground falls further away. When Bond arrives on the top floor, the structural elements now work in his favor as he moves from the dark hallway, dimly lit blue from an electric billboard outside of a window, to a series of offices that are enclosed with glass walls. The lights from the large external electric billboard not only illuminate the room but they also reflect on the glass and conceal Bond as he moves through the offices towards Patrice. Moreover, this scene is the epitome of Techno-Orientalism, as blue technology screens and electric lights define the city. At one point, Patrice turns around as the image of a white electric jellyfish appears on a blue screen the background. Not only does this frame Patrice as being as dangerous as the sea creature, but the jellyfish has also been used to describe the typology of the Internet.[15] As John Evans once wrote "The internet is like a giant jellyfish. You can't step on it. You can't go around it. You've got to get through it" (qtd. in Wood and Smith 2014, p. 3). Thus, Shanghai is not only defined as being hi-tech but its information infrastructure (signaled through the casting of communications logos on the glass) is set up as a barrier, like Patrice, that Bond has to overcome.

After Patrice shoots his target in an adjacent building, he looks up to see the reflection of Bond, cast in a blue light, on the glass. Much like a Trojan horse, Bond has snuck in from behind to disable his target. As the two men start to fight, Patrice shoots and cracks the window, rendering it translucent (like a shoji) and unable to reflect light. Instead, it becomes a matte blue backdrop against which the two men depicted in silhouette fight. This recalls the aesthetic approach utilized in the Bond opening credit sequences (as well as the aesthetic design of a fight sequence in *Kill Bill Volume 1* [Tarantino 2003] in the House of Blue Leaves). After the pair smashes the window with the gun during their scrummage, the unfiltered image from the billboard—that of the electric jellyfish—becomes the background framed by the window pane (Fig. 5.3).

Fig. 5.3 *Skyfall* (Eon Productions et al. 2012)

As the two men continue to fight, their faces are momentarily illuminated by the flashes of yellow light from the barrel of the gun. As Bond wrestles the man to the ground and pushes him out the window, the camera tracks up to Bond and tilts down over his shoulder to show him hovering over the dangling man whose body is framed by four glass skyscrapers in the shape of a quadrilateral. When Bond's arm gives out thereby dropping the man to his death, the film cuts to an image of Bond laying on the ground from the point of view of Severine in the adjacent building. Located behind the glass, his image is covered by electric blue Chinese characters momentarily before the billboard goes dark and when the light returns he is gone. Bond is set up as the force that can rival Chinese technology. The scene closes with a final aerial shot of Shanghai before cutting to M working on her computer in Britain and viewing the leaked list of British agents on YouTube. Thus, the film creates a diegetic connection between Shanghai and the cyberwarfare being waged against Britain.

The film depicts Macau in a different light in both a literal and figurative sense. The city is introduced through an establishing shot of the nightscape in which the buildings are partially illuminated by warm yellow lights (rather than being outlined by fluorescent ones). Bond spends his time in a luxury hotel and casino on the water, spaces defined by their wealth and their positioning on the periphery of the metropolis. Through their design, these spaces are rooted in Chinese tradition or the past rather than its high-tech future (like Shanghai) and this creates the sense that Bond is going back in time. On the one hand, the film presents Bond, as a hero, stepping back into the past. The film not only constitutes the conclusion of the orphan origin trilogy but also presents Bond returning to his roots particularly through the setting of the climax at his childhood home in Scotland. However, the hotel scene in Macau forwards a similar impression as it constitutes the space of Bond's transformation through his close shave from which he emerges looking youthful and revitalized (Dodds 2014, p. 121). Even Moneypenny helps to facilitate this change and it is here (and only here) in this traditional space that their flirtatious attraction plays out. On the other hand, the scene with the casino presents the impression that Bond is going back in Chinese history through his venturing into the underbelly of the city. This is conveyed through the more ornate and traditional Chinese architecture as well as dim lighting provided by Chinese lanterns. The casino also contains a pit filled with komodo dragons and while these creatures are not native to Macau their presence creates the sense that this building is rooted in pre-modern history. Moreover, the scene features the first encounter of Bond with Severine whose representation also seems 'pre-historic' as it relies on antiquated racial stereotypes of Asian femininity (Funnell 2015b, p. 86). Much like in *You Only Live Twice*, Bond re-asserts his masculinity and sexuality in these traditional East Asian spaces that exist on the outskirts or are hidden underneath the surface of the modern city.

Bond travels by boat to an abandoned island off the coast of Macau. Following an establishing shot of the crumbling buildings, Bond can be seen walking along a dirt road past debris. As Severine explains, Silva wanted the island and used "his computer" to convince the workers that there was a chemical leak. Bond is then taken to a room filled with computer servers and monitors where Silva interrogates him. While the island seems to embody the one Silva mentions in his metaphor (about how his grandmother controlled the rodent infestation on her island by capturing and changing the nature of two surviving rats, which he likens to Bond and himself), it also works to connect him to China. Formerly stationed in Hong Kong, Silva was an MI6 agent who was turned over to Chinese authorities in 1997 after they discovered that he hacked into their computer system; M handed over Silva in exchange for a dozen British agents and this agreement assured a peaceful handover. It contrasts with the experience of Bond in *Die Another Day* who was handed over by North

Korean intelligence forces in return for some of their agents. As with Silva, Bond was tortured and the opening sequences of the film relay the nature and extent of his suffering.

After a failed attempt at suicide, Silva emerges a number of years later as a cyber terrorist seeking revenge. While the details of his life during this interim period are not discussed, the film suggests that Silva traded British intelligence for his freedom and is somehow still connected to China even though his quest for revenge is deeply personal. And yet, the technology that he uses is distinguished from the blue screens featured throughout Shanghai, on the cellphones of Bond and M, and the computer interfaces in MI6. The screens on Silva's computers are black (which clearly suggests villainy) while the servers are comprised of metal frames covered in colored wires and red lights. Much like the abandoned city, Silva's command center is unpolished and makeshift, and this can be interpreted in two ways. First, it suggests that Silva's hacking skills are far superior as he can build up his own command center on an abandoned island and establish his terrorist network in the darkest corners of the Internet (hence the black screen). Second, it helps to mask his technological know-how and true purpose, as he intends to get captured in order to release a virus into MI6. Thus, the abandoned Chinese city serves as a staging ground for Silva's plot.

Although the remainder of the film takes place in London, one key element from Shanghai is carried forward: the electric blue screen. This is evident in Q's underground laboratory in which his workstation is set up in front of five large screens displaying blue data. This contrasts greatly with Silva's laptop, which features a black screen. When Q plugs the laptop into the system, the data is interpreted by the system and projected in the common format. Q mentions that Silva is using obscure codes to mask his true intent: "security through obscurity." When Bond locates the key to decrypt the files—"Grandborough," the name of an old underground station—the images on screen reconfigure and the blue graphics turn red to display an underground map of London. The red graphic can be read as a metaphor for the body as the lines are like veins that travel to and from the heart of the city. They also reflect Silva's cyber attack on MI6's electronic infrastructure as the color is linked to his other programs as well as the server system on the abandoned island off of Macau. Finally, the color provides a link to "Red China," a term used during the Cold War to emphasize the country's connection to the communist bloc. This 'red' invasion results in the release of Silva and his subsequent attack on

London. Through the representation of Chinese cities and emphasis on Techno-Orientalism, the film connects Silva's single-minded revenge plot to China.

CONCLUSION

In the Bond franchise, Asian citizens and cities are depicted through the Western gaze in Orientalist terms. Although *Die Another Day* does not dwell on any Korean cities, its depiction of the main Korean characters reinforces that racial and geographical imaginary.[16] Released at a time when President George W. Bush identified an 'axis of evil' involving Iran, Iraq, and North Korea, the film features the demilitarized zone (DMZ) of the Korean peninsula, and sets up a narrative involving renegade North Korean officers who take pleasure in exposing Bond's belief that the "British still have the right to police the world". Bond's humiliation and subsequent torture by North Korean agents set up a mission and a moral geography, which resurrects the Anglo-American special alliance while presenting the renegade officers as freakishly engaging in post-DNA replacement therapy so that they can disguise themselves as white. Throughout the film, the two Koreas are denied any semblance of modernity except when they import high-tech weaponry and access Cuban post-DNA replacement therapy. As Jodi Kim notes, "Even South Korea, a US ally, is depicted through Orientalist tropes. The film contains shots of South Korean farmers standing in a rice paddy (complete with an ox-plow), who stare confusingly at two Italian sports cars that have dropped from the sky. This primitivist and anachronistic rendering of contemporary South Korea is coupled with a scene in which an American general issues an order to 'mobilize the South Korean troops'" (Kim 2015, p. 131).[17]

In the main, East Asian cities are presented as highly modern spaces through their skyscrapers and/or underground developments, florescent lights and signs, and reflective and metallic surfaces. These are highly selective images that relay powerful impressions about the relationship between Britain (i.e. the Western white self) and particular East Asian cities (i.e. the Asian Other). While defined by their technological and economic progress (as evidenced by their shimmering nightscapes), cities like Tokyo and Hong Kong are depicted in a positive light as Bond can utilize their resources for missions from which they will benefit while Shanghai is depicted as a perilous space, as their technology threatens the national security of Britain. In comparison, South and Southeast Asian cities are framed as pre-modern spaces through their limited architectural design, use of natural and less durable buildings materials, and lack of electronic technology from computers and billboards to transit systems. Bond's street-level interactions in Bangkok, Udaipur, and Ho Chi Minh City are not only facilitated by foreign/imported automotive technology, but they are also highly destructive and demonstrate his sheer disregard for the value of these cities. His operations recall the historical occupation and conflicts instigated by foreign agents who inserted themselves into these spaces. The Asian/European city of Istanbul arguably sits some-where in between—a city defined in part by Bond's street-level encounters and simple modes of transport while Bond's relationship with the city is negotiated with the helping hand of a cosmopolitan head of station. As a result, the Bond franchise presents the impression that South and Southeast Asian cities are not on par with their East Asian counterparts and can be exploited by Bond and Britain as there will be limited geopolitical ramifications.

NOTES

1. *You Only Live Twice* is notable for situating Bond in a single location for the longest period of time across any Bond film.
2. For a detailed description, see Lee (n.d.).
3. The use of metal here recalls the interior design of Dr. No's underwater lair, which features a lot of mixed metals like copper and stainless steel. While located off the coast of Jamaica, the lair reflects the Chinese/Asian heritage of the villain.
4. Blofeld has built his rocket launching station inside a dormant volcano. Both he and his workers move through the base using an underground rail. The design and particularly the use of metals reflects the style of the offices of Osato and Tanaka. It creates the impression that SPECTRE is techno-logically advanced and the organization can only be brought down by national agencies that are comparable.
5. For a detailed discussion, see Chap. 7.
6. While the club is located on the Kowloon side of Victoria Harbor, a line of dialogue (incorrectly) suggests it is located on Hong Kong Island.
7. *Octopussy*, an American jewelry smuggler, resides in a floating palace in Udaipur, India.
8. For a detailed discussion of the Sino-Vietnamese alliance, including Chinese troop deployment in North Vietnam, see Zhai (2000).

9. For a detailed discussion of shifting American perceptions about the Vietnam War, see Appy (2015).
10. For a detailed discussion, see Turse (2013) and Appy (2015).
11. In *The Man with the Golden Gun*, MI6 set up a base on board its own ship off the coast of Hong Kong Island.
12. In one shot, the SUVs stand out against a sea of bicyclists in the center of the city.
13. The real yacht club is featured in *You Only Live Twice* as the site from which an enemy agent watches Bond's fake funeral.
14. Wai Lin was originally designed to be his local contact in Hong Kong but actor Michelle Yeoh declined the part and the scene was rewritten. For a detailed discussion, see Funnell (2014)
15. For a detailed discussion, see Siganos et al. (2006).
16. For a detailed discussion, see Kim (2015).
17. For a discussion on how *Die Another Day* stimulated considerable audience resentment in Korea see Chung (2007).

CHAPTER 6

Resourceful Bond

Classical/material elements—earth, air, fire, and water—play an important role in shaping the Bond film genre, as does the struggle for resources
such as gold, diamonds, and oil. From their definition of secret lairs to their
association with male sexuality[1] to their employment in action sequences,
Bond's negotiation of 'the elements' has long defined his heroic capacity and mobility (see Chap. 7), the people with whom he interacts, and
the international geopolitics and relations that frame the narrative. The
elemental is intrinsic to the Bond aesthetic with fire and ice being used
in multiple films including *Live and Let Die*, *Die Another Day*, *Quantum
of Solace*, *Skyfall*, and *Spectre*. In the case of *Skyfall*, for example, Bond's
body endures the icy waters of a Turkish river and later plunges through
an ice-covered Scottish lake after surviving an inferno that has engulfed
his childhood home.

Bond's knowledge and even sensual appreciation of the earth's physical environment including its natural resources and atmospheric system is
vital to his survival and those that accompany him. He is able to negotiate
extreme heat (e.g. *Dr. No*), ski and slide through ice and snow (e.g. *Die
Another Day*), endure water depths and pressures (e.g. *Thunderball*), and
glide through the air (e.g. *The Spy who Loved Me*) with spectacular endurance. At times, Bond literally has the fate of Britain and the world in his
hands when he touches, directs, and mobilizes these elemental aspects;
they both constrain and enable him. The elemental is generative of Bond

© The Editor(s) (if applicable) and The Author(s) 2017
L. Funnell, K. Dodds, *Geographies, Genders and Geopolitics of
James Bond*, DOI 10.1057/978-1-137-57024-6_6

and his capacity to improvise with his body, to negotiate demanding spaces, to master environments, and to inhabit unusual or remote places.

However, classical/material elements are also gendered and often associated with women. This relationship is established in the opening title sequences, which typically feature women in shadow or silhouette moving through and mobilizing elements against male figures, one of which represents Bond. Often, the elements featured in the title sequences play an important role in the narrative proper. For instance, the watery and/or wave-like elements in the title sequences of *Thunderball* and *For Your Eyes Only* anticipate the underwater sequences in the films and the decisive role that Bond will play in them. Bond's immersion in water proves critical in forging sexual and strategic alliances with women in both films—meeting Domino Derval while swimming in the Caribbean and diving with Melina Havelock in the Mediterranean, respectively. As noted by Sabine Planka, the Bond title sequence has become a trademark of the franchise and relies on female bodies and sexuality to attract/seduce viewers to the films (2015, p. 142; Hines 2011, p. 169). Moreover, the feminizing of classical/material elements creates a narrative in which Bond's mastery of and control over earth, air, fire, and water takes on gendered connotations and has patriarchal significance. Much like Bond's seduction and manipulation of women (oftentimes away from the villain) helps to ensure the success of his mission, his control and deployment of feminized elements frames his masculine superiority over the villain in gendered and heteronormative terms. Bond's performance is framed within a narrative that justifies and naturalizes his access to and negotiation of both women and material elements, which often threaten to overwhelm him.

The films also use gender in conjunction with geopolitics to demarcate who and what (in terms of objects and technology) can access certain renewable and nonrenewable resources, and how they should be used. Various Bond films incorporate contemporaneous resource conflicts into their narratives, which favor the needs and geopolitical strategies of Britain. Through the figure of Bond, Britain is placed at the center of the gold standard exchange, African blood diamond trade, and the energy crisis in the 1970s, as well as international conflicts over oil and water. Moreover, given the gendering of these resources, as women are both associated with and control access to them, the films emphasize the importance of Bond's libidinal masculinity to put the elemental/resourceful to work in order to make safe the economic and political security of Britain. In the discussion that follows, we will examine the nature of the elements/resources being sought, the motivation of the villain and the benefit of possession, the potential to disrupt Britain and even global systems, and how specific properties of elements/resources shape the gendered geopolitics of James Bond.

Gold

Gold is a chemical element and precious metal that has long been used in coinage, jewelry, and art, and has for long periods of human history been associated with evil, idolatry, spirituality, divine power, reward, and recognition. It naturally occurs in both nugget and flake forms, and is often found in rocks, their veins, and alluvial deposits (Krebs 2006, p. 166; Obaje 2009, p. 124). Gold is not only a coinage metal but also a store of value and has historically provided a basis for monetary systems via the gold standard.[2] Although most nations in the twentieth century have abandoned the gold standard as the foundation for their currency, many still possess substantial gold reserves that are housed by a central bank or unit. One of the best known is Fort Knox (or the United States Bullion Depository), which is located in Kentucky and stores a good portion of the United States gold reserves as well as other precious items belonging to the federal government. Fort Knox is so well fortified that there has yet to be an attempt to break in. As Thomas L. Norman explains, Fort Knox has "countermeasures including a formidable building and complex, heavily armed guards, layered detection systems, [and] automatic weapons (oh, and do not forget that it sits next to the largest assembly of U.S. Army tanks and tank crews in the world)" (2009, p. 249). This layered protection is designed to safeguard the gold inside the vault, which remains a central asset of the US government. Despite its reputation as a repository for gold, the actual amount of gold has been the subject of conspiratorial speculation in the past and present, with some suggesting that the popular cultural representations of Fort Knox are misleading because the United States' gold supplies are actually secured in and dispersed across multiple locations.

The role of gold in Cold War geopolitical imaginations has varied from being a material to be coveted and protected as a financial resource to a substance that was associated with one of the most audacious US-UK spying operations (Operation Gold) designed to penetrate the Soviet Army Headquarters in Berlin via a secret underground tunnel; this was subsequently discovered by the Soviets in 1956 thanks to the help of the British traitor and former spy, George Blake. Ian Fleming was also fascinated with gold, and wrote his novels on a gold-plated typewriter, which he purchased after the commercial success of *Casino Royale* (Fleming 2015, p. 5). Gold smuggling features in his novel *Live and Let Die* (1954) and several Bond films use gold as a substance and plot device to develop geopolitical dramas affecting Britain, the United States, the Caribbean, and areas of gold production such as South Africa.

Goldfinger

Gold plays a central role in Ian Fleming's novel *Goldfinger*. The story centers on gold smuggler Auric Goldfinger whose obsession with the metal is suggested by his name (as 'auric' refers to something that is derived from gold thus making him 'Golden Goldfinger'). The figure's unhealthy obsession with gold is described in vivid detail by sisters Jill and Tilly Masterson. For instance, Jill tells Bond that Goldfinger carries a million dollars in gold on his person at all times (except when passing through customs): "'He knows that gold will buy him anything he wants. It's all twenty-four carat. And anyway he loves gold, really loves it like people love jewels or stamps or – well', she smiled, 'women'" (1959, p. 39). Goldfinger's attraction to gold is framed, more explicitly, in sexual terms when Tilly describes Goldfinger's fetish for painting women in gold:

> He hypnotizes them. Then he – he paints them gold [...] he's mad about gold. I suppose he sort of thinks he's – that he's sort of possessing gold. You know – marrying it. He gets some Korean servant to paint them. The man has to leave their backbones unpainted [...] I found out it's so they wouldn't die. If their bodies were completely covered with gold paint, the pores of the skin wouldn't be able to breathe. Then they'd die. Afterwards they're washed down by the Korean with resin or something. Goldfinger gives them a thousand dollars and sends them away. (1959, p. 173)

In the novel, gold is depicted in gendered and sexual terms, and Goldfinger's seemingly unquenchable thirst for it is framed as a (sexual) perversion. Importantly, it is two women/sisters who describe Goldfinger's fetish before being killed (separately) by Oddjob on orders from the villain and their deaths have patriarchal implications. They are killed for siding with Bond—and refusing to be possessed (only) by Goldfinger—and working against Goldfinger thereby standing in the way of his gold mania.

Gold also plays an important role in the narrative, characterization, and imagery of the film adaption. *Goldfinger* explores the great lengths to which the villain goes to acquire gold and his use of the metal for a variety of purposes. Early in the film, he smuggles Nazi German gold[3] across European borders by way of his gold Rolls Royce and the film shows that the metal is highly malleable and ductile. It is a substance that can be smelted with ease and, as Goldfinger demonstrates, it is durable, divisible, and portable.[4] He also uses it to deadly effect after his companion, Jill Masterson, betrays him in a card game and then sleeps with Bond; he has her covered in gold paint and she dies from skin suffocation. Her body is overwhelmed by the materiality of the substance itself. It is also a substance for which he can demonstrate most cruelly his patriarchal power ('till death do us part') while also explaining to Bond that there is an aesthetic value to gold ("All my life I have been in love with its color, its brilliance, its divine heaviness"). He might have added "and its murderous capabilities" but the inference to Bond by that stage was clear. Financial reward underpins his sense of eminence and his master plan (Operation Grand Slam) consists of irradiating the American gold held at the Fort Knox repository in order to secure his domination of the global gold market. Moreover, his operation is multinational in scope and nature. He operates out of Switzerland, is protected by a Korean henchman (Oddjob), and is supported by a Chinese nuclear scientist (Dr. Ling) alongside a coterie of Chinese men.

The film presents the impression that gold smuggling in the 1960s has severe economic and geopolitical consequences. As noted by the British banker, Colonel Smithers, who is sent to brief Bond and M, gold is linked to British national economic security. Bond is warned that there are "unauthorized leakages" of gold across international borders including Britain and he is tasked with finding the source (which is Goldfinger). The 'gold exchange standard' was bound up with the international financial system and the Bretton Woods post-war settlement. Under this settlement, countries could fix their exchange rates with due reference to the US dollar and central banks such as the Bank of England could then exchange their dollar reserves into gold at a rate pegged at $35 per ounce. Only nation states and their central banks could access this arrangement and hence a gold smuggler like Goldfinger was outside the gold exchange system. If a national currency was pegged to the dollar it also enjoyed a fixed value with regard to gold and in the case of post-war France, for example, a decision was taken to accumulate gold and in exchange reduce dollar holdings.

The gold exchange standard ended in 1971 but was still operational at the time *Goldfinger* was released in 1964.

Despite the scale of Operation Grand Slam, Bond is still successful in killing the villain and thwarting his master plan. He does so after being transported to Fort Knox and handcuffed to the nuclear bomb inside the vault. After freeing himself, Bond uses a gold bar as a weapon to fight off Oddjob (who possesses superhuman strength) in the heart of the repository and removes the physical threat so that the bomb can be defused (albeit by another man). His touch also facilitates his successful seduction of Pussy Galore (who the film suggests might be lesbian), Goldfinger's private pilot, who sides with Bond and supports his mission. This golden/ tanned woman is the linchpin in Goldfinger's plan and controls access to the vault. As noted earlier, she commands a squadron of female pilots tasked with neutralizing the military threat surrounding Fort Knox. Ross Karlan likens Galore to a magician's assistant who "does the majority of the work allowing Bond to swoop in as the hero" (2015, p. 207). After sleeping with Bond, she warns the CIA of Goldfinger's plan and exchanges the poisonous nerve gas for a harmless substance. Karlan writes that "much like the magician's assistant, her actions take place off-screen and away from the view of the audience; she is the woman behind the curtain who manipulates the outcome of the trick" (ibid. 207). Thus, it is Galore who grants and revokes access to the gold at Fort Knox for Goldfinger, Bond, and the CIA.

In the film, gold has both a material and metaphorical quality. As a material it is clearly something that Bond has to secure in the face of the threat posed to Britain and the United States via Operation Grand Slam. While Bond has personally witnessed its murderous qualities he has also felt a gold bar and seen firsthand the transplantation economy underpinning Goldfinger's wealth creation. But gold has a metaphorical element as well. The association between gold and particular standards of purity, moral worth, and monetary value matters here. Goldfinger not only lacks moral character—as evidenced by his cheating at cards and golf—but he flaunts his gold: he uses it in material objects such as cars and planes, dresses in gold-colored clothes, and collects golden women like Jill Masterson and Pussy Galore. He not only deploys gold to kill Bond's lover but he also employs the heat used to smelt gold to try to castrate Bond with a laser beam aimed at his groin. While Goldfinger wants to steal gold and show it off, actions that are reflective of his sense of immorality, Bond steps in to safeguard it and by extension British and American economic security and moral probity. In the end, it is Bond who adheres to the 'gold standard' in order to maintain the status quo: he remains loyal to his American allies, he does not cheat or steal in gold, and he does not murder women. His touch and feel for gold (and the woman who helps to control access to it at Fort Knox) has been purely professional and generative of the 'good' British citizen.

DIAMONDS

A diamond is an extremely hard form of carbon that is mined and polished. While this stone is most frequently used in jewelry, it is also incorporated into cutting and engraving tools, x-ray machines and lasers, and other electronic devices due to its hardness and thermal conductivity. Given their value, diamonds are not only precious commodities that are traded through legal channels (via the international diamond market) but they are often associated with criminal activity as some individuals and organizations go to great lengths to possess them. Diamonds underwrite British regal and imperial authority, with Queen Victoria being presented in 1850 with the Indian diamond, the Koh-i-Noor. The diamond was later set in the British crown jewels in the 1930s. When not being taken or even gifted to royal figures, diamond smuggling was an area of interest to Ian Fleming and he incorporated it into his 1956 Bond novel *Diamonds Are Forever* (the title of which was taken from the marketing slogan first used by De Beers in 1948). He subsequently published a non-fiction book in 1957 on the subject, *The Diamond Smugglers*, which focused on the role of Sierra Leone as a source for illegal diamonds. As a result, diamonds play an important role in the filmic *Diamonds Are Forever* as well as the later production *Die Another Day*, which is explicitly referential of the former and other Bond films. Through his defeat of the villains and recovery of the diamonds, Bond symbolically restores British authority over the international conduct of the diamond trade particularly in postcolonial nations in Africa and the main European diamond-trading hub of Amsterdam.

Diamonds Are Forever

As suggested by the title, diamonds play an important role in the film *Diamonds Are Forever*. Following the title sequence, Bond and M meet with Sir Donald Munger, chairman of the Diamond Syndicate, who describes diamond mining in South Africa and the growing problem of international smuggling. Although similar to *Goldfinger* in this respect, the location of the element is different as is the nature of its rootedness. This time the problem involves the management of diamond mining infrastructure in South Africa rather than the identification of a master smuggler with a risky and outlandish plan. His description of the safeguards set in place to discourage theft is countered by a series of images that highlight a transnational smuggling operation and the key players involved. Unlike Goldfinger, there is no suggestion that one person alone is hoarding gold in order to secure market advantage. According to the film, local miners place the diamonds in their mouths, which are removed by a dentist (Dr. Tynan) who brings them to a middleman (Joe) for transport to a local contact (Mrs. Whistler) who ships them to a professional smuggler (Tiffany Case) who facilitates their sale and transfer.[5] Bond is tasked with uncovering the smuggling operation in order to stabilize the world diamond market and safeguard British interests. Although Bond does not have any expertise in the area of diamonds—a point reiterated by M who comments that it is "refreshing to hear that there is one subject you are not an expert on"—he has extensive knowledge of women and his ability to seduce them plays a central role in achieving his mission objective after posing as British 'transport consultant' Peter Franks who is charged with moving diamonds from Amsterdam to the United States. He ends up improvising and uses the real Peter Franks' corpse as a secret repository for the stolen diamonds.

Diamonds are strongly associated with women in the film (rather than dead male bodies). This is established by the title track, "Diamonds Are Forever," in which the gems are described as being a woman's best friend.[6] They have an enduring quality, as if to suggest that a woman can trust and take comfort in that rather than, say, in the arms of (unreliable) men. As noted in the lyrics sung by Shirley Bassey: "Diamonds are forever. They are all I need to please me. They can stimulate and tease me." The song is paired with images of naked women in shadow wearing diamonds and caressing the stones sensually.[7] And at one point, a woman in silhouette shimmers like a diamond as she dances inside an emerald cut jewel. This explicit feminization of the resource and its material qualities is sustained early in the film as two women are presented as key figures in the smuggling ring. The first is Mrs. Whistler, an elderly woman who serves as the primary contact in South Africa and uses her elementary school as a front for the diamond smuggling ring. A sweet and maternal figure, Mrs. Whistler is unassuming as she collects the diamonds in her bible (which itself makes reference to diamonds and their hardened qualities) while speaking fondly about the children in her care. The second is Bond Girl Tiffany Case, a much younger woman who coordinates the operation in the diamond-trading hub of Amsterdam and facilitates the transportation of the diamonds to Las Vegas. Dressed in lingerie, she uses her sexuality to distract her business contact as she checks Franks' identification. Early in the film, it is women who use their femininity, intersected by age and sexuality, to conceal the fact that they control the mobility and the access to the diamonds.

The association between women and diamonds is even more pronounced with Case. Like most Bond Girls, she has been given a double entendre for a name—a figure of speech that can be understood in two different ways, one obvious and the other requiring some thought. According to Umberto Eco, Case's name reflects her vanity and suggests "the beauty case of a mannequin" (2009, p. 47), which Boel Ulfsdotter notes is fitting given that "Case is a diamond smuggler in need of different identities that a beauty box can provide" (2015, p. 20). Her name also has a more literal interpretation that suggests a stronger relationship with the stone. The word "Tiffany" is a direct reference to the American jewelry retailer Tiffany & Company (as she was born in one of their stores) while "Case" refers to the (glass) boxes in which jewelry is housed and/ or placed on display. Through naming (in addition to her profession), the film creates a strong association between Case and the diamonds, which helps to further feminize the stones. Bond's mission takes on patriarchal significance as his ability to acquire the stones for Britain relies on his ability to access and manipulate Case. The killing of Franks (with whom Bond switches IDs) in the presence of Case proves crucial in the mobilization of the international movement of the diamonds and subsequently Bond's access to them.

In the film, the diamond smuggling operation is linked to Blofeld and is part of a much larger plot designed to destabilize geopolitical relations. The villain uses the diamonds to create a laser satellite or "sun gun," a theoretical orbital weapon that was conceptualized and researched in Nazi Germany during World War II. The "sun gun" was designed to harness solar energy using a concave mirror and reflect it onto a concentrated point on earth. It was thought to be 100,000 times more powerful than the mythical "death ray" conceptualized by Archimedes in 212 BC. While the "sun gun" was never completed, research from Hillersleben Germany was commandeered by American intelligence agencies (via Operations

Overcast and Paperclip) and subsequently utilized by American scientists (Bellows 2009, pp. 234–36). The film presents the impression that Blofeld commissioned the completion of the weapon using the stolen diamonds and tests the "sun gun" by destroying nuclear weapons in China, the Soviet Union, and the United States. While the United States is partially implicated in allowing this weapon to be developed and used against them, Britain (through the figure of Bond) is presented as playing an important role in maintaining global order through the defeat of a megalomaniac like Blofeld whose plot, at least in part, appears to mirror that of Adolf Hitler even though a direct connection between the men is never made in the film.

The denouement of the film occurs on an oil rig somewhere off the coast of Baja, California, which serves as an appropriate infrastructure for a film preoccupied with the elemental. Like oil, diamonds owe their carbon origins to earthly burial, heat, pressure, and cooling. Although Bond is not able to save the diamonds per se, he does disrupt the plot of Blofeld by blowing up the oil rig and sending it, as well as everything on it, to the bottom of the seabed. Since "diamonds are forever," the viewer can only speculate as to whether they will ever be recovered and who might actually claim them as they are left in outer space.

Die Another Day

In addition to smuggling, diamonds are also the focus of resource conflict. Conflict (or blood) diamonds are stones that are mined in areas controlled by belligerent forces and whose sale funds the purchase of arms and other military materials to fund their actions (Levy 2003, p. 2). The mining and sale of blood diamonds has contributed to conflicts in various parts of Africa including Angola, the Democratic Republic of Congo, and Sierra Leone (ibid. p. 2). While the violence is local/national, the conflict, according to Arthur Levy, is regional/international as "the possibility of gaining access to diamond wealth appears to have motivated foreign actors—including governments, private security-cum-mining firms, and mercenaries—to become party to each of these conflicts in exchange for diamond mining rights" (2003, pp. 2–3). While the Bond franchise does not criticize the (legal) diamond industry or the worldwide monopoly of the British diamond retailer De Beers in *Diamonds Are Forever*, it condemns the blood diamond trade by incorporating it into the plot of *Die Another Day*.

While diamonds are used to fund arms shipments in *The Living Daylights* and feature in a stunning diamond necklace worn by Elliot Carver's wife Paris in *Tomorrow Never Dies*, *Die Another Day* is the first Bond film to explicitly discuss issues surrounding the circulation of conflict, as opposed to commercial, diamonds. The film opens with Bond, who is impersonating a Dutch diamond smuggler, infiltrating a North Korean military base and intercepting the sale of weapons for African conflict diamonds. As Bond tries to escape, he sets off numerous explosions, one of which results in a handful of conflict diamonds being embedded into hench person Zao's face. This permanent deformation serves as a consistent reminder across the film of the material and mobile link between North Korean military extremism and the African blood diamond trade; they are embedded with one another. The remaining diamonds survive the explosion and Gustav Graves (formerly Colonel Moon) tries to pass off the stones as a natural find from Iceland. Much like Blofeld, Graves uses the stones for his new orbital mirror satellite, "Icarus," which can harness solar energy into a laser beam. He intends to use this sun gun to carve a path through the Korean Demilitarized Zone and allow North Korean troops to invade South Korea. The elemental, if the plan succeeds, is going to be put to work to literally remake the 'geo' in geopolitics as well as geography, as Korean relations in addition to its landscape are re-engineered.

Although satellites are frequently featured as weapons in the Brosnan-era films,[8] *Die Another Day* intertextually references the plot of *Diamonds Are Forever* and reworks some of the narrative points in key ways.[9] Much like Blofeld, Graves uses the diamonds he illegally acquires from West Africa to develop a "sun gun" that he will use to destroy military defense systems. However, the geopolitical context surrounding the development of this technology has changed. Unlike Blofeld, Graves is not using his "sun gun" to fundraise for his terrorist organization or reignite the Cold War per se. Instead, his goal is to reverse the outcome of the Korean War (1950–53) and reunite North with South Korea under his military control. His actions are also a response to the election of President George W. Bush in 2001 who rejected the Sunshine Policy that was re-establishing inter-Korean relations and was suspicious that the North was developing its nuclear arsenal (Fruchart-Ramond 2013, p. 147). The film taps into this geopolitical conflict by pitting Graves, a rogue North Korean agent, against Bond and his NSA-affiliated partner Jinx Johnson. Their defeat of Graves has particular geopolitical significance, as it helps to restore the peace that Britain and the United States fought for in World War II, and their collaboration together in a UN force involved with the Korean conflict in the 1950s. As with *Goldfinger*, the Anglo-American special relationship proves vital as both countries seek to prevent diamonds from being used to overturn the uneasy if not fixed geopolitical division of the Korean Peninsula.

In addition, the rhetoric surrounding the diamond satellite technology in *Die Another Day* is distinct. While Graves intends to use the Icarus satellite as a weapon, he initially markets the technology as large-scale geoengineering (or climate engineering). During an event he holds at his ice palace in Iceland, Graves describes how his satellite can provide year-round sunshine for crop growth. Although the technology featured in the film resides in the realm of science fiction—such as gene therapy that restructures a person's DNA, thereby changing their appearance and identity[10]—the rhetoric surrounding the Icarus satellite conveys messages about power and technology in the twenty-first century. The use of African blood diamonds to build a satellite that will alter the climate in the north—either to grow crops or to attack a country—taps into a long history of colonization and exploitation in which southern resources are extracted for the use and benefit of the north. Moreover, the film reflects the emerging social discourse on climate change by depicting a villain who is masquerading as a philanthropist and manipulating the public by pressing his environmental/food security agenda. In *Quantum of Solace* this theme of resource security is resurrected through the figure of Dominic Greene, and his alleged plans for water security in central South America.

Unlike *Diamonds Are Forever*, there is no female smuggler in *Die Another Day* who has to make a choice between her (illegal) profession and her feelings for Bond. Instead, the film features two women on opposite ends of the spectrum who are linked to the diamonds in different ways. This contrasting is suggested in the opening credit sequence that features silhouettes of women in the forms of ice and fire, and reflects Bond's contrasting (sexual) relationships with Miranda Frost and Jinx Johnson, respectively. On the one hand, Frost is a double agent who works for Graves as a hench person. As her name suggests, she has an icy demeanor and her first sexual encounter with Bond takes places on a bed made of ice; her chilly and slippery nature prevents her from falling for Bond and siding with him. In addition, as Ron Edwards and Lisa Dickie note, "Diamonds are sometimes called 'ice' because a typical diamond is clear and cold to the touch" (6). Through both her name and characterization, Frost is associated with the conflict diamonds and this aids in feminizing and demonizing the stones. The film relays the impression that Frost's heart, much like Zao's face, is compromised. This renders Frost another "gem" that Graves has collected and one that Bond struggles to crack/claim/possess. On the other hand, Bond works with NSA agent Jinx Johnson to recover the jewels and take down the villain. Unlike Frost, Johnson is associated with the fire and heat (as previously described) and her only direct contact with the diamonds takes place at the end of the film. After killing Graves, the lovers hide away in a cabin. Johnson can be seen lying on her back as Bond dumps diamonds onto her body and hovers over her lustfully (Fig. 6.1)

Travis Wagner writes that the "implications of this scene are troubling, especially in light of the fact that the blood diamond trade in Africa is rooted in colonialism, violence, and genocide" (2015, p. 57); but it is also one that the film never dwells upon, as Africa is barely mentioned in dialogue and not represented visually until *Casino Royale* in the context of being used to fund international terrorism.

The final scene in *Die Another Day* contains powerful messages about gender, race, and (British/colonial) power that reinforce the importance of Bond and his libidinal masculinity to ensuring the (military and resource) security of Britain. The film, however, has also been heavily criticized particularly by South Korean commentators for its depiction of North Korea

Fig. 6.1   *Die Another Day* (Eon productions et al. 2002)

and South Korea: its use of South Korean and Chinese (in addition to American) actors to portray North Korean characters, the treatment of South Korea as an American 'colony', and the depiction of both sides of the Korean peninsula as being backward/pre-modern (Lee 2007, p. 208; Kim 2015, p. 126). The film relays a limited and troubling impression of North and South Korean in order to justify the mission of Bond and bolster the geopolitical standing of Britain and America in the film.

CRUDE OIL/PETROLEUM

Crude oil or petroleum is a black liquid that is found below the Earth's surface and sold to refineries to be processed into various types of fuels including gasoline (or petrol). It is formed when large deposits of organic matter (such as dead plant and animal material) are buried in sedimentary rocks and subjected to intense heat and pressure over a long period of time (Hyne 2012, p. xiii–xiv). This fossil fuel, which is largely collected through oil drilling, is a non-renewable (or finite) resource that cannot be replenished for sustainable/consistent extraction within a human time frame. Given the increasing social dependence on oil, the depletion of the world's oil supply and rising cost per barrel have led to economic crises and regional/international conflicts, as well as the development of new renewable energy technologies. Explicit geopolitical conflicts over oil can be traced across three Bond films: *The Man with the Golden Gun*, *The World Is Not Enough*, and *Quantum of Solace* while an oil rig and oil storage tanks feature briefly in *Diamonds Are Forever* and *Goldfinger*, respectively.

The Man with the Golden Gun

In the 1970s, major industrial nations like Britain and the United States experienced an energy crisis that threw their economies into turmoil. This stagflation was the result of oil shortages, caused by disruptions to oil importation from the Middle East (made worse by an OPEC oil embargo in 1973) and the inflation of prices as a consequence of oil becoming more expensive. This not only led to global competition over the dwindling oil supply but also the consideration of other, and preferably local, energy sources from fossil fuels acquired through domestic drilling to the development of renewable resources (Vawter 2013, pp. 125–126). During this time, research on green energy technologies excelled and solar power in particular "was hailed as the alternative energy of the future" just as nuclear power had been in the 1950s and 1960s (Peacock 2008, p. 24). However, when energy prices came down by the 1980s, solar power was largely abandoned in favor of fossil fuels, which were cheaper and considered more plentiful and reliable (Peacock 2008, p. 24).

The energy crisis mediates the narrative conflict in *The Man with the Golden Gun*. The film opens with Bond receiving a threat from the assassin Scaramanga in the form of a gold bullet. M responds by formally removing Bond from his current assignment to track down a missing British scientist named Gibson who possesses information about a solar device that could "solve the energy crisis." When Bond tries to entrap the assassin in Hong Kong, he witness him murder Gibson and steal the "solex agitator"—a fictional device that transfers solar power into energy and is, as Q noted in a briefing, 95 % efficient—which he plans to sell the highest bidder. Bond eventually tracks down Scaramanga to his private island where the villain has set up a sample solar power station. In the end, Bond kills Scaramanga and destroys his island, but not before removing the device and returning it to Britain's protective custody.

The film not only reflects British and American interest in solar power during the energy crisis, but it also does the imaginative work of culture by exploring contemporaneous social anxieties associated with the development of solar energy and the role that western-trained scientists might perform. The film projects concerns that the development of green technology might fall beyond Western reach, especially if British scientists can be persuaded to share their expertise with non-Western others. This is initially suggested by having a British scientist develop the saving technology while working for Thai industrialist Hai Fat. Although Gibson tries to return to Britain by promising delivery of the device in exchange for immunity, Hai Fat has him killed and the device remains in the possession of Scaramanga in Asia. While the Middle East holds the UK and its allies to ransom, another part of the 'East' is now playing a pivotal role in a new era of resource geopolitics.

For his part, Scaramanga develops the solar power plant on his private island, which is located in "Red Chinese" waters. While the People's Republic of China (PRC) does not play an explicit role in the film, the mere mention of China taps into a broader vilification of "the East" as established in the early Bond films when China is associated with rogue nuclear weapons and the interference of the US-Soviet space program.[11] In addition, Scaramanga not only harnesses solar energy on the island but also weaponizes it through his development of a solar-powered laser (or "sun gun"). As a result, the close proximity of the island to China could provide "the East" and not "the West" with energy security and enhanced weaponry.[12] The film addresses these concerns by having Bond return the device to Britain but not before he destroys the island and with it, the solar plant and weapon.

In addition to being framed through resource geopolitics, the acquisition of the device and by extension solar power is clearly gendered. The film pits Bond against a comparable male assassin whose success depends on his libido—as Bond explains early in the film, Scaramanga has sex in order to increase his accuracy in shooting. The two men not only do battle to determine who will possess the device but they also compete for the affections of two women who control access to it. Andrea Anders is Scaramanga's lover and the one who sent the gold bullet threat to MI6 in order to bring Bond to East Asia. She not only provides Bond with critical information but she also agrees to give him the device in exchange for him killing Scaramanga. Although her change in affiliation (signaled by her sleeping with Bond) results in her death—as Scaramanga shoots her in the heart at the kickboxing match—she upholds her end of the deal by bringing the device to Bond who hands it off to Lieutenant Hip who gives it to Mary Goodnight, Bond's MI6 contact in the field. Goodnight unwittingly takes over the roles of gatekeeper and lover when she is kidnapped by Scaramanga and brought to his island to take the place of Anders. After Bond kills Scaramanga, Goodnight is set up as a foil who challenges Bond's access to the device by accidentally turning on the solar laser (with her bikini-covered butt) as he tries to remove the solex agitator.

This sets up a tense scene in which Bond has a brief weather window (due to prevailing cloud cover) to defuse the weapon and demonstrate his mastery over both the weapon and its energy source, the sun. Interestingly, this takes place after the death of the villain and is positioned as a second (or maybe even true) climax of the film with Bond battling against the weaponization of the sun. In the end, Bond not only demonstrates the superiority of his libidinous masculinity over Scaramanga, but also over the female gatekeeper who controls access to the device. This not only works to feminize the solar power but also naturalizes British/Western access to it via a patriarchal discourse that aligns the device with control of the female body.

The World Is Not Enough

Following the collapse of the Soviet Union in 1991, Western nations began investing in the oil industries of former Soviet states like Kazakhstan and Azerbaijan. Located in Central Asia and bordering the Caspian Sea, these countries contain significant oil endowments in addition to other energy reserves in coal and natural gas (Curtis 2003, pp. 65–66). In order to increase their production and export of oil and connect to the world energy market, new pipelines needed to be built to bypass Russia and its pipeline monopolies (Wakeman-Linn et al. 2003, p. 340). In 1995, both Kazakhstan and Azerbaijan joined consortiums of international oil firms to help develop new export pipelines. Describing the agreement for Kazakhstan, Glenn E. Curtis notes that

> Chevron and Mobil Oil of the United States, British Gas, Agip of Italy, and Russia's LUKoil enterprise were to fund the entire pipeline project in return for a 50 percent share in the pipeline. The governments of Kazakhstan and Russia were to receive the other 50 percent. However, pipeline construction was delayed amid further international negotiation over alternative routes. (2003, p. 66)

After the fall of the iron curtain, the oil fields of Kazakhstan and Azerbaijan offered the promise of energy security and became sites of geopolitical and resource conflict by the late 1990s.

Azerbaijan is the primary location of *The World Is Not Enough*. The film opens with the assassination of British oil tycoon Sir Robert King. Bond is assigned to protect his daughter, Elektra, who has taken over his company, King Industries, and is overseeing the plan to build an oil pipeline across Central Asia. Elektra, on meeting with Bond, explains to him the geographical and geopolitical significance of Central Asia and the Caspian Sea region. A computer-generated map shows Bond the different pipelines crisscrossing Asia and Europe and Elektra explains to him why the stakes are so high. When Bond accompanies her on a high altitude skiing tour of the proposed pipeline route, the couple is attacked (by paragliding snowmobilers) and this threat increases Bond's emotional attachment to King. As it turns out, King killed her father (as revenge for not securing her release when she was kidnapped as a teenager) and attacked her own pipeline to detract attention away from her real plan to bomb a Russian pipeline in Istanbul in order to increase the value of her own oil. Bond's attempt to save King's pipeline from being destroyed brings to the fore the material dimension of resource geopolitics as he races inside the pipeline itself to prevent further damage being done to the network. By stopping King and her partner/lover Renard, Bond reestablishes the conventional geopolitical order in order to ensure that oil continues to flow to the West, and protects the interests of newly independent Russia.

Gender factors into the geopolitical conflict over oil in Central Asia. Although King inherits the company from her father, she tells Bond that the oil field actually belongs to her mother: "My father was nothing! His kingdom he stole from my mother, the kingdom I will rightly take back." This emphasis on matrilineality (or her mother's lineage) helps to feminize the oil and its export pipeline and implicitly challenges her patrilineal surname (King). This is initially suggested in the opening credit sequence, which features silhouettes of naked women dancing while covered in oil. Moreover, it works to frame the management of oil in both colonial and patriarchal terms as the resource claimed through the Western/British masculine conquest of the Eastern/Asian feminine (King's mother and her oil). This renders the actions of King dangerous as she strives to subvert (if not invert) the gendered and geopolitical order structuring the world of Bond and Britain.

The deviant nature of King is represented in two key ways. The first is through her name, which recalls a figure from Greek mythology— Electra, the daughter of King Agamemnon. Years after her mother killed her father, she and her brother (Orestes) conspire to commit matricide in order to avenge his death (Claybourne 2005, p. 470). *The World Is Not Enough* adjusts this story (as signaled by the different spelling of her name) to feature a daughter conspiring with her lover to commit patricide to avenge her mother. While Electra is considered a hero for defending her father's line,[13] Elektra King is vilified for assaulting it and aligning with her mother. Her deviant nature is also demonstrated through her sexuality, which challenges Bond's phallocentric masculinity. In a reverse of the typical Bond narrative, it is King who pursues and seduces Bond in order to align him with her revenge 'mission'. Analyzing the sex scene, Alexander Sergeant writes (Fig. 6.2)

> King reaches across the bed and grabs a container of ice used to chill a bottle of champagne. So often a symbol of Bond's phallic prowess, King rejects the unopened bottle, which in previous movies Bond has been so keen to uncork and pop, in favor of the ice itself. She places the blocks in her mouth, and enjoys the sensation of them melting. King has transferred

Fig. 6.2   *The World Is Not Enough* (Eon Productions et al. 1999)

Bond's traditionally phallic display of male sexuality into a metaphor for her own desire: replacing the bottle with ice and the popping with a sense of wetness. (2015, p. 133)

The emphasis on wetness in this and other sex scenes helps to connect the sexual desires of King with her aspirations for her oil, a resource that is defined by its own liquid nature.[14] It also works to further gender the geopolitical conflict over her oil by framing it within the phallocentric discourse that has historically underpinned the series. This not only renders the death of King inevitable, as her sexuality threatens the heroic identity of Bond, but it also naturalizes the access of Britain/the West to her resources via patriarchal and colonial logic.

Quantum of Solace

In the twenty-first century, energy security remains a primary concern of major industrial nations and plays a central role in shaping their domestic and foreign politics. For instance, the United States has maintained a significant military presence in the Middle East in the 2000s and 2010s. It has used its military to safeguard its strategic partnerships with certain oil-producing nations (like Saudi Arabia and post-Saddam Iraq) while waging war against threats to its national and energy security (like Afghanistan). While American foreign policy in the Middle East is largely centered on oil (Azar 2011, p. 98), the same can be said about Britain and other European nations who also have a presence in the region. As a result, the prospect of acquiring fossil fuels from alternative sources (like the tar sands in Alberta Canada) with limited/less local resistance and geopolitical conflict is greatly appealing.

Quantum of Solace explores the geopolitical maneuvering associated with the discovery of a new oil field in Bolivia. The villain, Dominic Greene (who is not quite as ecologically minded as his surname might suggest), acquires the land through an agreement with an exiled Bolivian general, Medrano: Greene will help Medrano seize control of the Bolivian government in exchange for a section of land and the right to any resources he might find. When word gets out, the United States tries to secure a stake in the presumed Bolivian oil field by agreeing not to interfere with the political coup. This is negotiated through the South American branch of the CIA by the agents Gregg Beam and Felix Leiter. Although Britain is also interested in making a similar deal, Bond complicates matters by investigating Greene and meddling in his operation. This is noted when a British parliamentary minister says to M

> Say you're right. Say Greene is a villain. If we refused to do business with villains, we'd have almost no one to trade with. The world's running out of oil, M. The Russian's aren't playing ball. The Americans and Chinese are dividing up what's left. Right or wrong doesn't come into it. We're acting out of necessity. Bond is running wild. Who's to say he hasn't been turned? Pull him in or the Americans will put him down.

In spite of the collusion between Greene and the CIA, Leiter trusts in Bond more than his American colleagues and gives him enough warning to escape capture. The films presents a complicated and shifting web of geopolitical relations in which allies like the United States and Britain compete against one another for energy security. Moreover, through the figures of Bond and Leiter, the film questions the morality of these policy decisions, which are driven in response to the demands of Greene and his multinational corporation.

Unlike other Bond films, *Quantum of Solace* does not strongly associate oil production with women. This might be due, in part, to shifting generic and gendered conventions in the Craig-era Bond films. For example, *Quantum of Solace* does not have a Bond Girl proper as Bond does not interact sexually or romantically with his partner Camille Montes. In addition, this character is more strongly associated with fire due to a childhood trauma that has left her physically and emotionally scarred: her father was shot, her mother and sister were raped and then strangled, and her home was set on fire with her in it. The only female character linked directly to the oil is Strawberry Fields, an MI6 agent who works at the Bolivian consulate and serves as Bond's contact in the field. After Bond antagonizes Greene at a fundraiser, he returns to his hotel room to find Fields murdered, face down on his bed, with her naked body covered in crude oil.[15] These scene recalls the iconic death of Jill Masterson in *Goldfinger* who is covered in gold paint in Bond's hotel room the morning after he seduces her. While the death of Fields, like Masterson, serves as a warning to Bond not to meddle in the villain's affair, it is also designed to be a misdirection that will deceive MI6 into believing that Bond is interfering with their energy policy. Unlike Goldfinger, Greene is not interested in acquiring the resource he uses to kill Fields and this works to disjoin the link between women and oil in the franchise. It also suggests a reworking of the resource geographies in the Craig-era films.

WATER CONFLICT

Water is a critical resource to the sustainment of human, plant, and animal life. While water is plentiful on earth, only 3 % of it is freshwater and more than half is inaccessible as it is frozen in glaciers. Moreover, freshwater is not equally distributed on earth and six countries account for more than half of the world's fresh water supply: Brazil, Russia, Canada, Indonesia, China, and Columbia (Krapivin and Varotsos 2008, p. 495). Although water is a renewable resource,[16] the world's supply of fresh water is steadily decreasing due to contamination and overuse (via industrialization and agriculture),[17] and nearly a billion people worldwide lack access to safe drinking water. As a result, water has increasingly become a source of conflict as nations, regions, and groups fight to control water resources. And it is the conflict over water, and not oil, that is at the heart of *Quantum of Solace*.

Quantum of Solace

Bolivia is not only the setting for the film but it is also provides the best historical example of the fight over water privatization. In 1999, the World Bank recommended the privatization of the municipal water supply in Cochabamba and El Alto/La Paz, Bolivia's two largest cities. As noted by Jim Shultz "the World Bank argued that handing water over to foreign corporations was essential in order to open the door to needed investment and skilled management" (2008, p. 126). In Cochabamba, this led to a four-year contract with an American consortium, Bechtel Corporation of California, who doubled the price of water upon taking it over, leaving many poor families with the choice between buying water or food. This increase led to citywide protests and eventually the government revoked its water privatization legislation, after first attempting to protect the agreement by instituting martial law (McPhail and Walters 2009, p. 171). A similar uprising in 2005 led to the Bolivian government's cancellation of a water privatization deal in El Alto/La Paz with the Suez Corporation of France (Shultz 2008, p. 126).

Water privatization in Bolivia is the central objective for the villain, Dominic Greene, in *Quantum of Solace*. Greene masquerades as an environmentalist and philanthropist who espouses water and environmental conservation. He is the founder of Greene Planet, an environmental corporation that buys up large portions of land for ecological preservation. During a fundraiser in Bolivia, he describes his Tierra Project as "one small part of a global network of eco-parks that Greene Planet has created to rejuvenate the world on the verge of collapse." This project, however, is really a Quantum initiative designed to covertly establish water privatization in Bolivia. When Greene describes the processes by which deforestation in Bolivia has led to desertification and an increase in the price of water, he is referring to the actions that he has set in motion through his multinational corporations. What he does not mention is the way in which he collected and stored the freshwater underground by erecting dams that have stopped the resource from flowing to the rest of the country. Through the vilification of Greene and his corporation, the film strongly criticizes water privatization and the foreign acquisition of domestic freshwater reserves (while appearing more ambivalent on oil rights). Moreover, the film positions Quantum, an international terrorist organization, in the role of the World Bank and condemns their capital programs in developing nations like Bolivia. Importantly, it is Bond as an agent of Britain who restores geopolitical order and returns oversight of local resources back to the Bolivian government.

In *Quantum of Solace*, water conflict takes on gendered connotations. Water has long played a critical role in the Bond films. Bond is frequently immersed in water: he fights in and under water, travels on and under water, and sometimes has to prevent water from overwhelming places (e.g. *A View to a Kill*). He understands the role that water pressure can play on the immersed body (e.g. *For Your Eyes Only*) and is adept at adjusting his behavior to take constraints and opportunities offered by water such as impromptu water-skiing (e.g. *License to Kill*). Although Bond frequently operates in water, the element has historically been associated with women due to the reproductive capacity of the female body and its link to the 'waters of life;' in various art and written texts, the female body is described as a vessel/container and women have largely been essentialized in relation to their wombs in both society and culture. This association is forwarded in the Bond films in many of the opening credit sequences, which feature women underwater moving around (and seducing) men. According to Eileen Rositzka, these women "conjure up images of the nymphs from Greek or Latin mythology—beautiful maidens filling nature with life. A nymph is also regarded as a siren who lures a man—to his death" (2015, p. 153). As such, these anonymous women are presented as being threatening to Bond as they distract him from his mission. The Bond Girls in the film proper are also strongly associated with water and depicted as water nymphs and sirens. This connection was established in the inaugural *Dr. No*, which features Honey Ryder emerging from the sea while singing (Piotrowska 2015, p. 171). The combination of her image and voice are so appealing that they attract the male gaze of Bond and his helper Quarrel who stop and stare thereby halting narrative progress in order to look at her. Moreover, it is Ryder's knowledge of the island and its waterways that facilitates their escape from capture. Ryder is the first in a series of Bond Girls that Bond first sees (e.g. Jinx Johnson), meets (e.g. Domino Derval), kisses (e.g. Wai Lin), and works with (e.g. Melina Havelock) underwater in the series. The film enrolls patriarchal sentiments by associating women with the feminine element of water and Bond's subsequent use and mastery over them (both separately and combined).

As revisionist films, the orphan origin trilogy recalibrates many elements characteristic of the series including the association of water with women. In *Casino Royale*, it is Bond and not his lover Vesper Lynd who is envisaged through Bond Girl iconography. On two occasions, Bond emerges from the sea in a bathing suit and his body is positioned as the object of the gaze for two female onlookers: Solange Dimitrios watches

Bond swim along the coastline while Lynd waits for him to exit the ocean on the beach (Funnell 2011a, p. 467). Through the intertextual referencing of Honey Ryder, Bond is depicted through the well-known iconography of the Bond Girl: he is positioned as the object of the gaze and associated with water. This connection is carried into the climax of the film in which Bond is unable to save a drowning Lynd from a building that has collapsed into the Venice canal; by locking herself in the elevator carriage, Lynd commits suicide by drowning and it is Bond who lives and carries on. This effectively works to dissociate women with water while masculinizing the element. This relationship is carried over into the next film, *Quantum of Solace*, as the first three Craig-era films are more serial in nature and constitute a trilogy (with *Spectre* possibly being the starting point of a 'Blofeld trilogy') that conveys the orphan origin story of Bond, which is concluded in *Skyfall*.

In *Quantum of Solace*, Bond's association with water is both literal and symbolic. On the one hand, Bond uses his instincts and skill set to discover the man-made aquifer underground and deduce Greene's master plan. After Bond explains the situation to Camille Montes, shots of the pair walking through the mine shaft and then through the desert[18] are intercut with images of the local villagers congregating around a small water tower that is empty and discussing the situation (Fig. 6.3). Interestingly, the majority of villagers are men even though in most developing countries where water is collected outside the home it is women and girls who carry out the task. The foregrounding of men in this scene emphasizes the threat of water shortage on the community (rather than individual households) and in most patriarchal societies it is men who engage in social dialogue about local issues. However, the scene does not contain subtitles and most audiences will not be able to discern the concerns relayed through this exchange. As a result, these voices are rendered less important, like background noise—a symbolic representation of their limited power and lack of involvement in water privatization—as they cannot be accessed and understood. And it is Montes, a rogue Bolivian agent, who stands in and speaks out for the Bolivian people (and not the Bolivian government).

The relationship that develops between Bond and Montes can be read in both geopolitical and elemental terms. On the one hand, Bond as an agent of Britain intervenes in the Bolivian water conflict through his collaboration with Montes, and their growing friendship stands in for the strengthening of British and Bolivian relations. Although the government of Bolivia is in flux, Bond supports the people who are represented by

Fig. 6.3 *Quantum of Solace* (Eon Productions et al. 2008)

Montes in the film. On the other hand, Bond and Montes are associated with the antithetic elements of water and fire respectively (see earlier in the chapter), and their collaboration is necessary to relieving the drought in Bolivia. After Montes kills Medrano in the climax of the film, the eco hotel becomes engulfed in fire and she requires rescue from Bond who makes his way through the inferno untouched by the flames and carries her to safety. As a result, Bond is metaphorically associated with "the waters of life" as he saves Montes from the fiery danger inflicted by Medrano and Bolivia from the water collection and privatization of Greene.

Bond's association with water continues into the denouement when he travels to Russia to confront Lynd's former lover, Yusef Kabira, a Quantum operative who seduces women working in intelligence agencies in order to gain access to government information. After Bond interrogates the man, he leaves the apartment complex and indicates to M that he has received closure as he throws Lynd's necklace to the ground. The film relies on pathetic fallacy to externalize the emotions of the stoic Bond through the falling snow. Not only does the scene convey a sense of closure, but the snow represents the freezing or hardening of Bond's heart, a necessary step to ensuring his physical and emotional safety as a secret agent. In literal and symbolic ways, Bond resolves the conflict associated with water in both the geopolitical and personal realm.

Conclusion

Elemental qualities of the earth and conflicts over resources such as oil and water play an increasingly prominent role in the Bond franchise. While early Bond films explored gold theft, diamond smuggling, and (fictional) technology solutions to the energy crisis, the Brosnan- and Craig-era films, through the figure of Bond, explore Britain's geopolitical struggle for energy and resource security. While oil and water are depicted as conflict resources in the later films, developments in green energy technology are being incorporated into the world of Bond as they provide energy without the dependence on non-renewable resources. *Quantum of Solace* offers the best example as the hotel in the desert runs on hydrogen fuel cell batteries. While General Medrano criticizes them for their lack of aesthetic appeal, the film presents the impression that they offer a greener energy option for a structure built in an unsustainable environment. For his part, Bond uses these hydrogen fuel cells as weapons to blow up the ecohotel and destabilize the plot of Greene (who dies shortly after in the desert). In addition, Bond can be seen driving a hydrogen fuel cell car at the end of the film. Although this vehicle is depicted as a greener option, it is highly unlikely that it would be accessible in Bolivia given its high cost and limited availability. Instead, this scene reflects the social privilege of Bond who has access to advanced technologies that are not readily available in the global South.

The geopolitical conflict over resources is presented as the prerogative of major industrial nations whose claims over foreign resources is bound up in discourses of colonialism and patriarchy through the location and gendering of these elements. While Bond steps in to (re)establish international order, he does so at the behest of Britain and his actions help to safeguard the interests of his country and its allies. The moral authority that Bond demonstrates is thus an expression of his privilege as a white British man and while the conflict resources change—from diamonds and solar power to oil and water—the representational politics remain the same. As depicted in the films, Bond's colonial masculinity remains a consistent and dominant force that is needed to maintain global order and that authority is quite literally elemental. As the embodiment of a country with extra-territorial reach and global authority, Bond's feeling and understanding of ice, water, fire, and the earth strengthens his and Britain's virility and vitality.

NOTES

1. A good example is the castrating laser in *Goldfinger*.
2. For a detailed discussion see Bayumi et al. (1996).
3. This takes on even greater significance as Gert Fröbe, who plays Goldfinger, was once a member of the Nazi Party.
4. This stands in sharp contrast with *Dr. No* where the presence of bauxite as a cover story for the villain is never explored in any detail and underplays the central role Jamaica played in the US aluminum industry and indirectly its military and space program.
5. The opening chapter of the novel *Diamonds Are Forever* (1956) describes the pipeline through which the stones are being smuggled out of Africa. Fleming consulted De Beers and spoke to the Head of the International Diamond Security Organization (Sir Percy Sillitoe) as part of his background research for the novel. Sillitoe later helped Fleming with his nonfiction account, *The Diamond Smugglers* (1957).
6. This sentiment is reaffirmed by Bond who describes diamonds as the "hardest substance found in nature, they cut glass, suggest marriage. I suppose it replaced the dog as the girl's best friend."
7. Shirley Bassey's "Diamonds are Forever" was later used by American rapper Kanye West in his song "Diamonds from Sierra Leone," which was featured in a 'blood diamond' public campaign designed to enlighten US consumers on the relationship between diamonds and violent conflict in Africa.
8. In *GoldenEye*, the goldeneye satellite can send an electromagnetic pulse that disrupts/damages electronic equipment. In *Tomorrow Never Dies*, Carver's satellite transmits his propaganda around the world. And in *Die Another Day*, the Icarus satellite is a "sun gun" that can direct concentrated solar energy to a specific point on earth.
9. Released on the 40th anniversary of the Bond franchise, *Die Another Day* references various Bond films. In the scene with Q, Bond finds a number of gadgets from his previous missions that are being held in storage from the jetpack he used in *Thunderball* to the alligator submarine from *Octopussy*. In addition, the introduction of Bond Girl Jinx Johnson emerging from the sea is a homage to Honey Ryder in *Dr. No* and her torture via laser recalls Bond's interrogation in *Goldfinger*.
10. This is also a reference to *Diamonds Are Forever* in which the arch-villain changes his identity. In the opening scene, Bond tracks down Blofeld to a facility that is producing lookalikes of the villain. Bond believes he killed his arch-nemesis by drowning him in hot mud only to discover that Blofeld and one of his lookalikes survived.

11. In a similar way, while the Soviet Union does not play a role in the film, the mention of Scaramanga's training as a KGB agent roots the energy crisis and race for solar technology in the Cold War conflict.

12. Concern over China dominating the solar market continues today as it is believed that the country currently manufactures more than half of all solar collection equipment (Gonzalez 2012, p. 9).

13. According to Anna Claybourne, "The ancient Greeks valued the ideals of loyalty and justice, and Electra was seen as a hero for her devotion to her father and her obsessions with avenging his wrongful murder. Women were meant to be faithful and obedient to men, and Electra showed the loyalty and patience her mother should have exercised" (2005, p. 472).

14. This is not the first film in which a woman manages a pipeline. In *The Living Daylights*, Bond transports a defecting Soviet general from Czechoslovakia to Austria through the Trans-Siberian Pipeline. His "inside man" is actually a woman named Rosika Miklos. She not only sets up the transits system, but also uses her sexuality to distract the security guard as Bond engages the machine.

15. Bond avenges her death by killing Greene in a similar manner: he strands him in the desert with only a quart of motor oil that the villain ingests when he becomes thirsty.

16. A renewable resource is one that "can be replenished through a natural process in the environment" (La Bella, 2009, p. 9). Through the hydrologic or water cycle, freshwater can be replenished (ibid. 10).

17. The American lifestyle demands 1800 gallons of water per day, which is more than twice the global average (Myers and Spoolman 2014, p. 283).

18. The film intertextually references *The Spy Who Loved Me*, which features Bond and Anya Amasova walking through the desert in formal clothing. Only here, the figures are dirtier and located in a much more dire situation.

CHAPTER 7

Smooth Operator: Space, Mobility, and Social Rituals

In *On Her Majesty's Secret Service* (*OHMSS*), Bond meets with Sir Hilary Bray from the Royal College of Arms and is informed that his family motto is "*Orbis non sufficit*" ("The world is not enough"). This maxim was subsequently used as the title for the 1999 Bond film and is referenced explicitly during a conversation between Bond and the villain Elektra King:

> King: "I could have given you the world."
> Bond: "The world is not enough."
> King: "Foolish sentiment."
> Bond: "Family motto."

This motto is significant as it provides a rare glimpse into his ancestry (prior to the Craig-era films, which relay his orphan origin story). It can be interpreted in a few different ways and offers insight into the development and definition of his character. On the one hand, the family motto suggests a lack of satisfaction with the present condition and a desire to improve the current situation. It draws attention to Bond's drive to protect Queen and Country against threats from an ever-changing world. On the other hand, this motto encourages a sense of movement beyond existing physical and mental limitations perhaps echoing a sense of dissatisfaction that Bond might have experienced as a child and young adult with sources and spaces of foster parental authority governing his formative years. It provides insight into Bond's astonishing skills in dealing with

© The Editor(s) (if applicable) and The Author(s) 2017
L. Funnell, K. Dodds, *Geographies, Genders and Geopolitics of James Bond*, DOI 10.1057/978-1-137-57024-6_7

both strangers and extraordinary situations. In both cases, the world—geopolitically and geographically—plays a central role in delineating the heroic identity of Bond.

As a corporeal hero, Bond is defined by the ways in which he operates within and moves through various sites and spaces. Bond is a man who might be thought of as 'on the move' as opposed to being stationary like the people in his professional life—older men (M and Q) and women (Miss Moneypenny and Dench's M).[1] Cultural geographers like Tim Cresswell argue that movement and mobility are central to everyday life but Bond's social and geographical mobility are strikingly important to his character development (2006, p. 47). His ability to move is defined by physical and social rules that not only demarcate access but are also frequently gendered, and Bond's performance in these spaces is invested with patriarchal significance. Moreover, his actions in various physical and social spaces have geopolitical significance as they convey messages about power, access, movement, and management. Bond uses his "license to destroy" the structures erected by villains while safeguarding the cultural artifacts and national monuments of ally nations. While Bond traverses great distances via train, plane, and automobile, these technologies are defined by traditional gender roles and Bond's mastery over them signals his dominance in the field. Although Bond is not presented in suburban spaces—as marriage and domesticity are at odds with him being an agent, a fact he discovers after the tragic shooting of his wife Tracy in *OHMSS*)—he does appear in spaces of socialization. While he looks out of place in tourist traps and venues of mass entertainment like the carnival and circus, he is able to navigate his way through higher-brow social spaces like the casino, the club, the luxury hotel, the theatre, and the opera house. His interactions in these various spaces help to define Bond as a largely mobile hero who is able to simultaneously manage his own mobility, the mobility of others (and particularly wealthy villains), and the mobility of dangerous objects such as missiles and satellites.

These movements, with varying speeds, durations, and intensities, are noteworthy and lead to an array of consequences, both planned/expected and unplanned/unexpected, in the course of missions around the world. Even when Bond is not able to move, he can often use immobility as a tactical advantage such as encouraging the villain to reveal more about their plans, safe in the apparent knowledge that Bond cannot threaten them. This occurs in *Goldfinger* when Bond's comment about "Operation Grand Slam" unsettles Goldfinger's confidence in the secrecy of his plan; instead of killing Bond, Goldfinger brings him 'along for the ride' and provides Bond with an opportunity to discover and stop his plot. Moreover, in *The World Is Not Enough*, Elektra King's hubris proves to be her downfall after she reveals her plot to a captive Bond who eventually escapes, shoots her, and thwarts her plan to destroy a Russian oil pipeline. Even when he is anchored to the spot, the viewer is left with the prospect that Bond will recover his mobility by feeling his way out of demanding and dangerous situations.

LICENSE TO DESTROY

In *The World Is Not Enough*, Bond states that, "Construction isn't exactly my specialty" to which M replies "Quite the opposite, in fact." This exchange draws attention to the fact that Bond is a destructive hero who is not only armed with a "license to kill" but also with a "license to destroy." He makes claims on a range of spaces and his ruination of physical property plays a central role in shaping his heroic identity and professional prowess. While Bond sets out to destroy the villain's expansive lair (usually in an explosive fashion), he rarely damages cultural artifacts and national monuments. In that sense the demolition and explosive work he engages in appear measured and proportionate. Importantly, Bond is rarely shown causing harm to animals/wildlife and takes care to rescue any person who is associated with him. His explosive capacity is thus targeted and when is he not able to destroy the villain's lair he takes out specific elements of the villain's portfolio. However, as the series progresses, Bond becomes increasingly destructive and his license to destroy is amplified in the Craig-era films that feature action scenes in construction zones—spaces that are (partially) built or destroyed. Through the corporeal adventures of Bond, the franchise conveys powerful messages about Bond's heroism and Britain's geopolitical/destructive power.

Villain's Lair

In each film, James Bond is tasked with bringing down a villain and dismantling his organization. As Bond investigates his target, he usually uncovers the villain's lair and base of operations. While these spaces vary in terms of design and function, they share many common traits. These spaces are usually new and elaborate constructions that are developed and erected by the villain to suit his particular agenda. At times, the villain also takes advantage of existing structures and cover organizations like SPECTRE, whose headquarters in central Paris is located inside an international refugee organization called The International Brotherhood for the Assistance of Stateless Persons. Moreover, these lairs serve as visual signifiers of the strength of the villain and his access to wealth, resources, and technology. In *Thunderball*, for example, this is illustrated straightforwardly when SPECTRE operative Emilio Largo was initially chastised by a police officer for parking outside the refugee organization in Paris. As soon as the police officer sees that it is Largo, he immediately apologizes for challenging his right to park his car there. In a similar sort of way, MI6 as 'Universal Exports' (UE), much like other government organizations, often retrofits and repurposes preexisting spaces for their covert bases. In *Dr. No*, for example, M's UE office in London is located in a building shared with lawyers and insurance underwriters. It is an anonymous looking place with an outer/secretarial office occupied by Miss Moneypenny and an inner sanctum for M. MI6, like SPECTRE, enjoys multiple office locations. They operate their Hong Kong base out of a partially submerged ship (the RMS *Queen Elizabeth*) in *The Man with the Golden Gun* and relocate their operations to underground chambers/offices after a terrorist attack in *Skyfall*.[2] When the villains detect professional similarities with Bond, there is some truth to this observation not least in the way that their respective operating environments are disguised and at times footloose.

The villain's lair often serves multiple purposes. Aside from the living quarters, it also contains a command center from which the villain oversees his/her operation. This space is high-tech (for the time period) and usually contains some visual representation of the scale of the plot as depicted through maps, globes, models, and/or computer graphics. These visuals not only relay important information to the viewer about the hubris of the villain, but they also provide Bond with a strategic advantage when he discovers them. In the case of the former, the large yellow colored globe stationed with Karl Stromberg's super-tanker in *The Spy Who Loved Me* serves to emphasize the scale of his lunacy, as his proposed nuclear attack on Washington and Moscow is made clear. It is also evident in *Goldfinger* and *Diamonds Are Forever* when Bond finds the scale models located in the floor of the office and he quickly determines a plan of action. And in the latter, Bond accidentally discovers the offshore oil rig of Blofeld.

These spaces are also isolated and insulated, which makes them difficult to discover let alone access. They might be built on top of a mountain (e.g. *OHMSS*), in a volcano (e.g. *You Only Live Twice*), on an island (e.g. *Man with the Golden Gun*), underwater (e.g. *The Spy Who Loved Me*), and even in outer space (e.g. *Moonraker*). They might also be mobile and located on such vehicles as trains (e.g. *GoldenEye*), ships (e.g. *Thunderball*), and planes (e.g. *Die Another Day*). These spaces are heavily fortified and access to and through them is limited by hench people and guards (rather than technology). In order to reach the inner sanctum, Bond utilizes a variety of approaches such as taking on a cover identity (e.g. posing as Hilary Bray in *OHMSS*), sneaking past a barrier (e.g. scaling the wall in *For Your Eyes Only*), or organizing a full-scale military attack (e.g. *The Spy Who Loved Me*). Bond's ability to access the heart of the operation emphasizes his mastery over people, elements, objects, and technology. In *Moonraker*, Bond's access to Hugo Drax's launch center is made possible when he manages to kill a crocodile, which was assumed to have killed him, after he was tricked into falling into its lair. This is one of the few moments in the series when Bond is shown killing an animal (that is attacking him) in order to reach a villain's lair.[3]

By the end of each film, Bond usually kills the villain and destroys his lair in an explosive finale. He often has little time to escape (with his Bond Girl) before the space is demolished. But there are a few occasions when Bond does not "get his man" and these films end on a different note. *OHMSS* and *Casino Royale* end with the death of Bond's lover and not the primary villain; while Blofeld drives away with his hench person Irma Bunt in the former, Mr. White is taken into Bond's custody in the latter only to escape at the beginning of the next film, *Quantum of Solace*, with the help of a treacherous British agent. Both films end with a cliffhanger rather than the expected denouement with the heart of Bond rather than the inner sanctum of the villain being destroyed. Unlike his opponents, this destruction does not weaken Bond but rather strengthens his resolve as a hero (as it removes his emotional attachments) and reaffirms his sense of purpose in the next mission.

Preserving Monuments

Although Bond destroys the buildings erected by the villains, he is careful not to damage cultural artifacts and national monuments. This is evident in *The Spy Who Loved Me* when Bond's mission takes him to Egypt. Although he fights against Jaws at the pyramids, there is only minor damage to the scaffolding and the historical site is preserved. While he quips about 'Egyptian builders', it is Jaws who uses a part of an ancient Egyptian column to hurl at Bond and his Soviet counterpart. Bond moves carefully and even respectfully through the site itself, and does so again when listening to an evening lecture for tourists about the history of the pyramids. In *Moonraker,* Bond fights against Chang in a Kendo-inspired fight sequence in the Venini glass shop in Venice, which serves a cover for Drax's secret biological laboratory. While most of the glassware inside is shattered during their encounter, the building is preserved and Bond does not ruin the infrastructure of the historic waterfront building. Even when he is fighting Chang, Bond is reluctant to use a particular glass artifact as an improvised weapon because he accidentally overheard a lecture about its value from a tour guide earlier in the day. He later drives the specially converted gondola carefully around St. Mark's Square. Finally, in *A View to a Kill,* Bond chases May Day through Paris. Although he destroys his car and others, and literally crashes (onto) a wedding on a boat, he does not deface the Eiffel Tower, a cultural icon of France, as this would be an egregious act against one of Britain's allies. Even though he is later admonished by M for his driving in pursuit of May Day, it is clear that Bond has nonetheless been mindful of the iconic significance of the Eifel Tower. These are but a few examples of the ways in which Bond preserves spaces of national, cultural, and historical significance in order to maintain diplomatic relations with their respective countries. In *A View to a Kill,* more generally, it is the villain who is willing to destroy the cultural and social life of San Francisco including torching city hall.

There are a few exceptions to the rule and mainly when Bond is in very particular spaces. In *GoldenEye,* Bond tries to secure the release of Natalya Simonova by chasing after General Ourumov's car with a tank. He leaves a trail of destruction as he makes his way through the streets of St. Petersburg. He runs over cars, crashes into walls, and even destroys a few bridges while in pursuit. At one point, he crashes through a monument at the center of town and the statue remains on the top of the tank as Bond drives on. The artifact is an ironic extrapolation of the Bronze Horseman statue of Peter the Great that is located in St. Petersburg. The addition of wings to the horse (to create a Pegasus) transforms the statue into the emblem adopted by British Airborne Forces during World War II. Thus, the sight of this British symbol moving through the streets of St. Petersburg sends a message about Britain's access to a newly independent Russia after the Cold War (Fig. 7.1).

Such a scene might have seemed fantastical to viewers in the 1960s and 1970s, and even in the 1980s Bond only manages to access the Russian Arctic.

Fig. 7.1   *GoldenEye* (Eon Productions et al. 1995)

Another particularly destructive scene takes place in the opening of *Casino Royale*. After tracking down Mollaka to the Nambutu Embassy in Madagascar, Bond takes the man hostage and drags him through the halls of the building while sustaining gunfire. He is clearly indifferent to the 1961 Vienna Convention on Diplomatic Relations, which asserts that the embassy should be treated as sovereign territory of Nambutu. Bond then exits the building and moves to the back property before shooting the hostage and setting off an explosion. In this scene, Bond not only destroys the building but he also disregards international diplomatic architecture in order to obtain information about a terrorist attack. Although Bond and his boss are reprimanded, his actions are presented as justified and necessary to ensuring the safety of Britain, and if anything the security staff attached to the Nambutu Embassy are depicted as largely ineffectual. Much like *GoldenEye*, the film provides insight into the subtle geographies of the series in which Bond is far more destructive in certain places like Russia and Madagascar. Had this taken place in France or the United States, the consequences would be far more serious as Bond would have jeopardized Britain's relationship with a strategic partner. Only in *A View to a Kill*, does Bond receive a formal reprimand for his behavior in Paris but the admonishment does not prevent Bond from continuing his mission.

Construction Sites

As the series progresses, Bond is increasingly destructive as the films become more action oriented. The Craig-era films amplify the damage by setting a number of action sequences in construction zones—spaces that are partially built or destroyed, depending on how you look at it. In *Casino Royale*, Bond engages in a parkour-inspired chase sequence through the construction zone of a high-rise building in Madagascar. While Mollaka navigates his way over and around various obstacles, Bond rams through and destroys them in the process. This scene emphasizes Bond's positioning in the Craig-era films as a 'blunt instrument' whose approach to fieldwork is physical and forceful rather than subtle and nuanced. Moreover, the construction zone can be read as a metaphor for the character of Bond. Monika Gehlawat argues that the placement of Bond in construction zones "accentuates his own attempts to emerge from underdevelopment" (2009, p. 133). Over the course of three films—*Casino Royale*, *Quantum of Solace*, and *Skyfall*—Bond learns how to be a superspy and experiences growing pains as he learns from his physical, emotional, and psychological mistakes. The aforementioned sequence is part of Bond's first mission after attaining his license to kill. While his desire to capture Mollaka is evident, he lacks the skill set to capture him quickly and efficiently. As a consequence, he ends up killing Mollaka and violating diplomatic protocols leading to his escapades being widely publicized in the media.

As a hero, Bond is a work in progress and this is symbolized through the use of construction sites to bookend *Casino Royale*. The final action sequence takes place in a partially renovated building in Venice. In her detailed analysis of the "aesthetics of demolition" in *Casino Royale*, Gehlawat draws attention to the movement and instability of the structure itself:

> Stairwells and landings crumble and drop into the floors below and, eventually, into the canal. Light fixtures, balustrades and random objects (as well as people) seem to detach from the context and slide helplessly downward [...] All the while the atmosphere of the scene is dark, confused and foreboding. The scene's liminal quality manifests not only because it occurs in a space that is neither building nor rubble, but also because of the watery world that soon consumes it. (2009, p. 137)

Gehlawat argues that this scene, in combination with the aforementioned chase in Madagascar, can be read as metaphors for the broader changes taking place in the Craig era as Bond is refashioned and updated (2009, p. 137). This scene can also be read diegetically. After discovering that his lover, Vesper Lynd, has betrayed him, he tracks her down to the building and fights her captors. Although this space is relatively empty, the construction equipment presents a new danger as it is mobilized as weapons for attack rather than pursuit. Unlike *Moonraker*, the conflict destroys the structure of the building, which collapses into the water below. Lynd eventually drowns after she locks herself in the elevator and refuses to be rescued. This scene can also be read as a metaphor for Bond as his faith in Lynd has been shaken and his world, much like the building, has come crashing down.

This foundational instability continues into the next film, *Quantum of Solace*, which opens with Bond transporting Mr. White to be interrogated by M in Siena, Italy. During the examination, M's bodyguard Mitchell, who is working as a double agent for the Quantum organization, frees Mr. White. Bond's pursuit of Mitchell leads them to a bell tower that is under renovation. The men crash through the glass on the roof and fall onto the scaffolding where they begin to use building materials as weapons. When Bond gets caught up in a rope, he swings upside down and struggles to reach his gun in time to kill Mitchell. Not only does the construction site increase the tension of the scene (as the viewer questions if Bond has what it takes to get the job done), but it also reflects the instability of MI6 as an organization, which has traitors in its midst—first Lynd and now Mitchell.

Skyfall also uses construction zones and equipment to signify the end of the Bond's orphan origin story. In the pre-credit sequence, Bond uses a backhoe loader to deflect bullets on the train (although he does get shot) and create an opening to enter the train car; Bond can be seen jumping from the boom of the backhoe onto the carriage just as the back of the car is being peeled away. His progress is short lived as he is accidentally shot by Moneypenny and falls into the river below. This sets in motion a resurrection narrative in which Bond rebuilds himself physically, emotionally, and psychologically over the course of the film. Bond comes across another construction zone while pursuing Silva who has escaped from MI6 custody. It is here that Bond discovers Silva's plan but not before the villain blows up a wall and causes an underground train derailment. Although Bond is a few steps behind Silva, he races through the streets of London in pursuit as M recites a poem by Tennyson: "We are not now that strength which in old days moved earth and heaven, that which we are, we are. One equal temper of heroic hearts, made weak by time and fate, but strong in will. To survive, to seek, to find, and not to yield." This sequence creates a visual and narrative contrast between Silva, a former MI6 agent who deconstructs the system from the inside, with Bond, a hero who shores up the agency from the outside. And in the end, Silva cannot destroy the will of Bond or the ideals of MI6 despite destroying part of the MI6 building. In the final scene of the film, Bond enters into the office of M, retrofitted to match the design of the early Bond films. Both Bond and MI6 have been rebuilt as the last line of defense for Britain.

TRAINS, PLANES, AND AUTOMOBILES

Bond is a world traveler. His experiences of and in various modes of transport add greatly to character and narrative development. In the case of trains, they provide opportunities for conversational set pieces notably in *Casino Royale*; violent confrontations in *The Spy Who Loved Me, Octopussy,* and *Skyfall*; and a romantic getaway for Bond in *Live and Let Die*. The Simplon-Orient Express in *From Russia with Love* combines all three as Bond and his companion make the journey from Istanbul to Venice. But as *Skyfall* demonstrates, a train leaving Istanbul is also the site of one of his closest brushes with death, the result of an accidental shooting by Miss Moneypenny. In the case of planes, Bond's travel is either fleetingly hinted at with shots of Pan Am jets in *Dr. No* and *Live and Let Die* and/or used to add a thrilling element to the narrative arc. Bond's relationship to the aircraft has been a mixed one; he has been thrown out of a plane (*Moonraker*), kidnapped and transported on a private jet (*Goldfinger*), shot at while flying an aircraft (*Quantum of Solace*), tussled with a villain while hanging out of a transporter plane (*The Living Daylights*), and flown in other crafts including auto-gyros and helicopters (*You Only Live Twice*). Finally, as we discuss in further detail, Bond's relationship to cars is essential to the Bond formula, especially the Aston Martin in the Connery, Dalton, Brosnan, and Craig eras and Lotus Esprit in the Moore era. Other car makes such as BMW are used in films such as *The World Is Not Enough*. While Bond is adept at driving motorbikes, trucks, and buses, his mobility is perhaps most clearly registered in his own customized car, equipped with a range of specialist extras. In all three cases, these vehicles are feminized and Bond's mastery of/over them has patriarchal significance as it works to validate his heroic and libidinous masculinity.

Trains

Prior to the development of mass airplane travel in the 1960s, trains provided a primary form of international transit. According to Simon Ward, "the train is an emblem of industrial modernization and civilization. It generally conveys its passengers through regions that have already been 'explored'" (2003, p. 1189). As such, it was featured prominently in literature and film as a way to depict spatial, temporal, and social relations. Trains not only signal mobility across locations and time, but they also provide a confined and even claustrophobic space within which narrative meaning can be accentuated. As Steven Spalding and Benjamin Fraser note in their analysis of Émile Zola's *La Bête Humaine* (1890), "the ceaseless movement of trains leaving and arriving serves as a continuous backdrop for a series of halts, stoppages, and interruptions that mark narrative time, that, like stops on a train line, punctuate the novel's narrative trajectory" (2012, p. 188). Given the degree to which train travel captured popular imagination in the late nineteenth and early twentieth centuries from *Arrival on a Train* (Lumière and Lumière 1896) to *North by Northwest* (Hitchcock 1959), it is no wonder that trains factor into the early Bond films.

Train travel plays an important role in both the novel *From Russia with Love* and its film adaptation. It not only facilitates the transportation and subsequent defection of Soviet Bond Girl Tatiana Romanova, but also functions as the site of her conversion from a Soviet citizen to a Western woman.[4] In the film version, the progress of the train via montages of train wheels and carriages is superimposed over a map tracing the journey from Istanbul across Greece and Yugoslavia. Scheduled stops at stations along the route provide Bond and his adversaries the opportunity to re-group and re-plan their nefarious activities. More generally, as noted by Ward, "As the bearer of modernization, the train is linked with imperialism—trains in different colonies may have been built by the same company—and the imperialist gaze is evident in rail travel accounts from the Shoemaker down to Charles Small in *Far Wheels* (1955)" (Ward 2003, p. 1190). The depiction of Bond's seduction of Romanova both sexually and geopolitically from the East/communism on the Orient Express (a train service that was featured in a fair share of films including *Murder on the Orient Express* [Lumet 1974]) helps to further emphasize the importance of Bond's libidinal masculinity, which serves as a visual signifier of the strength of MI6 and Britain at large.

The train ride from Istanbul to Paris via Venice takes up nearly one third of the film (and approximately one quarter of the source novel). While traversing time, the trip also straddles it. Thomas Barrett writes,

> As a Romanova, that is with a name that links her to the imperial royal family, she harkens back to an earlier era when Russian royals and nobles fled the revolution to a West where they were always a bit out of place; she too escapes, but with her youth, beauty, and contemporary sheen, she points to the future, and there is no doubt that she will fit in comfortably. (2015, p. 42)

A similar reference is included in *Octopussy*, which centers on the theft and transportation of the Russian Crown Jewels and specifically the Romanov Star out of the Soviet Union by train. However, in the Moore-era films, which encourage Anglo-Soviet cooperation,[5] the actions taken by General Orlov are framed as extreme, nationalistic, and a threat to international peace. As a result, Orlov is killed on the train tracks immediately after he runs past the guards on the border of East and West Germany, and Bond is tasked with returning the Romanov Star.

In addition to facilitating the conversion of Romanova, the train ride is also the setting for the altercation between Bond and Red Grant, an assassin for SPECTRE. Prior to their meeting on the Orient Express, the film draws parallels between the two men. Like Bond, Grant is a trained killer with ties to Britain (as he escaped Dartmoor Prison). He is shown to be physically fit and sexually attractive as depicted in a scene in which he is shirtless and receiving a massage from a beautiful woman.[6] The two men meet briefly on the platform before boarding the train with Grant masquerading as Bond's contact that he has just killed. The two men spend time in the dining car[7] before Grant pulls a gun on Bond in his quarters. In the end, it is Bond who outsmarts his opponent by using a specialty case designed by Q and then strangling Grant with his own garrote.[8]

Importantly, it is the moving train (rather than the immobile platform) that serves as the setting for the first significant test of Bond's masculinity in the film franchise from an opponent who is physically, mentally, and sexually comparable. According to Spalding and Fraser, the word 'locomotive' is feminine and the relationship between 'man' and 'train' has been defined via gender. This is most notable in *La Bête Humaine* through Zola's depiction of Jacques Lantier's train as his lover: "He loved her deeply, his machine, through the four years he had driven her...he loved that one because she truly had the qualities of a good woman. She was mild, obedient, easy to start up" (qtd. and trans. in Spalding and

Fraser 2012, p. 188). Interpreting this work, Spalding and Fraser argue that "for the train, Lantier ensures smooth functioning, achievement of required speeds and times, and satisfaction of the train's basic needs...this is Lantier's fantasy of becoming machine-like, mixing characteristics of the train and projecting gendered, even sexualized, qualities" onto it (ibid. 188). In *From Russia with Love*, although Grant does not compete with Bond for the affections of the Bond Girl, he does challenge Bond's masculinity (in the cabin and dining room) and dominance in a space that is often feminized. Thus, Bond's defeat of Grant on the train takes on patriarchal significance and can be linked to his seduction of Romanova and mission recovery, after being forced to leave the Orient Express prematurely.

A decade later, *Live and Let Die* includes a similar (albeit shorter) train sequence only this time race rather than nationality is at the forefront. Midway through the film, Bond seduces Solitaire away from the villain Kananga, a significant act given that she is his tarot card reader and her power resides in her virginity. The film presents a clear double standard with respect to miscegenation: not only does Bond have sexual access to both white and black women (Solitaire and Rosie Carver, respectively), but he is also set up as the (colonial) savior of the white woman from the sexual threat of the potent black man. After Bond kills Kananga, he gets on a train with Solitaire and the two prepare to make love in the train car after Solitaire models some lingerie (Fig. 7.2).

Fig. 7.2   *Live and Let Die* (Eon Productions et al. 1973)

Before they can do so, Tee Hee, Kananga's hench person with a metal arm and pinchers for a hand, attacks Bond before he is thrown off the train—a scene that mirrors Bond's dispatch of Jaws on a train in *The Spy Who Loved Me*. Through the intersection of gender and race, the train sequence in *Live and Let Die* underscores the superiority of the white hero over the black man in physical and sexual terms.

With the exception of *Octopussy*, trains do not factor largely in the narratives of Bond films in the 1980s and 1990s (as the villain's train features only briefly in *GoldenEye*), and it is not until *Casino Royale* that train travel reappears with any narrative substance. Not only does the train sequence help to connect Bond films of the Connery and Craig eras, but it also serves as the location for the first meeting between Bond and Vesper Lynd, his bankroller from the Treasury. According to Ward "With the advent of mass airplane travel…the decision to travel by train becomes an aesthetic choice…the focus is less the land to which the train takes the traveler… but rather the trains themselves and, in particular, their passengers" (Ward 2003, p. 1190). Sitting in the dimly lit dining car, the encounter between Bond and Lynd is expository and intimate. The two 'size each other up', surmising the ancestry and the qualities of the other. It is here that Lynd deduces the origins of Bond:

> By the cut of your suit, you went to Oxford or wherever. Naturally you think human beings dress like that. But you wear it with such disdain, my guess is you didn't come from money, and your school friends never let you forget it. Which means you were at school by the grace of someone else's charity, hence that chip on your shoulder. And since your first thought about me ran to orphan, that's what I'd say you are…And that makes perfect sense since MI6 looks for maladjusted young men, who give little thought to sacrificing others in order to protect Queen and Country…Now, having just met you, I wouldn't go so far as calling you a cold-hearted bastard… but it wouldn't be a stretch to imagine. You think of women as disposable pleasures rather than meaningful pursuits. So as charming as you are, Mr. Bond, I will be keeping my eye on our government's money—and off your perfectly formed ass.

In this scene, Lynd provides (the most) significant insight into the upbringing and character of Bond. She also inverts traditional gender dynamics in the series by establishing her dominance over Bond. This creates the impression that it is Lynd who seduces Bond and not vice versa. A woman who challenges Bond in the arena of mass transit has historically peaked his interest and captured his heart.

The train also factors into the narrative of *Spectre* and the sequence is explicitly referential to previous Bond films. First, the film features an expository scene in a dining car in which Bond discusses an important (and personal) topic with a potential love interest. Here, Bond discusses the nature of choice with Dr. Madeleine Swann—that neither is beholden to fate or familial circumstance, and each can decide the direction of their life. Second, the film features a fight on the train after Mr. Hinx attacks Bond in the dining car and the conflict eventually shifts into a second dining car and the kitchen before ending up in a pantry/storage unit. Unlike other Bond films where the Bond Girl is separated in some way from this conflict—Romanova is drugged in *From Russia with Love* and Solitaire is trapped in a foldaway bed in *Live and Let Die*—Swann inserts herself into the fight and gets beat up in the process; she hits Mr. Hinx on the head with an object and later shoots him in the arm. Bond eventually dispatches of the hench person by pushing him out of the train car (and literally out of the film), saving the Bond Girl in the process (like his predecessors). The pair subsequently consummates their relationship in their sleeping quarters. Through the intertextual referencing of previous Bond films and the Bond Girls featured in them, *Spectre* positions Swann in this traditional role while accentuating how she is (supposed to be) different from Bond's previous lovers. As the daughter of an assassin (Mr. White), Swann is set up in the film to be the best romantic match for Bond and this is first indicated through the reworking of the Bond train sequence.

Planes

Bond is sent on missions throughout the world and airplanes offer the most expedient form of transportation. Bond is depicted boarding planes (*The Living Daylights*), travelling in flight (*Goldfinger*), and exiting airports (*Dr. No, Live and Let Die*). Bond has battled hench people on the runway (*Casino Royale*) and in the air (*Spectre*), and been debriefed by allies on the tarmac upon deplaning (*Tomorrow Never Dies*). He demonstrates his knowledge of aviation technology by flying various aircrafts on his missions (*You Only Live Twice*) and has brought wayward planes under his control (*Die Another Day*). He has been the target of aircraft attacks while in the air (*Quantum of Solace*), on land (*From Russia with Love*), and even under water (*The Spy Who Loved Me*). While airplanes are frequently featured in Bond films in both practical and innovative ways, they are not neutral technologies and are bounded by social identities and particularly notions of nationality (for large airliners) and gender (for light and small aircrafts).

The plane has proven to be an iconic object for reminding audiences of the Anglo-American special relationship. When Bond flies commercially, his airline of choice in the 1960s appears to be Pan American (Pan Am). The choice was apposite for as Denis Cosgrove notes, "Not tied to an imperial network as state-operated European operators were, the free-enterprise American international airlines adopted a consciously global market strategy, reflected in their names and logos—Trans-World Airways, Pan American Airlines" (2001, p. 254). By the time Bond was shown arriving in Kingston (*Dr. No*) and Istanbul (*From Russia with Love*) courtesy of Pan Am, the Boeing 707 in particular was bringing long-distance travel into the purview of business and tourist travelers. Bond is shown travelling again with Pan Am in *Live and Let Die* on a brand new Boeing 747, and as it turns out aborting his travel plans with the airline in *License to Kill*.

In the early Bond films, while Pan Am is associated with the global travel plans of Bond, light and small aircrafts (but not helicopters, as they are always flown by men until Naomi pilots a helicopter in *The Spy Who Loved Me*) are feminized and largely associated with female pilots. This is established in *Goldfinger* with the introduction of Pussy Galore and broadened in *You Only Live Twice* when flying technology is explicitly feminized. In the latter, Bond submits a request for "Little Nellie and her father" to be sent to Japan. Little Nellie is the codename for the gyroplane developed by Q. Bond frequently refers to aircraft using feminine pronouns and even calls it a "girl." The notion of girlhood is one that is sustained throughout the Bond franchise as evinced by the description of the lead female protagonist as a Bond Girl and not a Bond Woman. In the world of Bond, a girl is a relatively young and single woman who is sexually available to the male hero and usually requires his saving. In comparison, women in the franchise tend to be older like Judi Dench's M and are often referred to as "ma'am" and "mum." These polite forms of address relay the impression that womanhood is associated with marriage and maternity, which is a problematic and limiting sentiment. Little Nellie's youthfulness—due to her size and newness as a technology—is signaled through her familial relationship as a daughter with a father rather than being a parent/mother herself.

Language also helps to draw parallels between the gyroplane and the Bond Girl as Bond refers to both as "good girls." This is notable through his radio transmission following his success in an aerial fight: "Little Nellie got a hot reception. Four big shots made improper advances toward her, but she defended her honor with great success. Heading home." This description is aligned with the contrasting of Bond Girls and Bad Girls in the Connery era:

> Throughout the 1960s, the franchise both engaged with and recapitulated historical approaches to gender that situated female sexuality as suspect and dangerous when articulated outside the confines of heterosexual marriage [...]Thus, in order to be presented as a "good" character, the Bond Girl is expected to submit to the will and libido of James Bond, forfeiting her own liberated sexual identity for a domesticated one. By comparison, women who embrace their liberal sexualities and refuse to adhere to the "Bondian" standard of normative femininity are presented as "bad" and are violently punished. (Funnell 2011b, pp. 200–201)

Additionally, the term "girl" has been historically used as a way to diminish, deprecate, and trivialize women by labelling them as immature or inexperienced (Wood 2011, p. 123). As a result, the depiction of Little Nellie not only aligns her with the Bond Girl but also emphasizes the patriarchal role that Bond plays via touch. His heroic identity is defined not only through his seduction and domestication of the Bond Girl but also through his mastery of/over feminized technology like Little Nellie.

In addition to the feminization of aircrafts, flying is often presented as a female profession in the Connery era and Bond's ability to seduce the female pilot is a key factor in the success of his mission. This is most evident in *Goldfinger* as the villain has hired Pussy Galore to be his personal pilot. She is first introduced to Bond midflight as she is flying the private plane. When Bond inquires about the extent of her relationship with Goldfinger, she becomes offended and states "I'm a damn good pilot, period." She is also a flight instructor and the head of an all-female flying troupe comprised of five beautiful women dressed in black spandex uniforms that emphasize their femininity and attractiveness. These women will participate in Goldfinger's Operation Grand Slam by crop-dusting the military surrounding Fort Knox. Thus, Bond's ability to seduce Galore (and by extension her troupe) away from the villain proves to be the tipping point in his mission; after their sexual encounter, she exchanges the gas canisters and works with the CIA to foil Goldfinger's plan. But her sex with Bond and positioning as a Bond Girl also seem to reduce her effectiveness as a pilot as she cannot land the depressurized plane in the final scene. She has

to be ejected and the film ends with her kissing Bond underneath a parachute. Over the course of the film, the professional female pilot is seduced
and then subsequently domesticated through her romantic relationship
with Bond.

Extrapolating from the character of Galore, *You Only Live Twice* establishes the figure of the personal assistant pilot. Helga Brandt is introduced
as the secretary and pilot of Mr. Osato, a Japanese industrialist who is
affiliated with SPECTRE. While Brandt is a SPECTRE agent and number
11 in their hierarchy, she works in a supportive rather than management
role in the office. Although Blofeld orders Brandt to kill Bond, she is
seduced by him and this delays her assassination attempt. The next day,
she puts a plan into play that consists of strapping Bond into a small plane
and parachuting out, leaving him to die in the crash. After Bond escapes,
Brandt is punished for her failure by being dropped into a pool of piranhas
where she is eaten alive. As instituted in the Connery era, the seduction
of the personal assistant pilot is pivotal to the survival of Bond and the
success of his missions, and usually occurs at her expense—professionally
and/or personally.

In the Moore and Dalton eras, female pilots are presented as either a
personal assistant to the villain and/or Bond Girl pilots who work with/
for Bond. For instance, in *The Spy Who Loved Me*, the bikini-clad Naomi
works for Karl Stromberg and is tasked with killing Bond. Although Bond
gazes at and flirts with Naomi, he cannot sleep with her since he is already
romantically involved with his Bond Girl, Anya Amasova. As a result, she
quickly loses her standing in the narrative and is killed off when Bond
shoots down her helicopter as it hovers over his location. In *Moonraker*,
the scantily clad Corinne who works for Hugo Drax becomes an asset to
Bond soon after she gives him a flying tour of the Drax personal estate
and space shuttle testing institution; after he seduces her, Bond tricks her
into revealing the location of her employer's safe. After Bond leaves, she is
killed by Drax who sends his Rottweilers to chase her down in the forest.
Dressed in a high-collar white lace dress, which emphasizes her youth and
innocence, her attack is stylized like a scene out of a horror film. In both
instances, the personal assistant pilot is a highly sexualized and disposable
object of desire that is killed off as soon as she loses usefulness to Bond
and/or the villain.

In comparison, the Bond Girl pilot plays a pivotal role in the success of
Bond's mission. In *Moonraker*, Dr. Holly Goodhead is introduced as an
astronaut and scientist working for Drax. Although Bond initially assumes

that Goodhead, like Corinne, is a personal assistant pilot he can seduce, he soon discovers that she is an undercover CIA agent and changes his approach by suggesting they work together platonically. While Goodhead flies them into space, Bond demonstrates an intuitive understanding of aeronautics and astronautics that allows him to use the technology.[9] And it is only after the mission has been completed that Bond finally seduces Goodhead and their zero-gravity lovemaking session is accidentally transmitted to the base back home. In *License to Kill*, Pam Bouvier is presented in a similar way, as she is a pilot and CIA agent who assists Bond on his mission. She flies Bond to Isthmus City for the undercover mission and Bond introduces her as his personal assistant, a cover identity that does not go over well with her as she would rather be *his* boss. Bond tells her that she needs to look the part and Bouvier undergoes a makeover to increase her sex appeal: she returns with a slick haircut and formfitting dresses that support her cover as a personal assistant pilot. Although Bouvier offers tactical support in the air, she operates on the periphery of the final action sequence as she flies in a crop-dusting aircraft (which if anything trivializes her professionalism) and out of the conflict while Bond performs the majority of the heroic labor by confronting Sanchez in a tanker-truck chase. And like Goodhead, she consummates her relationship with Bond once the mission is complete when he chooses her over his Latin lover, Lupe Lamora.

In the Brosnan era, the female pilot is reimagined as a central antagonist through the figure of Xenia Onatopp in *GoldenEye*. Onatopp is initially presented as being a personal assistant pilot to General Ourmuov for whom she steels the Tiger helicopter in order to transport him to Siberia. This role is suggested through costuming, as she wears revealing clothes such as a low-cut dress and a bathrobe, as well as Bond's interest in seducing her at the casino albeit with no success. It is later revealed that Onatopp is actually working for Alec Trevelyan and no longer functions as a potential conquest and tipping point for Bond. This is signaled through a change in costuming as she wears a black military-styled uniform when she abseils from a helicopter to attack Bond. She is subsequently killed when Bond shoots at the aircraft, which leads to her suffocation against a tree. As the last female pilot appearing in the franchise, Onatopp highlights the dangerous role that female pilots play when they cannot be seduced or domesticated by Bond.

The intersection of gender with nationality draws attention to the geopolitical significance of the gendering of light and small aircrafts and the representation of female pilots. Importantly, only American women serve as Bond Girl pilots (Galore, Goodhead, Bouvier) while women who lack an obvious national affiliation take on the secondary role of personal assistant pilot (Helga Brandt, Naomi, Corinne). This highlights the central role the United States has historically played in aeronautics and astronautics, and Bond's ability to fly helicopters, light planes, fighter jets, and military transport aircraft helps to counter-balance that aerial/aeronautic dominance. In comparison, the only female antagonist pilot (Onatopp) was once affiliated with the former Soviet Union and her theft of this technology along with Bond's inability to seduce her renders her as a genuine threat. Through its representation of female pilots, the Bond franchise appears to reiterate an antiquated message that was once relayed to American and Soviet female pilots after World War II through the reestablishment of gender roles. As Amy Goodpaster Strebe writes, "the women pilots in both nations found that their place in society was not in the cockpit of a military airplane, but in the home as wives and mothers. The airwomen had fulfilled a temporary need created by the war and were expected to return to their prewar roles in society. There was seemingly no room for women pilots in postwar military aviation" (2007, p. 2). Through his seduction of female pilots, Bond orients them away from the cockpit and towards the domestic sphere with his loving touch.

Automobiles

Cars are a central aspect of the James Bond brand. Beyond their practical function, cars play a key role in shaping the heroic and mobile identity of Bond as well as defining his relationship with women. As Ian Fleming explains in the second Bond novel *Live and Let Die*,

> Bond liked fast cars and he liked driving them. Most American cars bored him. They lacked personality and the patina of individual craftsmanship that European cars have. They were just "vehicles" […] All the fun of driving had been taken out of them with the abolition of a gear-change, with hydraulic-assisted steering and spongy suspension. All effort had been smoothed away and all of that close contact with the machine and the road that extracts skill and nerve from the European driver. (1954, p. 125)

Although Bond drives a variety of domestic and international cars, he is most strongly associated with the vehicles produced by British carmaker Aston Martin.[10] Bond first drives an Aston Martin DB5 in *Goldfinger*, which has been retrofitted with weapons, navigation aids, and other gadgetry by Q.[11] The car appears again in the opening sequence in *Thunderball* with additional modifications. As noted by Stephanie Jones, in the Connery era the Aston Martin became such a transcendental symbol of the franchise that it established the vehicle as a core component of the (mobile) Bond formula. Aston Martins have appeared in eight additional Bond films including those featuring the inaugural performance of a new actor in the role of Bond (with the exception of Moore)—for Lazenby in *OHMSS*, Dalton in *The Living Daylights*, Brosnan in *GoldenEye*, and Crag in *Casino Royale*. Moreover, the Aston Martin DB5 has been featured in *Die Another Day* and *Skyfall* to commemorate the fortieth and fiftieth anniversaries of the franchise, respectively (2015b, p. 207).

Car culture contains a pronounced gender ideology that informs the relationship between Bond and his vehicles. Generally, cars tend to be feminized through the use of feminine pronouns and female names in their descriptions (S. Jones 2015b, p. 206), as well as the perception of the interior as being womb-like (Lupton 1999, p. 60). As a result, the ability to construct, maintain, sell, and/or operate these vehicles takes on patriarchal significance due to a culture that discourages and excludes women from participating in this sphere. This is most evident in the depiction and description of the BMW 750iL in *Tomorrow Never Dies*. In addition to the use of feminine pronouns, Q's choice of a female voice for the operational computer and Bond's ability to move her around with this touch help to frame Bond's relationship with the car as inherently sexual. Bond later destroys the German car (by driving it off a car park), drawing attention to the disposability of some automobiles as well as some women in the franchise as he is always given a new one—a car and a girl—in the next film. Interestingly, villains destroy his British cars such as the Aston Martin (e.g. *Skyfall*) and Lotus (e.g. *For Your Eyes Only*) but never Bond.

The car is considered to be a part of male culture and the driver's seat has largely been perceived as "a naturally male position" (O'Connell 1998, p. 45). This notion is built into the design of cars through the placement of the pedals, which accommodates a male rather than female physique. The passenger seat, by comparison, was reserved for the woman and presumably the romantic partner of the driver in a heteronormative sense. Jones notes that "a vast amount of rhetorical work [has been] expended on making these roles seem natural and incontestable" (2015b, p. 206). Moreover, Sean O'Connell writes that the car arrived "at a time of great controversy over the issue of women's role in society" and the woman driver emerged as "a powerful symbol of potential equality" (1998, p. 45). As a result, Bond's vehicular interactions with women convey messages about mobility, gender, and heroic competency in the franchise.

It is not unusual for Bond to be picked up by Bond Girls who provide him with a quick escape from impending danger (see Chap. 2). However, Bond does not like being "taken for a ride" and rarely appears comfortable as a passenger. He can be extremely critical of women drivers like Anya Amasova in *The Spy Who Loved Me* when she struggles to start the van and free the vehicle from the clutches of Jaws in Egypt. He makes similar condescending comments to Eve Moneypenny in *Skyfall* and even pulls at the steering wheel to spin out the car they are pursuing; his actions demonstrate that her driving skills are not up to par and this is the beginning of a much larger criticism of Moneypenny's aptitude as a field agent. Bond takes similar action in *For Your Eyes Only* and asks Melina Havelock to switch places after she rolls her car. These interactions are much different from Bond's equal-weighted partnership with Wai Lin in *Tomorrow Never Dies* as evinced by their performance in driving a motorcycle while handcuffed together. In the Bond franchise, the competency of women as heroic allies is often signaled, if not partially embodied, by their driving skills and those who do not measure up (in Bond's eyes) are deemed inferior agents and allies.

Bond also meets, flirts with, and tries to "pick up" women on the open road. It is not uncommon for a woman to peak Bond's interest by speeding past him. This happens in *Goldfinger* while Bond is tailing Auric Goldfinger through Switzerland. Tilly Masterson honks her horn before zooming past his car and Bond, who is clearly intrigued and (sexually) excited, has to tell himself to stay focused on the task at hand. He says aloud "Discipline, 007. Discipline." He later picks up the pursuit after Masterson almost shoots him and he runs her off the road. In the 1959 source novel, Bond says to Masterson "If you touch me there again you'll have to marry me" (p. 155) as they inspect the damage to his Aston Martin. This draws attention to the flirtation and even courting Bond does while driving on the open road. The women Bond encounters are presented as enigmas based on the mystery surrounding their driving skills. And while mystique plays a central role in female characterization, as noted by Eileen Rositzka, "once the (female) enigma is solved, she is rendered unremarkable and new enigmas are produced to take her place" (2015, p. 156). After Masterson is killed by Oddjob, Bond quickly moves on to pilot Pussy Galore. Much like the cars he uses and discards, women drivers are passing fancies who are easily replaced by a newer and flashier model.

On occasion, Bond encounters a woman driver who poses him grave threat. In *Thunderball,* Bond is picked by Fiona Volpe who drives him to his hotel. She begins to accelerate and Bond looks nervous as the car travels at a dangerous speed. The camera pans to the speedometer as if to suggest that his physical discomfort is not unreasonable. Her reckless driving is connected to her rampant sexuality and during their sexual encounter Bond even comments that she should be locked in a cage. Xenia Onatopp is presented in a similar way in *GoldenEye.* Bond first meets her as they flirtatiously chase each other along a winding road. Her driving, however, is far more reckless as she drives off the road, spins out, and even helps to knock over a group of cyclists. Her driving is also related to her sexuality as she screams wildly in bed and asphyxiates her lovers with her legs. Both women challenge Bond on the road and in the bedroom: while Volpe resists domestication and mocks Bond's libidinal masculinity, Onatopp attacks Bond and insists that she will be the one to experience pleasure. For female villains, their driving skills serve as an indicator for their sexual performance and the relative threat they pose to Bond and mission success.

High Versus Low Culture Spaces

In addition to being a mobile hero who traverses space and time, Bond is defined by the ways in which he moves and operates in various social environments. Social mobility is something of considerable significance to Bond's subjective position. Implicit in the depiction of these spaces are value judgments of relative worth that tap into the high versus low culture debate. On the one hand, high culture refers to that which the socially elite can access/appreciate such as classical music, art, and literature. On the other hand, low culture refers to that which is mass produced and is presumed to cater to base tastes (Sturken and Cartwright 2009, p. 60). This debate creates a hierarchy in which the socially elite are viewed as more refined and civilized than the disreputable popular consumer. It also informs our impressions of these spaces particularly when a figure like Bond, who resides in the upper-middle/upper class, moves through them.

Bond's social mobility and even 'snobbery' has been a perennial feature of his reception. Critics like Paul Johnston have famously noted that "sex, sadism and snobbery" lay at the heart of the Ian Fleming novel *Dr. No.* He remarks that there are "three basic ingredients, all thoroughly English... the sadism of a schoolboy bully, the mechanical two-dimensional sex-longings of a frustrated adolescent, and the crude, snob-cravings of a sub-urban adult" (Johnson 1958, p. 430). The early Bond films are predicated on a conspicuous form of social consumption, as Bond travels the world, drinks expensive and branded champagne, and accesses exclusive clubs and hotels. His geographical mobility goes hand in hand with this social mobility. *Dr. No* telegraphs this relationship early on from his appearance at an exclusive card playing club in London to his demeanor at Kingston Airport when he walks confidently out of the building and takes the first available taxi oblivious of the fact that some flight attendants were actually ahead of him in the taxi rank queue. As it turns out, he does not need that taxi and gives way to the waiting women. *Dr. No* establishes the social mobility and snobbery of Bond, which is carried forward in subsequent films.

Tourist Traps

As a super spy, Bond has the ability to stand out from the crowd but he is also presented as being vulnerable in some crowded places and specifically tourist traps. Carnivals, circuses, and street festivals in particular become more complicated spaces for the secret agent to navigate, precisely because the mobility of others is not tightly controlled. These spaces are defined by what Mikhail Bakhin describes as the four categories of the carnivalistic sense, in which the term "carnival" refers to "the sum total of all diverse festivities, rituals, and forms of a carnival type" (1998, p. 250). First, the carnival promotes free and familiar contact among people who are typically separated socially via hierarchal barriers. Second, it encourages eccentric and unacceptable behaviors without social consequence. Third, the carnival promotes mésalliances by combining "the sacred with the profane, the lofty with the low, the great with the insignificant, [and] the wise with the stupid" (ibid. 251). Fourth, it allows for profanation and sacrilegious events to occur without the need for punishment (ibid. 251). Imbued with the carnivalistic sense, these tourist traps become complicated spaces for a hero like Bond to navigate.

In the Bond franchise, travelling carnivals and fairs are depicted as chaotic spaces that can both help and hinder an agent. This is evident in *OHMSS* when Bond escapes from Piz Gloria and tries to blend into the crowd at the Grand Ice Carnival. The film emphasizes Bond's experience of chaos through editing as the film cuts between brief shots of Bond and his pursuers making their way through the crowd. When Bond finds himself cornered, he begins to walk backwards and turns when he bumps into something. The film conveys his point of view and presents, through a low-angle shot, a man in a polar bear costume growling and taking his picture. Both Bond and the viewer are startled by the bear and the camera flash, and the film cuts quickly between images of the bear and Bond's face to emphasize his terror. As Bond sits on a bench to collect himself, the film continues to intercut images of his pursuers through brief shots, which now includes the polar bear in addition to Irma Bunt and her hench people. Bond looks exhausted and exasperated by the situation until he is approached by Tracy di Vicenzo who guides him out of the carnival. The film conveys the impression that Bond struggles to operate in a chaotic space that contains unforeseen social threats that are beyond his control.[12] He even appears claustrophobic.

Bond is more comfortable in structured environments where he can utilize/manipulate physical and social elements. While the nightclub might be one such space, it is sometimes evident in other spaces, even dangerous ones. This is best demonstrated in *The Man with the Golden Gun* when Bond enters into Scaramanga's fun house, which contains various devices designed to surprise, challenge, and distract Bond as he attempts to locate the villain. Bond initially struggles to make his way through all the smoke and mirrors until he finds the edge of a glass pane and climbs underneath the obstacle course. Bond's ability to maneuver himself through the metal rafters and emerge at the other end of the course provides him with the element of surprise and affords him with the opportunity to shoot an unassuming Scaramanga. In this scene, Bond circumvents the carnivalistic sense by working his way through the underlying structure rather than chaotic veneer.[13] And it is Bond's unwillingness to play "the game" and search for physical and social order that allows him to emerge victorious.

Scaramanga's comfort level with the carnivalistic sense is rooted in his upbringing. Early on, it is revealed that Scaramanga was born in the circus: his father was a ring-master and his mother was a snake charmer. He became a trick shot artist before he was recruited by the KBG and then worked freelance as a million dollar assassin. In addition, he also has a supernumerary or third nipple, a physical deformity by which he can be identified. His accomplice, Nick Nack, is a little person who he presumably met while in the circus and their relationship is so close that Nick Nack will inherit Scaramanga's wealth when he dies. The film relies on negative stereotypes associated with the circus and particularly "freak shows" to further vilify the two men. As noted by Debbie Rodan et al., there is a long literary tradition in which disability is associated with evil and it is the combination of danger/risk and human curiosity that helped to establish the "freak show" as a popular entertainment in the 1700s. People with disabilities "were styled and presented in a certain social context to *appear as freaks*" in the travelling circus, which "constructed them as not normal and subjected their bodies to a particular gaze" (2014, p. 22). It is these physical differences that help to visually connect these men (in a sort of brotherhood or family unit of Otherness) while isolating them from the rest of society.[14]

Other characters in the franchise are also associated with the circus. Although Jaws first appears in *The Spy Who Loved Me*, he is featured in *Moonraker* and re-introduced in relation to the circus. After pushing Bond out of a plane and chasing after him in the air, Jaws pulls the rip cord and it detaches without deploying his parachute. The scene intercuts shots of Jaws freefalling with those from inside a circus as "circus music" plays. The film then cuts to a long shot of the circus tent and a drum roll as Jaws crashes down. His ability to survive this fall not only emphasizes his abnormal strength and size, but it also works to define him in relation to the other strong men and "freaks" featured in the circus. Later in the film, it is this Otherness that compels Jaws to turn on the villain and work with Bond. Hugo Drax intends to destroy all human life and re-populate the world with a perfect race. When Bond points out to Jaws that neither he nor his spectacled girlfriend fit the mold, the two men combine forces and destroy the space station. In *Moonraker*, Jaws is reimagined and humanized through this romantic subplot.

Octopussy also contains a reframing of the circus. The film opens with British agent 009 transporting a fake Fabergé egg to the British embassy in East Berlin while dressed as a clown. He is tracked down and mortally wounded by Mischka and Grischka, identical twin knife-throwing hench people. This pre-credit sequence presents the impression that the circus is a dangerous place for secret agents. The narrative centers on Octopussy, a business woman who uses her travelling circus as a front to smuggle jewelry across the border. However, her partner, Kamal Khan, along with his associate, General Orlov, plan to use the circus to transport a bomb that they will destroy the US Air Force base. And it is up to Bond, who is dressed in the same clown costume as 009, to disarm the weapon during the show. Bond accomplishes this by establishing order in the circus tent: he speaks with the American general, appeals to reason with showrunner Octopussy, and then uses his skills to disable the bomb. Much like Jaws in *Moonraker*, he crashes the show and reframes the circus as the target rather than the origin of danger. *Octopussy* presents the impression that (Soviet) extremists rather than circus performers are the true danger as they work within rather than outside of the system.

In addition to travelling fairs and circuses, street festivals and celebrations are also potential sites of danger through their disordering of social and spatial relations. In *Thunderball*, Bond is pursued by Fiona Volpe and her hench people through the Junkanoo—a street parade held in the Bahamas featuring live music, dancing, and costumes (Smith 2011, p. 684)—via intercutting shots of Bond and his pursuers weaving through the performers, which evoke the chaos of the scene. Bond is eventually tracked down at the Kiss Kiss Club where Volpe is killed by a bullet intended for him. In *Live and Let Die*, two agents (one MI6 and the other CIA) are killed while watching an African American funeral procession in New Orleans. Both men exhibit social decorum by stopping on the sidewalk to let the funeral pass only to be killed by the organizers and placed in the coffin. The somber music is replaced by a celebratory tune as the funeral marchers begin to dance, effectively transforming the funeral into a street celebration. In *Moonraker*, Jaws attacks Bond's Brazilian contact Manuela during a street celebration (presumably Rio Carnival). Although he is over seven feet tall, he is able to blend in with the other performers by dressing in a costume and this enables him to get close to her. Bond is able to fight off Jaws, who is pulled back into celebration by other partygoers. Finally, in *Spectre*, Bond pursues a target in Mexico City during the Day of the Dead Festival. The crowd gradually serves as physical obstacles and potential witnesses to this assassination. In all four instances, the street festival serves as an exceptionally dangerous space for trained government agents.

While Bond struggles to navigate his way through carnivals, circuses, and street festivals due to their carnivalistic senses, his interactions in the latter are also coded by race. These festivals are structured around people of color whose bodies and cultures are depicted as both spectacular (to draw you in) and dangerous (to avoid you getting too close) for the white hero and, by extension, the presumed white spectator.[15] Unlike the reframing of circus performers in the franchise, there is no contradistinction for people of color who perform in these spaces. As a result, Bond's eventual success in navigating his way through these predominantly nonwhite spaces takes on colonial significance. Just as Bond tries to establish social and spatial order in other carnivalistic spaces, his movements and actions as a white man connote a sense of imperial order that has been historically forced upon the black colonial subject. As such, these tourist traps are not neutral spaces but rather are invested with social significance.

HIGHBROW SOCIAL SPACES

Unlike tourist traps that promote free contact between people from different social categories (such as class and race), highbrow spaces reduce access to those of particular financial means and cultural sensibility. Although those with privilege often enter into the spaces of those with less social power, the opposite is rarely true as this space is defined, maintained, and secured through physical means and cultural codes. Territoriality is particularly evident with respect to socioeconomic class as certain spaces are rendered inaccessible for those who do not measure up. In the Bond franchise, extreme personal wealth is often signaled through the spaces in which the villains operate. As explained earlier, most own residential estates and secret bases that are located in isolated areas. These villains also network and socialize in exclusive environments like the casino, symphony, and golf course. Although Bond is not excessively wealthy, he possesses a high degree of social and cultural capital that grants him access to these spaces and is frequently shown winning large sums of money at the card table. And his ability to successfully navigate his way through these places plays a central role in the success of his missions.

The Casino

The casino is a space in which Bond consistently operates across the franchise, and famously features in the opening pages of Fleming's 1953 novel, *Casino Royale*. Bond was first introduced in the inaugural *Dr. No* winning a game of baccarat against Sylvia Trench at an exclusive club in London. With his face hidden from the camera, Bond is initially defined by his style (as he is dressed in a black tuxedo and is smoking a cigarette) and skill set (as the film presents a close-up shot of his hands). When Trench asks for his name, the film cuts to a medium close-up of Bond who replies, "Bond, James Bond" as the Bond theme song begins to play. Since then, and echoing Fleming's novels, Bond has played at casinos around the world and has been defined by his ability to win at various games, including baccarat (*Thunderball*), craps (*Diamonds Are Forever*), sic bo (*The Man with the Golden Gun*), backgammon (*Octopussy*), blackjack (*License to Kill*), and Texas Hold'em poker (*Casino Royale*). Over the course of the series, the casino has served as a key site in which Bond defines his heroic identity and professional competence.

Bond establishes his libidinal masculinity in the casino. He not only meets beautiful women but also seduces them at the card table and his proficiency in gambling is linked to his abilities in the bedroom. For example, in *OHMSS*, Bond not only defeats Tracy di Vicenzo in baccarat but also offers to pay off her debt in the casino. This mirrors his previous attempt to save her when she tries to commit suicide in the pre-credit sequence in coastal Portugal.[16] She then sleeps with Bond to repay her debt and she begins to fall in love with him thus establishing her position as his Bond Girl and helpmate in the film. In *For Your Eyes Only* and *Octopussy*, Bond seduces women in the casino in order to forward his mission objectives: while Countess Lisl von Schlaf provides him with information over pillow talk, Magda is set up to steal a Fabergé egg that has been implanted with a tracker. In both cases, the casino represents the first step in the seduction of a key asset in the film.[17] Finally, in *Diamonds Are Forever*, Bond meets Plenty O'Toole while playing craps at a casino in Las Vegas, but she is thrown out of his hotel window (and ejected from the narrative) before they can have sex. She represents one of the many casino girls Fleming describes in his novels who help to warm up the tables (Ulfsdotter 2015, p. 25). She is a disposable object of pleasure whose sole purpose in the narrative is to confirm Bond's libidinal masculinity.[18]

The casino is also a space of networking for Bond. It is here that Bond introduces himself to the villain and/or his hench person, and defines himself as being equal, if not superior, to his opponent. For example, Bond introduces himself to Emilio Largo in *Thunderball* by inserting himself into Largo's baccarat game (Fig. 7.3).

While Largo is seated at the table, Bond is standing behind his hench person Vargas and this spatial orientation suggests that Bond needs to earn his spot at the table. After winning the hand, he is invited to sit down in Vargas' place and the two men are formally introduced. Over the course of the game, and again faithful to the source novel, Bond antagonizes Largo by frequently using the word "specter" to suggest his knowledge of Largo's affiliation with the terrorist organization (SPECTRE). After winning two hands, he leaves Largo at the table to win his money back and buys Largo's companion, Domino Derval, a drink. This is the first of a series of encounters—such as a shooting competition and their rivalry for Derval's affections—in which Bond proves himself to be superior to Largo. The dynamics of their relationship are established at the casino.

Bond's interactions within the casino are limited by the rules of the game as well as the social decorum expected from the establishment. Although

Fig. 7.3   *Thunderball* (Eon Productions et al. 1965)

the games are civil, they are not necessarily friendly and Bond "plays with fire" as he antagonizes violent figures like Xenia Onatopp (*GoldenEye*) who seek revenge later in the film. But in *Casino Royale*, Bond is placed in mortal danger while playing in the Texas Hold'em tournament when LeChiffre's girlfriend Valenka poisons him.[19] He deals himself out of the hand and stumbles to his car just as his heart stops beating; he is subsequently resuscitated and returns to the game looking refreshed, much to the surprise and dismay of LeChiffre. After some trial and error, Bond eventually defeats LeChiffre and wins the $115 million pot. Unlike other films, Bond is tasked with playing in the tournament and his defeat of LeChiffre is the objective of the operation designed to alienate the villain from his terrorist network. Bond is not only depicted as a superior card player but he is also defined as heroic by the way in which he navigates his way through the dangers of the casino.

Symphony and Opera

While the casino serves as a site of competition and commerce, the opera house and concert hall are spaces of high culture in which the affluent can appreciate classical music. Using acoustical engineering (which focuses on the science of sound and vibration), these spaces are designed to enhance sound while reducing unwanted noise. This is achieved through the building of tiered seating as well as the strategic use of particular materials that reflect or absorb sound. In addition to their physical qualities, these spaces are structured socially around a series of rules that prescribe proper etiquette. These include a dress code (which is often formal), signals (such as the bell that ends intermission), and the use of ushers (who control access to seating). As such, these spaces have long been associated with the gentry and/or notions of cultural refinement.[20]

Given their structure, these spaces serve as key sites for covert encounters in the Bond franchise. In *The Living Daylights*, the concert hall in Bratislava, Czechoslovakia is the location for the defection of Soviet General Georgi Koshov. Seated in the balcony beside fellow agent Saunders, Bond surveils Koskov who is seated below him on the floor flanked by guards. His gaze shifts towards a cellist, Kara Milovy, whose beauty and talent pique his interest. At intermission, Koskov enters the restroom while Bond relocates to the building across the street. When Koskov climbs out a window, Bond provides him with sniper cover and notices an armed woman in the window of an adjacent building. Through his sniper scope, Bond identifies the woman as the cellist and neutralizes the threat by shooting away her gun rather than killing her. Through observation and intuition, Bond deduces that Milovy is an artist (i.e. creator) rather than a killer and although he is initially criticized for sparing her life, he ends up turning Milovy into an asset who aids him in taking down the villains.

The concert hall is featured two additional times in *The Living Daylights*. Midway through the film, Bond takes Milovy to see the symphony in Vienna. This date helps to facilitate Bond's seduction of Milovy away from her boyfriend Koskov by appealing to her passion for classical music; this clearly works as she is captured in a close-up shot enjoying the performance. When she excuses herself to use the restroom at intermission, Bond takes the opportunity to meet with Saunders and requests some information. In the end, both actions prove to be critical to the success of Bond's mission. The final scene of the film also takes place in a concert hall, only this time in Britain with Milovy playing her cello. Following her performance, the gallery becomes a meeting place for a series of characters that represent a new alliance between Britain, the Soviet Union, and Afghanistan (see Chap. 4). And it is the concert hall—appearing at the beginning (Czechoslovakia), middle (Vienna), and end (Britain)—that serves as the space for these shifting geopolitical relations from cold war hostility to a new era of Anglo-Soviet relations.

In *Quantum of Solace*, it is an opera house in Bregenz, Austria, that functions as the location for a secret meeting between members of the Quantum organization. Up to this point, MI6 has gathered little information on the terrorist group.[21] Bond follows Dominic Greene into the opera house and surveils the gallery from a second floor balcony. He discovers that a small number of people are being given a special gift bag containing an ear piece and microphone. After commandeering a set, he listens in to the Quantum meeting as he climbs up to the rafters backstage and surveys the patrons trying to locate the members. Unable to locate them in the audience, he flushes them out when he interrupts their conversation by stating "Can I offer an opinion? I really think you people should find a better place to meet." His comment startles the Quantum members, most of who stand to leave the performance. As the music begins to swell, Bond takes their photos and sends them to MI6 where they are identified. While tactically effective, his comment also chastises the group for not acting appropriately during the performance.

As Bond tries to leave the opera house, he runs into Greene in the lobby and is chased by his hench people through the building. The film intercuts shots of Bond running through the gallery, kitchen, and hallways with images of the opera unfolding on stage. Moreover, the opera remains at the forefront of the soundtrack while the sound of gunshots, screams, and breaking glass can be heard more faintly in the background. The stylization of the scene effectively connects Bond with, if not inserts him into, Giacomo Puccini's opera *Tosca*. This is appropriate given the nature of the piece as evinced by Burton Fisher's summary of the opera:

> *Tosca* is a high-voltage, powerful, and sensationalist thriller crammed with action, containing intense and sometimes ferocious, supercharged dramatic confrontations: it delivers an abundance of violent cruelty, and it contains an ingenious blend of sex, sadism, jealousy, and religion. It is true melodrama with raw emotion, and Puccini masterfully uses his music to savagely assault the emotions as the action generates into a feverish pitch as it moves from one climax to another. (2005, p. 26)

The opera, in addition to the opera house, provides a social, structural, and stylistic context for Bond's infiltration of the Quantum organization and invests additional meaning into the conflict that ensues.

Although Bond does not reside in the upper class, he possesses enough social and cultural capital and even chutzpah (turning up to the opera in

Austria without a ticket) to successfully navigate his way through these spaces in order to bring down the villain and his organization. The films suggest that he understands these social milieus without being part of them. In doing so, Bond increases the popular appeal of his character as most action heroes typically come from the middle class and are figures with whom audiences can relate. While extreme wealth is often linked to notions of greed, criminality, and evil, Bond is able to (respectfully) step into this space without being fully defined by it. As a British agent motivated by duty, Bond acts on behalf of Britain for the common good rather than on behalf of himself for selfish purposes.

CONCLUSION

Across 24 films, there are only three scenes of Bond in his home. In *Dr. No*, we get a brief glance at his flat after his chance meeting with Sylvia Trench. In *Live and Let Die*, M drops by Bond's flat in the early morning to send him on his next mission. The encounter is humorous as Bond attempts to direct M away from the place where his female companion is hiding; he moves them from his bedroom into his kitchen (where he makes him a cappuccino using an avant-garde coffee making machine) and then back into the hallway towards the front door. Although Bond is a jet-setting spy, the film highlights the fact that Bond does have a home in Britain, which curiously is never attacked by the villain.

Bond's flat is not mentioned again until *Skyfall* when Bond "returns from the dead" to resume active duty. He is informed by M that as per regulations his flat was sold and his belongings were put into storage.[22] This transforms Bond from a mobile to peripatetic hero and his uprooting leads him to seek refuge at his childhood home in Scotland, Skyfall manor. This becomes the site of Bond's last stand against Silva. Moreover, it is the first time that Bond's home is attacked and destroyed by a villain, who is a former MI6 agent no less. Unlike the villain, Bond does not perish in the assault (although M does) and emerges a stronger and more reserved hero. The film ends with Bond entering into the new M's office, which has been redesigned to match those of her predecessors, and the film conveys the impression that Bond is back and ready to work. But we have no idea where his new home is, a point that *Spectre* picks up when Bond invites Moneypenny to his flat early in the film. Bond can be seen sitting on a couch while examining secret information in order to gain insight as to who is responsible for setting up the Quantum network. His new flat has few obvious touches of homeliness, and the only ornament on display is a bulldog figurine left to him by the late M in her will. Bond has not even had time to unpack when again the mission intrudes into the prospect of a more immobile let alone anchored domestic life.

NOTES

1. If they do travel to brief/aid Bond 'in the field', they either bring with them a 'replica office' or retrofit spaces using Western décor and/or technology.
2. In *You Only Live Twice*, the Japanese secret service builds their base underneath a subway line.
3. Sharks frequently appear in the early Bond films. The villain's lair/base is often surrounded by a moat that contains these sea creatures. And yet, Bond is able to avoid the sharks and/or direct them towards others as in the case of *Thunderball* and *The Spy Who Loved Me*. His adversaries (like hench people in *Thunderball* and *For Your Eyes Only*) and allies (like Felix Leiter in *License to Kill*) are not as lucky.
4. See Chap. 4 for more details.
5. See Chap. 4 for more details.
6. The source novel opens with a detailed description of SMERSH and its plot against Bond. A large portion of "Part One: The Plan" is dedicated to relaying the backstory of Red Grant in order to position him as a threatening adversary to Bond. Fleming emphasizes the size and strength of Grant's body through the perspective of a female masseuse who is horrified by the strength and perfection of his body (1957b, p. 4).
7. The physical appearance of Daniel Craig in *Casino Royale* looks a lot of like Robert Shaw who plays Red Grant in *From Russia with Love*.
8. This encounter unfolds differently in the novel with Bond anticipating Grant's shot in his sleeping car and pretending to be dead in order to gain a tactical advantage (1957b, p. 254). The encounter in the novel is more violent than in the film and emphasizes Bond's physical and instinctual prowess over his abnormally strong and intelligent attacker.
9. In *Live and Let Die*, for example, Bond hijacks a plane from a flight school in order to evade hench people in pursuit. An elderly woman named Mrs. Banks is already seated in the aircraft awaiting her lesson and she brings humor to the scene by reacting to Bond's maneuvers. While Bond demonstrates an intuitive use of aviation technology via his "trial and error" approach, Mrs. Banks describes the mistakes he makes along the way such as over-revving the motors. Although Bond's approach turns out to be effective in the end, it is at the expense of the plane, which is severely damaged, and Mrs. Banks, who looks shaken and stirred by the experience.

And since the female student is too old to serve as a love interest and/or tipping point in the film, she becomes an object of ridicule who is discouraged (by Bond through his actions) to take up flying.

10. Bond's association with Aston Martin is so prominent that the company features a picture gallery outlining the history of the cars in the Bond franchise on its website. See Aston Martin (n.d.).

11. In the novel, Bond selects the Aston Martin DB3 over the Jaguar 3.4 because it "had the advantage of an up-to-date triptyque, an inconspicuous colour – battleship grey – and certain extras which might or might not come in handy" such as multicolored front and rear lights, a steel bumper, and a Homer device (1959, p. 72).

12. A similar impression is conveyed in *Diamonds Are Forever* as Bond conducts surveillance of Tiffany Case in Las Vegas. A portion of the ground floor in the hotel is designed for children and contains a variety of carnival games. Case receives a toy filled with diamonds after she wins a water balloon game. She tries to shake her tail by joining a group of children to watch an exhibit of a woman transforming into an ape. Much like *OHMSS*, the animal jumps out and scares a group of children who flee from the room, and Case is able to escape amidst the chaos.

13. In *The Living Daylights*, the carnival is shown to be a place that is dangerous for secret agents. Midway through the film, Bond meets with his MI6 ally Saunders in a restaurant at a carnival in Vienna. As Saunders leaves the building, he is killed by the hench person Necros who has programmed the glass sliding door to crush him. Bond is unable to apprehend the killer who escapes into the crowd.

14. Nick Nack lives up to his name when he blends in with the trident statues in Hi-Fat's garden, a place Bond refers to as "Grizzly Land." This scene emphasizes both the Otherness and evilness of Nick Nack.

15. In *Diamonds Are Forever*, a scene involving a funfair provides an unlikely sounding opportunity to show a freak show involving a black woman transforming into a simian. The scene has no narrative value and appears to associate race with freakery.

16. Bond similarly tries to save Elektra King from herself in *The World Is Not Enough* when she gambles against Valentin Zukovsky, and his efforts serve as an expression of his growing affection for her.

17. Even outside of the casino, Bond uses card games to connect with women in order to gain an advantage. This is notable in *Live and Let Die* when Bond "stacks" Solitaire's deck of tarot cards so that "The Lovers" card will be flipped. Believing that sex with Bond is her destiny, she gives in to his advances and loses her power of sight. Through his manipulation of the tarot cards, Bond has seduced Solitaire away from his target Kananga and renders him vulnerable for attack.

18. Plenty O'Toole does not appear in Fleming's novel but rather was developed by screenwriter Tom Mankiewicz to serve as a peripheral love interest for Bond (Ulfsdotter 2015, p. 25).

19. The physical danger of the game is suggested "in the opening credit sequence, which presents card suits as weapons striking down male silhouettes" (Funnell 2011a, p. 463).

20. This is suggested in *GoldenEye* through an encounter between Bond and Moneypenny late at night before he steps into a meeting with M. Bond inquires about her appearance, as Moneypenny is dressed in an evening gown, and she responds that she was "on a date…with a gentleman" at the theatre.

21. During his interrogation at the beginning of the film, Mr. White laughs at M and exclaims "You really don't know anything about us! The truth is you don't even know we exist."

22. She also refuses to put him up for the night and tells him he needs to leave.

CHAPTER 8

Heartland Geopolitics

As an MI6 agent, Bond travels the world on missions aimed at ensuring Britain's physical, geopolitical, and resource security. The political geographies of Bond's world are anchored in London and specifically in what used to be Universal Exports but is now more straightforwardly identified as the MI6 building in central London. When Bond first made his appearance on the silver screen, it was customary to deny the existence of the UK security services as well as to refuse to confirm or deny the senior leadership of MI6 and its domestic counterpart, MI5. The lingering shots of the MI6 building in *The World Is Not Enough* were a first for the Bond franchise; they signal a shift in the geographical and geopolitical terrain of the Bond films. For the first time, the franchise dispensed with the fiction of a 'Universal Exports' and the fleeting glimpses of London including Parliament and Trafalgar Square, which were more prevalent in the Roger Moore era. Only a decade earlier was MI6 first publicly acknowledged in UK political life via the Intelligence Service Act 1994, which outlined a statuary mandate for the agency (Gill and Phythian 2006, p. 98).

Since the 1990s, MI6 has had a more material rather than disguised presence, at a time when the conventional cartographies of the Cold War were becoming looser in their imaginative grip. Dench's M was far more inclined than her predecessor to warn of the 'shadows', complain about public and parliamentary oversight and scrutiny, and, famously, condemn Bond for being a Cold War misogynist and "dinosaur." She had a new and modern-looking office and worked in the MI6 building

© The Editor(s) (if applicable) and The Author(s) 2017   199
L. Funnell, K. Dodds, *Geographies, Genders and Geopolitics of
James Bond*, DOI 10.1057/978-1-137-57024-6_8

in Vauxhall/London, and, as *Casino Royale* demonstrated, she took her work home with her. British intelligence and its management appears to be a 24/7 activity in the Craig era, which blurs the distinction between the public and private lives of its senior operatives, in a way that was commonplace for spies such as Bond.

This was a decisive shift from earlier incarnations of Bond. Prior to the Dench era (1995–2012), which highlights a rather different periodization to the one that privileges the male actors who have played Bond, 007 collected his mission from M's wooden paneled office. There was the customary flirty interaction with Miss Moneypenny both before and after the meeting with M. Once briefed, Bond's world was decidedly outward facing. The dialectic of an inside and outside, here and there, and safe and unsafe was defined and punctuated by enemies located elsewhere. While these threats might project their power into UK domestic space (e.g. *The Living Daylights*), there was a persistent and almost rigid geography to threat and danger. Working with various allies (e.g. Americans, Chinese, Japanese, Russians) and operating in a range of geographical spaces and social contexts (e.g. Asian cities, casinos, outer space), Bond was presented as a loyal, mobile, and corporeal hero who uses his professional "touch" to neutralize threats (e.g. Cold War, nuclear conflict, oil shortage) before they affected London, Britain, the West, and even the world. Bond's unrivalled capacity to 'save' the world from an array of evil geniuses and their fiendish plans helped to make him an attractive and appealing British action hero (Winder 2011, p. 153).

Bond's role in protecting what British geographer Halford Mackinder refers to as the 'heartland' (1904, p. 421) was both abstract and embodied. In more abstract terms, his allies and foes alike identify him as a public servant (even specifically as a policeman) working for 'Queen and Country'. As Bond tells a lover in *The Spy Who Loved Me*, "England needs me." While some might quibble about whether Bond should have said the 'United Kingdom' rather than 'England', the dramatic escape via a Union Jack embossed parachute perhaps serves as a visual reminder that he was a British, rather than merely an English, spy. Bond's professional background as a Commander in the Royal Navy helps to reinforce his loyalty to former senior naval officers such as the male M and even to royalty. In a more embodied manner, Bond's relationships with M, Q, and Moneypenny act as his 'heartland'. Even though these interactions can be strained and even tetchy especially with both the male and female versions of M, Bond values their camaraderie and friendship highly, and clearly desires the approval of his boss. Although Bond's encounters with Moneypenny are framed as meaningless flirting, the two clearly care for each other and the introduction of younger women to the office and even in Q's laboratory in later films does not fundamentally alter their dynamic.

In the Brosnan and Craig eras, the heartland is defined further through distinct and clearly geographical and gendered terms. While Bond typically travels overseas on his missions, *The World Is Not Enough* and *Skyfall* present attacks on MI6 in London with Dench's M as the primary target. Up to this point, MI6, under male leadership, has never experienced a direct attack and even when the office has (temporarily) been moved to Hong Kong, India, and Egypt as well as to the back of a Hercules transporter plane flying somewhere over Gibraltar, they remain immune to direct assault; M's papers might be ruffled by air turbulence in *The Living Daylights* but that is the closest MI6 comes to any kind of calamity. By way of contrast, Dench's M requires saving from Bond both in London and in the field, and his ability to protect her is akin to his capacity to safeguard the nation state in a more embodied and direct manner than earlier films.

Under Dench's tenure as M, the previous geographies of safety and threat are overturned. London is no longer safe and suffers direct attacks. Allies, such as the United States, while significant in terms of logistical support and intelligence sharing, cannot help Bond and Britain. In the Daniel Craig era, Dench's M is increasingly depicted as both a lone and lonely figure with few allies to aid and abet her. American support, and even Chinese and Soviet/Russian assistance from earlier eras, is nowhere to be found. While Bond works with Felix Leiter in *Casino Royale* and *Quantum of Solace*, senior managers attached to the CIA and NSA are not involved in mission oversight as compared to the final Brosnan film *Die Another Day*. It is M who alone runs the operations and must take responsibility for their outcomes. And by *Spectre*, Bond and Britain are on their own, and Bond's personal pursuit of those responsible for M's death takes him to Mexico City, Rome, and North Africa in his quest to discover more. Back in London, the devastated edifice of the old MI6 building remains, still bearing the scars of a terrible explosion carried out by disgruntled operative Silva in *Skyfall*.

Across the Dench era, M seems to be carrying an immense burden that only gets heavier as her personal life is put under greater scrutiny than her previous male office holders. Her competency and decisions are questioned, as if to suggest that her 'fitness' for high office is something that needs to be monitored closely. At the same time, Dench's M shifts from being a public servant safeguarding the state to a figure embodying the state itself, a transformation that is made possible by changes in the gendered and generic contours from the Brosnan- to Craig-era films. This chapter explores how the heartland is (re-)imagined across the Dench era through a comparative analysis of the external versus internal attacks on MI6 featured in *The World Is Not Enough* and *Skyfall*, respectively. While the former requires Bond to travel away from London/Britain to neutralize the threat, the latter hits close to 'home' and requires Bond to combat the threat in his own backyard (both literally and figuratively speaking). As a result, *Skyfall* develops the concept of the heartland via gender (e.g. framing Dench's M as a maternal figure) and visuals (e.g. using the color palette of the Union Jack). *Spectre* picks up these elements through its depiction of Bond's home and the heartland ruins via the abandoned and decaying MI6 building that arguably stands in for the loss experienced by Bond/Britain through the death of Dench's M. Taken together, *Skyfall* and *Spectre* signal a significant reshaping of heartland geopolitics in the face of public visibility and scrutiny.

HEARTLAND UNDER ATTACK

Although released 13 years apart, *The World Is Not Enough* and *Skyfall* share the same basic premise. Both films feature an attack on MI6 in London in which a portion of the headquarters is destroyed by an explosion. Even at the height of the Cold War, MI6 (Universal Exports) was never subjected to a direct hit. As the leader of MI6, Dench's M is (one of) the target(s) and the villain is on a personal quest for vengeance that centers on manipulating and terrorizing her. This revenge plot is framed within familial terms and M's maternal qualities (be they real or imposed on her) prove to be her downfall. While Bond is responsible for safeguarding M, he injures his shoulder in the opening scene and should not have been cleared for duty. When he returns to the field, his injury proves to be a vulnerability that the villain exploits. In the end, it is Bond who rescues M and kills the villain thus restoring symbolic order to MI6. While he is clearly vindicated in *The World Is Not Enough*, his capacity to save the 'heartland' is frequently called into question in *Skyfall* as is M's judgment when she confirms that the injured Bond is 'fit for purpose'; Bond's inability to save M in the end casts a somber shadow over this redemption narrative.

While structured around similar narrative elements, the films contain notable differences that shape different readings of the British heartland. *The World Is Not Enough* is a decidedly female-focused film that centers on the betrayal of Elektra King by her father and her quest for revenge. The purpose of her attack on MI6 is to kill her father and M, and while the latter escapes unharmed she remains largely unaware that she is still in danger. If anything, M's conversation with Robert King in front of Bond in her office hints at an easy familiarity with the older man born out of being students together at the University of Oxford. She speaks of him with obvious fondness and perhaps might even have had an affair with him while they were students. The short conversation, however, is sufficient to introduce a scintilla of doubt about M's judgment in the aftermath of an explosion where King unwittingly acts as a suicide bomber.

The film presents a (surrogate/symbolic) mother-daughter relationship and M, for her part, frequently mentions her difficulty in ignoring her maternal instincts and acting impartially. After Robert King's death, M clearly feels responsible for his daughter's fate as she advised him on how to respond to the kidnapping years earlier. In the end, M is captured by Elektra King and requires rescue from Bond in Istanbul who removes an external threat to the energy security of Britain (embodied here by M). M's sentimentality and instinct as a mother are presented as generative of insecurity while Bond's expression of similar emotions is deemed to be necessary in saving M and Britain from disaster. In this iteration of 'heartland geopolitics', both M and Bond have to (re-)negotiate where the boundary between the inside and the outside lies, and to do so through their personal relationship with Elektra King. Bond is charged with protecting her while M assumes a guardianship role. Bond sleeps with King but is unable, tellingly, to prevent her from continuing her personal and professional relationship with Renard. Bond's loving touch fails him and he struggles to make sense of her relationship with M.

In contrast, *Skyfall* is a male-focused narrative that centers on the betrayal of Silva, a former MI6 agent, by M and his quest for vengeance. His attack on MI6 is not designed to kill M but to burden her with guilt for the deaths of her agents working in the building; she is not in MI6 during the attack but stands on a bridge and watches it occur. Her role as spectator is significant because it comes immediately after she speaks with her superior (Mallory) who urges her to retire from the service. M refuses and explains that she is determined to "get the job done". Unlike Bond whose determination is framed as praiseworthy, M is depicted as being stubborn rather than sentimental and her refusal to concede endangers the heartland. This is reinforced by M being defined through maternal qualities—as Silva frequently refers to her as "mommy"—and the competition between Silva and Bond is framed as brotherly/sibling conflict for the affections of their mother. In the end, Bond whisks M away to his childhood home, and in a final stand kills Silva, who has re-established himself as an internal threat to the security of Britain (embodied again by M).

In addition to being female-focused, *The World Is Not Enough* features a fairly broad female cast—a female assassin, doctor, scientist, and villain—in addition to M. Through his encounters with these women, Bond is shown to be fallible and unable to make sense of King's motives and movements, and has to redeem himself by the end of the narrative by causing King's death and saving another woman, the scientist Christmas Jones. While the female assassin is the source of Bond's injury, the female doctor prematurely clears Bond for fieldwork after he seduces her. Moneypenny is not fooled by the positive assessment, however, and makes it clear that she knows why Bond has been approved. Not only does King use this injury against him, but she attains plutonium for her bomb after Jones blows Bond's cover and facilitates the escape of Renard. Moreover, Bond's inability to seduce King results in the kidnapping of M. As a result, Bond has to overcome these female obstacles to re-establish his libidinal masculinity.

In *Skyfall*, by comparison, women (other than M) play relatively limited roles. After Moneypenny shoots Bond in the opening action sequence, she is demoted and relegated to the periphery of the narrative as a helpmate and someone who is brought back to the office, offering some limited field support to Bond in China. The femme fatale Severine also spends limited time on screen and is killed by Silva; she is presented as a disposable object of struggle between two (white) men.[1] This draws attention to the explicitly male focus of the narrative: the central conflict is fraternal, the NATO agents Silva exposes are male, the film sets up Mallory to take over as M, and Bond develops a working relationship with the new Q. Women are largely swept to the side, leaving only M at the heart of the narrative. And through her explicit connection to the Queen in the film—an association made by Silva in his emails in which he presents her portrait with a crown on her head paired with the phrase "God Save The Queen" as well as by his comments that Bond follows the orders of an "old woman" that helps to combine the figures—she stands in for the heartland over which the two men fight. Bond's redemption is thus framed in relation to his ability to protect her—M and Britain.

Finally, *The World Is Not Enough* contains character hybridity through the figure of King. She is depicted as a Bond Girl–Villain or at the very least a villain who masquerades as a Bond Girl. Her initial characterization shares much in common with Tracy di Vicenzo (who saved Bond's life in Switzerland) from *On Her Majesty's Secret Service* (*OHMSS*) who eventually becomes Bond's wife: she is depicted as troubled, develops an intense connection with Bond, and requires him to save her from herself (at the casino) and others (on the slopes). In return, Bond really loved di Vicenzo and, unlike other women, he did so unconditionally. In contrast, King uses her sexuality to attract Bond and render him vulnerable for attack, and wholeheartedly believes that Bond will not kill a woman he loves, an assumption that leads to her death. The film presents the impression that while Bond may be sexually attracted to and involved with villainous women, he will always remain loyal to his first/true love, Britain.

Skyfall also features character hybridity as M is not only presented as Bond's boss and mother (see later in the chapter) but is also framed as his primary love interest, which is the defining feature of the Bond Girl character type.[2] Christopher Holliday reads this hybridity through the typology of the Bond Girl (2015, p. 273) and particularly the "English Partner" phase prevalent in the Connery and Lazenby eras (1962–69) in which Bond was paired with English or Anglicized women ranging from the marginal figures of Sylvia Trench in *Dr. No* and the Masterson sisters in *Goldfinger* to Bond Girls like Tracy di Vicenzo in *OHMSS* (who is played by an English actress) and Domino Derval in *Thunderball* (who is Anglicized via voice dubbing; Funnell 2008, pp. 64–66). He argues that "[t]he partnering of Craig with Dench in *Skyfall* evokes something of the British 'male-female team' that inaugurated the Bond franchise, serving to re-establish an English national and cultural identity between Bond and his Bond Girl" (2015, p. 269). Moreover, he links the death of di Vicenzo (notably with the Anglicized name 'Tracy') in *OHMSS*, which brings about the downfall of the "English Partner" Bond Girl, with that of M in *Skyfall*, who similarly dies in Bond's arms as he weeps. Holliday argues that the films send the message that the women who get to close to Bond are destined to die since they divert his attention away from Queen and Country (ibid. pp. 269–72). However, another reading can be made. If M stands in for both the Queen and heartland, than her tragic death does not push away Bond but rather pulls him in and deepens his commitment to his first/true love, Britain.

Standing on the roof of the attacked MI6 building and overlooking the London cityscape on a clear day, Bond pledges himself more fully to Britain's security, after he receives from Moneypenny the porcelain bulldog M has bequeathed to him. His gaze lingers over the physical infrastructure of the heartland, while pondering his relationship to M and what she meant to him. Significantly, he is not overlooking the shattered remains of the MI6 building but rather the untouched rooftops of the surrounding structures. His physical stance, redolent of Casper Friedrich's oil painting Wanderer above the Sea of Fog (1818), invites speculation about what Bond's future might hold, and at once emphasizes Bond's mastery over the cityscape while reminding viewers that, however extraordinary his abilities and talents might be, he depends on others to save the heartland.

Rallying Around the Flag

The Union Jack is the national flag and an iconic symbol of the United Kingdom, which features most memorably in Bond's dramatic parachute escape in *The Spy Who Loved Me*. It is a composite of the earlier flags of England (St. George's Cross), Ireland (St. Patrick's Cross), and Scotland (St. Andrew's Cross), and signifies their amalgamation. Although Bond is presented as a distinctly British hero, he can be viewed as a figure of the United Kingdom (or perhaps even the British and Irish Isles) as the actors playing the character range from English (Moore, Dalton, Craig) to Scottish (Connery) to Irish (Brosnan) with an Australian (Lazenby) in an outlier film. And yet in *Skyfall*, both the Union Jack and its colors are woven into the visual landscape and associated with M. This works to further gender the geopolitical heartland and position M as the literal "heart" of MI6.

The flag, however, has another ideological role in *Skyfall*. Its presence signifies, by the end of the film, the restoration of 'heartland geopolitics'. While M had to witness the Union Jack over the coffins of dead agents (see later in the chapter), Bond's proximity to the national flag is quite different. The re-inscription of an inside and outside to the geopolitical and gendered order surrounding Bond is made manifest by London being safe and by M being replaced by a new male boss. The traitorous Silva has been killed and rooted out of London and Bond stands ready to protect the heartland from both foreign and domestic threats. But unlike

Captain America, where the red, white, and blue of the US flag is directly embossed on his outfit, the colors of the Union Jack work more discreetly to consolidate the British 'heartland'.

Blue

While Bond films like *OHMSS* and *License to Kill* depict Bond's struggle with love versus duty, *Skyfall* presents M grappling with it as she negotiates her personal feelings for Bond, the demands of her own family, and her job as the head of MI6. This conflict is depicted through the use of filters with the color blue standing in for M's professional role and her loyalty to MI6. This is established from the outset of the film to depict M running the field operation in Istanbul from her office in London. She spends most of her time behind her desk, first seated and then standing as she begins to pace. Three large windows that overlook the London cityscape frame her desk. Wearing a black dress with a grey sweater jacket, she remains focused on the task at hand, which is to recover a stolen file listing the identity of every NATO agent working around the world. Given the stakes, she directs Bond and Moneypenny verbally through the mission, telling Bond to leave a fellow agent to bleed to death and instructing Moneypenny to "take the bloody shot" at Patrice even though it will not be "clean." She demonstrates her willingness to protect MI6 and the UK at any cost and that includes sacrificing the lives her agents including Bond.

Through the use of filters, the film provides a visual contrast between the mission focus of M (cast in blue) and the emotional responses of her field agents in Istanbul (cast in a warmer yellow hue). Although M appears cold and stoic as the mission spirals out of control, she carries the weight of her decisions and shoulders the responsibility for the loss of the list as well as her field agents. Through pathetic fallacy, her emotions are relayed externally as she turns to stare out the window at the rain falling on the city below; the sound of rain turns to rushing water as the film cuts to a gravely injured Bond floating downstream and to the bottom of the river bed leading into the opening credit sequence.

The following scene at MI6 presents M in a different light, literally. It opens with a shot of the MI6 building at night, with warm yellow lights illuminating the exterior. The film cuts to a shot of M seated at her desk writing Bond's obituary as the rain pours down on the city visible through the wet windows behind her.[3] A single lamp on her desk casts a warm yellow light on her face, which dimly illuminates her office. The film cuts to a shot of her computer screen, which features an open Word document on the left that covers a portion of Bond's portrait; the right side of his face stares back at M as she struggles to compose the text. The film then cuts to a close-up shot of the porcelain bulldog on her desk, a figurine that comes to stand in for Bond (and his dogged determination) in the film. This visual stylization of M privately working her in office is brief and as she is transported to and from her meeting with Mallory the next day, she is depicted again through a blue filter. It is here that she receives her first message from Silva (aligning her with the Queen) before watching a bomb go off in her office as she stands helplessly on a bridge and forced to ask a policeman who has impeded her progress "Don't you know who I am?" It is through M that MI6, London, and Britain are being attacked, and it is this event caught on a television screen that cajoles a stupor-like Bond to return to Britain.

After viewing the caskets of the MI6 agents who perished in the attack, M returns home on another rainy night. The house is empty as her husband is no longer alive and her children have long since left home. In spite of the bad weather, both the exterior and interior lights of her home emit a warm yellow glow. As she pours herself a drink, the silhouette of Bond can be seen over her shoulder as he sits in front of her window. M is shocked at/by his appearance, and the pair engages in a conversation about the failed mission. While Bond appears overtly emotional, as his eyes water when he talks about her betrayal, M is more composed and seems rather relieved that Bond has returned when she/MI6 needs him the most. The mother-son relationship established here (after her prodigal son returns) extends into the next scene in which Bond is depicted through the same visual conventions as M. He can be seen looking out a car window on a rainy day as he travels to the underground MI6 station. Much like scenes with M where she puts on her professional face, Bond is also shot using a blue filter as he attempts to earn his way back into MI6. Through the use of filters, the film links the physical struggles of Bond with the professional struggles of M, and only together with Bond protecting M can they overcome the attacks of Silva.

The film also uses the color blue in costuming to depict the connection/union of agents working in MI6. For instance, Bond wears a grey suit in the opening scene and a brown leather jacket paired with beige pants when he visits M at her house; when Bond is operating on his own and outside of the context (or mission directives) of MI6, he wears neutral color clothes. His costuming changes upon his return to MI6; he wears a blue sweat suit embossed with the MI6 logo while completing the tests, a dark blue suit when he meets Silva, and a blue shirt and tie when first meets with the new M at the end of the film. Dench undergoes a similar process in which she wears black and grey costumes until she meets with the parliament near the end of the film.[4] Wearing a blue dress, she speaks about the importance of MI6 and the threats that face their country. Other figures like Mallory, Moneypenny, and Bill Tanner wear blue costumes while in MI6 and this becomes a uniform of sorts for the agency. Much like the use of blue filters, blue costuming helps to identify the figures in MI6 who are competent and loyal to the agency and committed to protecting Queen and Country, and in *Skyfall* that means protecting M who serves as a stand-in for the female monarch. And in the end, as Bond wears a blue shirt and tie while overlooking the city, the scene is shot using a blue filter and this saturated image conveys the impression that Bond is fully committed to MI6 and will fight in M's honor. This blue costuming is carried forward into *Spectre* to introduce and distinguish loyal MI6 personnel (Bond, M, Moneypenny, Tanner, Q) from imposters like C.

Red

In *Skyfall*, the color red is used strategically to emphasize particular elements that stand out against the blue iconography. First and foremost, it symbolizes blood. This is established in the opening credit sequence that begins with Bond, who has just been shot, sinking down into the water. A stream of blood flows from a shooting target designed in the image of Bond and provides a visual contrast with the blue water. Blood also surrounds a building (presumably Skyfall Lodge) and later converges to form a skull, which is the calling card for Silva. At the end of the sequence, the camera zooms into the bullet wound of Bond and enters his body; after passing veins it moves to the 'heart' of Bond, which turns out to be Skyfall Lodge and associated with M (see later in the chapter), upon which it is raining blood. Not only does the film foreshadow the events that will unfold in the narrative, it also stresses the sacrifices that will have to be made at Skyfall Lodge. And while the rain throughout the narrative symbolizes M's sorrow, the blood raining on the Skyfall Lodge in the opening credits is that of M who dies in order for Bond (and MI6) to be reborn.[5]

Red also symbolizes the sacrifice and patriotism of the MI6 agents who are killed in the explosion. When M visits the holding room, the scene opens with a high-angle close-up shot of a Union Jack flag laid on top of a casket. As the camera tilts upwards while tracking down, additional coffins come into view and the vertical portion of St. George's Cross forms a red line that leads up to M who is standing behind the last casket just left of center (Fig. 8.1).

From this shot, M appears quite small when compared to the coffins that loom large in the forefront, an image that emphasizes the magnitude of guilt she carries for their deaths. When Tanner enters the room to call on M, the film presents an over-the-shoulder shot of the back of M who is staring down at the row of coffins and the red line looks like a waterfall of blood leading to her as she is the heart of MI6. The film then cuts to a medium close-up of M who vows to find their killer. As both their boss and matriarch, M claims responsibility for their deaths and the film presents the impression that violence stops with her (death).

The Union Jack is also employed by Silva to criticize M for her actions. His email messages typically begin with a shot of M's face positioned in the center of the Union Jack. From there, graphics and text appear in red, white, and black before the message "think on your sins" scrolls across the screen. In one particular instance, a slot machine with red buttons appears and when M presses one of them Silva releases the first five names of the undercover NATO agents on YouTube. In addition, as discussed

Fig. 8.1 *Skyfall* (Eon Productions et al. 2012)

in Chap. 5, the color red is used to display Silva's computer virus that attacks the London underground leading to the heart of the city where M is giving testimony during a hearing. Just as M is positioned at the center of the flag, she also serves as his primary target and thus an attack on her constitutes an attack on the nation.

M herself provides a counter image of the Union Jack in the form of porcelain bulldog that sits on her desk. While the dog faces away from her, the Union Jack painted on its back remains in clear view and serves as a constant reminder that the security of the nation is her utmost priority. The image of the bulldog adorned with a Union Jack has long been associated with Winston Churchill, Britain's most celebrated Prime Minister who is known for his defense of the nation particularly against foreign aggressors. It is this legacy of defense that she passes onto Bond after she dies and bequeaths the statue to him. In response to Moneypenny's comment, "maybe it was her way of telling you to take a desk job" Bond states "just the opposite." Just like M stands in for the nation, Bond serves as the British bulldog protecting it and this vintage figurine, which miraculously survives the bombing of her office (just as Bond survives a near fatal shot in Istanbul), continues to endure. Although Bond might be likened to an old dog learning a new trick, his "old school" methods are the ones that bring about success and help to ensure the security of the nation state.

Homecoming

Home as both a space and a concept plays a key role in gendering the geopolitical heartland. While it designates a particular dwelling where a person lives (such as a house or an apartment), it also conjures up notions of family as it constitutes the place where kin live together. The Craig-era films place greater attention on the home(s) of M and frequently depict her in this domestic space. Aside from *OHMSS*, male versions of M are not depicted at home in the Connery, Moore, Dalton, and Brosnan eras. But in *Casino Royale*, Bond breaks into the female M's flat in order to use her computer and leaves a trail of digital breadcrumbs so that she can follow his actions in the Bahamas and the United States. This recalls the Brothers Grimm fairytale "Hansel and Gretel" in which the young protagonists drop bread/breadcrumbs in order to create a pathway home. Bond's trespassing comes after he botches the mission in Madagascar and blows up an embassy, and his return "home" to M is framed as one of a prodigal son seeking forgiveness and redemption. This in turn codes M (even more) as a maternal figure—as she appears more motherly in the Craig-era films—and her personal dwelling as the true home of Bond.

In *Skyfall*, Bond's homecoming is again framed in relation to M's domestic sphere. He returns from the dead—after being shot by Moneypenny and disappearing in Turkey—after the attack on M's office and breaks into her home where he waits in the dark for her to return. Their initial conversation is certainly framed in mother-son terms with M scolding Bond for not calling and Bond running away from 'home' in response to her unfair treatment of him. In true motherly fashion, she takes the opportunity to teach Bond a lesson when she informs him that she sold his flat—i.e. he has no other 'home'—and tells him he cannot stay with her; this renders Bond homeless (again) and increases his connection to her since "orphans make the best recruits." While her words are stern, they can be interpreted as a form of tough love designed to bring Bond back into the fold. Moreover, her actions are even more telling when she clears Bond for service after he fails every proficiency test. When she tells Bond that "we need you," she really means "I need you" and in the end only Bond, the "true son" of Britain, can protect his (Queen) mother from internal/fraternal threats.

Just as M's home provides a safe haven for Bond when he is in trouble, Bond takes M to his childhood home, Skyfall Lodge, when she is being pursued by Silva. Ironically, perhaps, he is able to take her in his prized Aston Martin DB5 because she clearly did not know about his lock-up garage in London where he stored the car. The pair drive 'under the radar', while leaving digital breadcrumbs for the symbolic brother/son to track them. Much like *Casino Royale*, the use of breadcrumbs creates a pathway 'home' and helps to emphasize the familial dynamics of the conflict. Moreover, the film emphasizes their isolation by including shots of them standing in front of the Aston Martin (first used in *Goldfinger*) on an empty roadway looking out onto a mist-covered rocky terrain in Scotland. This creates the impression that Bond is not only taking M back in time but also into a remote and disconnected environment where he can exert control because it is beyond the electronic grasp of Silva and his hench people.

When they arrive at Skyfall Lodge, the groundskeeper Kincaid takes M on a tour and before showing her a secret passage he comments "like all great ladies she still has her secret ways." This works to explicitly feminize the house, which takes on maternal connotations when Kincaid shows M the spot where Bond hid when his parents were killed and comments that

Bond was not the same when he came out. This womb-like metaphor works to frame the home (as well as the redemption narrative) in maternal terms and M's familial connection to the place is emphasized by the discovery of the grave of Bond's mother and the revelation of her name, Olivia Mansfield, which collapses both women under the signifier "M."

As a result, the attack on Skyfall Lodge and its fiery destruction can be interpreted as an attack on M and the nation she represents. While Bond manages to kill Silva and removes the internal/fraternal threat, M is mortally wounded by a shot to the stomach/womb, the locus of her identity in the film. As she lay dying in Bond's arms, she looks up at him and states "I did get one thing right." This comment is both sentimental and maternal, and her death (like the destruction of Skyfall) is deemed a sacrifice that is required in order to (re)build the nation state. Her legacy, however, will prevail as symbolized through the passing on of the British bulldog to her "true son," Bond. And a dying M has trusted Bond to continue to defend the heartland.

In *Spectre*, this responsibility weighs heavily on Bond as he sits in his austere-looking apartment with only the figurine of the bulldog on ornamental display; it sits on the left side of the coffee table watching/facing him as he reads material on the couch. The spatial arrangement of the room—with Bond seated along the back wall, the dog on the coffee table in front of him, and the TV that once held M's image along the fourth wall—reproduces the office setup of Dench's M in Bond's flat. On the one hand, this reinforces the idea that Bond is still a secret agent acting on behalf of M to safeguard 'Queen and Country.' On the other hand, it stresses the impression that MI6, particularly under the leadership of Dench's M, has always been home for Bond. He is now working in a very different environment with Mallory as the new M and the abandoned MI6 building lying in ruin (see later in the chapter). Bond's professional and personal heartland has changed and is changing. Bond and Mallory have to contend with a UK security actor, C, who is head of a new Joint Intelligence Service, following the merger of MI5 and MI6. C is not an advocate of the 00 program and is eager for Britain to join a new global intelligence sharing and surveillance grouping called Nine Eyes. If Bond remains in employment, it is conceivable that under C's leadership he might be co-opted into the Nine Eyes initiative or worse be dispensed with as an example to others who might be reluctant to embrace a new intelligence era. As such, Bond re-imagines the MI6 of old through the spatial arrangement of his flat to affirm his unending commitment to Queen and Country.

Spectre uses materiality to contrast the dangers of Nine Eyes with the traditionalism of MI6. For example, the Joint Intelligence Service is located in a modern and glass-clad building filled with bright and open planned offices devoid of wooden paneling and traditional oil paintings. While the glass symbolizes the inherent transparency of Nine Eyes and the fact that no one, including Bond, can hide from their view, it is also a substance that can be cracked, chipped, and broken if enough pressure is applied. In the end, it is revealed that C is an agent of SPECTRE who is using Nine Eyes—a name that rhymes with "nine lives" and hints towards Blofeld's involvement given his love for white cats—to strengthen the terrorist organization. Importantly, it is Mallory who takes out C quite literally when he shoves him out of his office window—an act of defenestration that has been associated with the killing of royalty and senior civil servants over the centuries. Unlike Dench's M, Mallory does not require the protection or rescue from Bond and survives the encounter thus proving that he is capable of protecting the British intelligence service from an internal threat like C. And crucially the film does not suggest that Mallory has any reason to fear any legal consequences from the death of C as he (like Bond) seemingly has a "license to kill." While Dench's M is associated with the heartland, Mallory is presented as another one of her protectors much like Bond given their closeness in age that effectively removes any parental overtones.

Heartland Ruins

As discussed in Chap. 7, action sequences in the early Craig-era films are often set in construction zones. These partially constructed/deconstructed spaces are located outside the UK—in Madagascar and Italy in *Casino Royale*, for instance—and Bond's struggle to perform within them can be read as metaphors for his development as a secret agent in the orphan origin trilogy. By comparison, in the later Craig-era films like *Skyfall* and *Spectre*, Bond moves through what we term 'heartland ruins'—a building or place that symbolizes the (national) identity and strength of Britain and/or its extraterritorial reach that has been fully or partially destroyed and are presumed to be unoccupied/abandoned. These sites and spaces were initially compromised by internal threats—weakening them from the inside-out—and subsequently claimed, mobilized, and repurposed by the villain in order to inflict further damage against the nation state. They represent an ongoing internal threat to the heartland and stand in as monuments to this struggle.

Bond first encounters heartland ruins midway through *Skyfall* when he travels to a small island off the coast of Macau now occupied by Silva. While Macau is not a current or former British protectorate (as it was once a Portuguese colony), it now a Special Administrative Region of China that lies in close proximity to Hong Kong. This is significant given the backstory of Silva who was captured by China for spying and abandoned by MI6 during the 1997 handover. Thus the island has geopolitical and narrative significance given its proximity to both Hong Kong (a former British colony) and China.

Bond first spies the island from the stern of a yacht, an image that recalls the depiction of the Hong Kong cityscape in various Bond films like *Man with the Golden Gun* and *Die Another Day* (see Chap. 5). While Hong Kong (Island) is frequently depicted at night to emphasize the electric skyline and thus its modernization, the island in Macau is presented during the day and even from a distance the architecture appears to be decaying. When Bond first enters the city, a high-angle long shot depicts the crumbling rooftops and walls of the various high-rise buildings that line the street. This is followed by a street-level view of Bond walking along a road covered in small- and medium-sized rocks as decaying buildings surround him on all sides. It is Severine who provides context for Bond (and the audience) when she explains that the city was abandoned after Silva manipulated the electronic infrastructure to signal a chemical leak. She states, "He wanted the island so he took it," and his claim of the island certainly has historical and colonial implications. Bond is then taken to a large and airy room filled with computer stations and hard drives; Silva has repurposed this space in order to attack the digital infrastructure of MI6. From these ruins, he can plot and plan his revenge.

It is here that Silva first speaks to Bond and draws parallels between them. He explains that they both have been betrayed by M and tries to recruit Bond to participate in his plan to attack the heartland. Silva further criticizes Bond for this loyalty when he states "England. The Empire. MI6. You're living in a ruin as well. You just don't know it yet. At least here there are no old ladies giving orders, and no little gadgets from those fools in Q Branch. If you wanted, you could pick your own secret missions, as I do." Silva not only comments on his bombing of MI6, but also foreshadows the depiction of the building in the following film *Spectre* where it is abandoned. Interestingly, Bond can be seen at the end of *Skyfall* on top of

MI6 and later meeting with Mallory in his new office styled like those of the male Ms of the past. The film ends with the impression that things will return to normal—just like *Die Another Day*, which does not reference the attack on MI6 in the previous film *The World Is Not Enough*—thus concluding the orphan origin trilogy.

Interestingly, *Spectre* does not change directions but rather doubles down on the heartland imagery featured in *Skyfall* and presents the ongoing internal threat to (the existence of) MI6 as symbolized by the decaying and abandoned headquarters. Bond first sees the decrepit MI6 building as he travels by boat along the River Thames. It is Tanner, Bond's colleague, who provides context for the heartland ruins when he explains that MI6 has been relocated and that this "poor old girl" of a building has been "rigged for demolition in a week." This personification and especially feminization of the building carries forward the gendering of the heartland featured in *Skyfall*. Much like the attack on Dench's (physical) office weakened the structure of the MI6 building, her death has left the (figurative) office and 00 program vulnerable to attack from internal forces. This is emphasized through the introduction of the new Internal Security Building located across the river in full view of the heartland ruins. Not only is the building sleek and modern, but it also features a large glass spiral staircase in the center, which is arguably phallic in nature, thus framing the contrast between MI6 and the Joint Intelligence Service in both material and gendered terms. While MI6 is loyal to Queen and Country (embodied by the late Dench's M), the Joint Intelligence Service and the Nine Eyes program they are promoting is a SPECTRE initiative (represented by both Blofeld and his protégé C). Moreover, while Dench's M warns of threats from the shadows in *Skyfall*, Bond and Mallory must confront an enemy who is hiding in plain sight (and on a grand scale) in *Spectre* through the overemphasis of transparency (via surveillance) and building construction (via glass). Through the gendering and materiality of these competing intelligence institutions of the past (MI6) and future (Nine Eyes program), *Spectre* frames Bond as an 'old school' spy who has to operate underground (like in Q's office), in the shadows (like at Blofeld's meeting), and on the margins (like in Tangiers) to remove a new and internal threat to the establishment with limited resources and justify the need for the 00 program.

Heartland ruins serve as the site for Bond's confrontation of Blofeld in the climax of the film. Bond enters the derelict MI6 building and follows the red arrows left for him by Blofeld. Along the way, Bond passes a list of fallen MI6 agents on which his name has been painted; this recalls the scene of M mourning the death of those who died during the explosion in *Skyfall* (see earlier in the chapter) (Fig. 8.2).

As Bond makes his way through the lower levels of MI6, it is clear that the building has been prepared for demolition as red wires hang from the walls and ceilings, and link to the explosives. Much like the imagery used in *Skyfall* in which the red underground map of London can be read as a metaphor for the body, the red wiring in *Spectre* can also be read as a metaphor that leads Bond to the heart of MI6. When Blofeld challenges Bond to find the kidnapped Swann before the building is destroyed, Bond runs directly to office of Dench's M, which has long served as the heart of MI6. It is here that Bond finds Swann in a hidden compartment and disconnects her from the many red wires holding her in place. This moment can be read in a number of ways. First, it represents a shift in Bond's affection from maternal to romantic love; it is Swann who has replaced Dench's M in Bond's heart. Second, it presents Bond being able to save his love from danger while thwarting a threat from a fraternal foe; unlike Dench's M in *Skyfall*, Swann does not die in Bond's arms but rather is (literally) carried to safety as his home, MI6, is destroyed. Third, it emphasizes the importance of love over duty as Bond chooses to leave with Swann rather than work with Mallory.

Fig. 8.2 *Spectre* (Eon Productions et al. 2015)

The film ends with the destruction of the old MI6 building as triggered by Blofeld. Importantly, the destruction is witnessed by the core/loyal MI6 personnel (Mallory, Moneypenny, Q, and Tanner) who have just defeated C and stopped the Nine Eyes program from initiating; while Bond chases after the external threat, the core personnel have removed the mole and internal threat. Through the demolition of heartland ruins, the film recalibrates the gender and geopolitical landscape of the franchise by removing maternal femininity and the last vestiges of Dench's M, leaving the franchise open to questions about the future. When Bond drives off with Swann (who has professed her love for him), is he (the character and/or the actor) stepping away from the service or does this signal a return to traditional male-centric Bond narratives and a reversionist turn in the franchise (as opposed to the revisionist nature of the orphan origin trilogy) in which romantic relationships are fleeting when compared to Bond's long-term fidelity to a male M? Moreover, with the removal of both internal and fraternal threats to national security, will the heartland be reimagined in subsequent films or will Bond return to confronting villains who threaten Britain's geopolitical and resource security from afar? Although *Spectre* asks the question 'do we need the 00 program' and answers with a definitive 'yes', the future (direction) of the franchise remains unclear. Bond should be back but what sort of future will he and his colleagues confront?

NOTES

1. For a detailed discussion, see Funnell (2015b).
2. For a detailed discussion, see Funnell (2008).
3. Much like Elektra King is defined by wetness in *The World Is Not Enough* (see Chap. 6), M is associated with rain and it comes to represent her sadness over the deaths of her agents.
4. Prior to this, M wears a blue sweater when the names of the first group of NATO spies are released by Silva. By the time she reaches Parliament a few scenes later, she is wearing a blue dress with a blue blazer and the strength of her commitment to MI6 is relayed through her costuming.
5. The opening credit sequence also features red dragons, which foreshadow Bond's trip to China and particularly his time in Macau. Red is considered to be a lucky color in China and is used frequently in Chinese clothing, interior design, and festivals. Moneypenny is wearing a red dress when she gives Bond his close shave and the color suggests that Bond himself might be getting "lucky." Severine wears a dark red dress after she has sex with Bond on the boat and is killed by Silva for her betrayal. It is clear the Bond's luck does not translate in *Skyfall* to other female characters.

AFTERWORD

This book offers up what we believe is a detailed, multifaceted, and interdisciplinary analysis of how James Bond as British super spy is co-constituted through the intersection of geographies, genders, and geopolitics. Our analysis ranges from an examination of these intersectional relationships and manifestations to an exploration of the material and elemental embodied experiences of James Bond. Although his superiors and co-workers might consider his everyday engagements, practices, performances, and relationships quite exceptional, Bond's gambling, card-playing, and dining habits help to hone his social capital while his frequent missions ensure that he is constantly confronted by a wide array of environments, landscapes, and sites. Indeed, the prequels to the main Bond mission (in the pre-credit sequence) remind us that Bond is never far from a parachute, a set of skis, an aqualung, or a high performance car. He does not spend a great deal of time in his various flats throughout the series and apart from films such as *Dr. No*, *Live and Let Die*, and *Spectre* he is rarely shown to be entertaining visitors. He appears most 'at home' in the field on missions and never complains about travelling overseas.

As we argue in this book, Bond's capacity to cope, let alone prevail on his missions, depends on his personal relationships with close allies including the American agent Felix Leiter, negotiating dangerous sites and spaces ranging from carnivals to the theatre to various nation states like Russia, crossing borders around the world, liaising with superiors, appreciating and understanding the challenges posed by environments and landscapes,

© The Editor(s) (if applicable) and The Author(s) 2017   219
L. Funnell, K. Dodds, *Geographies, Genders and Geopolitics of
James Bond*, DOI 10.1057/978-1-137-57024-6

and using everything at his disposal including his mobility and touch to overcome villains and resist almost certain death. Luckily for Bond, he has a head for heights and depths, and is not claustrophobic. He is not squeamish and is capable of using violence against women and children if necessary (even through Roger Moore was said to have regretted pushing a child into a river during the making of *The Man with Golden Gun*). He does not appear to suffer from illness, and his body, mind, and heart have extraordinary healing capacities.

Although Bond is an action hero with extraordinary abilities, we wanted to show that he is also an embodied figure who negotiates everyday relationships, happenings, and places in a way that contributes to the geopolitical and gendered order of the franchise. We explore the more-than-textual moments when Bond's body has to twist, contort, stretch, recoil, and endure pain, stress, and vicarious extremes as he negotiates the man-made structures of the construction site in *Casino Royale* and later the torture in the same film, where the audiences witnesses his exposed and vulnerable body. He is an action hero par excellence but his body, touch, and relationships with others can let him down occasionally.

For much of the book, we have performed a geopolitical analysis that explores the relationship between states, people, and forces such as the Soviet Union, General Gogol, and nuclear submarines, respectively, and charted how geopolitical landscapes have both embraced and shifted the spatial and political coordinates of the Cold War and later the War on Terror. The textual and intertextual references, along with objects and practices, have been used by the Bond franchise to hint at both continuity and change. It is the women closest to Bond who are most torn about broader geopolitical changes. Judi Dench's M can profess to "miss the Cold War" while condemning Bond for being a Cold War "dinosaur." And when Eve Moneypenny gets the chance to be a field agent in *Skyfall*, it is she who retreats back to a more Cold War work order where women managed the offices and the men served as field agents, at least in the British context. British women working in the 'field' were either attached to local embassies or shown to be less effectual when in the field. The same is true with American women who, while serving as Bond's allies, were more likely to be manipulated (e.g. Rosie Carver in *Live and Let Die*) and captured (e.g. Tiffany Case in *Diamonds Are Forever*) by the villain and/or require rescue from Bond (e.g. Octopussy in *Octopussy*) than their male counterparts like Felix Leiter and Jack Wade. Gender strongly impacts the nature of Bond's relationship with his American helpmates.

Bond as an action hero has often been interpreted as offering a celebration of Britain's role in the world and the UK-US 'special relationship' and/or a compensatory figure designed to make Britain's post-imperial decline less manifest. Such readings of Bond not only underestimate the global consumption of the Bond franchise but also the manner in which the films are capable of producing more ambivalent readings, where Bond's social and geopolitical superiority is challenged, constrained, undermined, and even ignored. In both *Skyfall* and *Spectre*, we have seen how screenplay development has changed to facilitate the return of Q and the role that a very different man can play in safeguarding Britain, and by extension Western interests. Q, physically smaller and sexually unchallenging to Bond, is nonetheless positioned as someone who has a skill set that eludes the traditional field agent (007). In order to preserve Bond's hegemonic masculinity, the films had to re-position Bond amongst the ruins of both his childhood home (Skyfall) and his professional home (MI6) as if to suggest that Bond's experiences and skills continue to be needed in a world where infrastructure and people can be destroyed by a touch of a computer keyboard or screen.

Genders, geographies, and geopolitics remain crucial to the activities and ambience of Bond in a franchise with no end in sight, operating in a contemporary climate where governments, around the world, warn of ever greater dangers and vulnerabilities from cyber-terrorism to irregular migration. As the latest films suggest, threat and danger can originate from anywhere and as such we continue to need field agents who are able to appropriate and inhabit a world that refuses to stand still. The world may not be enough but Bond cannot get enough of that world.

BIBLIOGRAPHY

Abbas, A. (2000). Cosmopolitan descriptions: Shanghai and Hong Kong. *Public Culture, 12*(3), 769–786.

Alexander, B. K. (2013). Br(other) in the classroom: Testimony, reflection, and cultural negotiation. In T. K. Nakayama & R. T. Halualani (Eds.), *The handbook of critical intercultural communication*. Malden: Blackwell Publishing Ltd.

Amis, K. (1965). *The James Bond dossier*. New York: New American Library.

Appy, C. G. (2015). *American reckoning: The Vietnam War and our national identity*. New York: Penguin.

Aston Martin (n.d.). 007 & Aston Martin. *AstonMartin.Com* [Online]. Available from: http://www.astonmartin.com/en/heritage/james-bond. Accessed 1 July 2015.

Azar, K. T. (2011). *U.S. foreign policy & its's link to terrorism in the Middle East*. Bloomington: AuthorHouse.

Bahun, S., & Haynes, J. (2014). *Cinema, state socialism and society in the Soviet Union and Eastern Europe*. London: Routledge.

Bakhtin, M. (1998). Carnival and the carnivalesque. In J. Storey (Ed.), *Cultural theory and popular culture: A reader*. Harlow: Pearson Education Limited.

Balio, T. (1978). *United artists: The company that changed the film industry*. Madison: University of Wisconsin Press.

Barrett, T. (2015). Desiring the Soviet woman: Tatiana Romanova and *From Russia with Love*. In L. Funnell (Ed.), *For his eyes only? The women of James Bond*. London: Wallflower Press.

Bayoumi, T., Eichengreen, B., & Taylor, M. P. (Eds.). (1996). *Modern perspectives on the gold standard*. Cambridge: Cambridge University Press.

Bellows, A. (2009). *Alien hand syndrome: And other too-weird-not-to-be-true stories*. New York: Workman Publishing Company, Inc.

© The Editor(s) (if applicable) and The Author(s) 2017
L. Funnell, K. Dodds, *Geographies, Genders and Geopolitics of James Bond*, DOI 10.1057/978-1-137-57024-6

223

Bennett, T., & Woollacott, J. (1987). *Bond and beyond: The political career of a popular hero*. London: Macmillan.

Bennett, T., & Woollacott, J. (2003). The moments of Bond. In C. Lindner (Ed.), *The James Bond phenomenon: A critical reader*. Manchester: Manchester University Press.

Beranek, L. (2003). *Concert halls and opera houses: Music, acoustics, and architecture*. New York: Springer.

Berns, F. G. P. B. (2015). Sisterhood as resistance in *For Your Eyes Only* and *Octopussy*. In L. Funnell (Ed.), *For his eyes only? The women of James Bond*. London: Wallflower.

Black, J. (2005). *The politics of James Bond: From Fleming's novels to the big screen*. Lincoln: University of Nebraska Press.

Bold, C. (2003). "Under the very skirts of Britanna": Re-reading women in the James Bond novels. In C. Lindner (Ed.), *The James Bond phenomenon: A critical reader*. Manchester: Manchester University Press.

Boyce, M. (2015). Property of a lady: (S)mothering Judy Dench's M. In L. Funnell (Ed.), *For his eyes only? The women of James Bond*. London: Wallflower Press.

Broccoli, B. (2008). The secrets of *Quantum of Solace*. *IGN.com* [Online]. Available from: 25 March 2015. http://www.ign.com/articles/2008/04/04/the-secrets-of-quantum-of-solace?page=2. Accessed 25 Mar 2015.

Brown, J. A. (2015). "Who is salt?": The difficulty of constructing a female James Bond and reconstructing gender expectations. In L. Funnell (Ed.), *For his eyes only? The women of James Bond*. London: Wallflower Press.

Burnetts, C. (2015). Bond's bit on the side: Race, exoticism, and the Bond 'fluffer' character. In L. Funnell (Ed.), *For his eyes only? The women of James Bond*. London: Wallflower Press.

Chapman, J. (2000). *Licence to thrill: A cultural history of the James Bond films*. New York: Columbia University Press.

Chapman, J. (2011). Reflections in a double bourbon. In R. Weiner, B. Whitfield, & J. Becker (Eds.), *James Bond in world and popular culture: The films are not enough*. Cambridge: Scholars Publishing.

Chung, H. (2007). From *Die Another Day* to 'another day': The South Korean anti-007 movement and regional nationalism in post-Cold War Asia. *Spectator, 27*(2), 64–78.

Cimbala, S. J. (2001). *Through a glass darkly: Looking at conflict prevention, management, and termination*. Westport: Greenwood Publishing Group Inc.

Clarke, J. (2001). *Gallantry medals and decorations of the world*. Barnsley: Pen & Sword Books Ltd.

Claybourne, A. (2005). Electra. In *Gods, goddesses, and mythology* (Vol. 4). New York: Marshall Cavendish.

Colley, L. (2002). *Captives: Britain, empire, and the world, 1600–1850*. London: Cape.

Connell, R. W. (2005). *Masculinities* (2nd ed.). Berkeley: University of California Press.

Cooper, H., Schembri, S., & Miller, D. (2010). Brand-self identity narratives in the James Bond movies. *Psychology & Marketing, 27*(6), 557–567.

Cosgrove, D. (2001). *Apollo's eye: A cartographic genealogy of the earth in the Western imagination.* Baltimore: John Hopkins University Press.

Cresswell, T. (2006). *On the move: Mobility in the modern Western world.* London: Routledge.

Cresswell, T., & Dixon, D. (Eds.). (2002). *Engaging film: Geographies of mobility and identity.* Lanham: Rowman and Littlefield.

Curtin, M. (2007). *Playing to the world's biggest audience: The globalization of Chinese film and TV.* Berkeley: University of California Press.

Curtis, G. E. (2003). Kazakhstan: A country study. In L. M. Buyers (Ed.), *Central Asia in focus: Political and economic issues.* New York: Nova.

Dixon, D., & Marston, S. (2013). *Feminist geopolitics: At the sharp end.* London: Routledge.

Doane, M. A. (1991). *Femme fatales, film theory, psychoanalysis.* New York: Routledge.

Dodds, K. (2003). Licensed to stereotype: Geopolitics, James Bond and the spectre of Balkanism. *Geopolitics, 8,* 125–156.

Dodds, K. (2005). Screening geopolitics: James Bond and the early Cold War films (1962–1967). *Geopolitics, 10,* 266–289.

Dodds, K. (2014). Shaking and stirring James Bond: Age, gender, and the resilient agent in *Skyfall* (2012). *Journal of Popular Film and Television, 42,* 116–132.

Dodds, K. (2015). "It's not for everyone": James Bond and Miss Moneypenny in *Skyfall* (2012). In L. Funnell (Ed.), *For his eyes only? The women of James Bond.* London: Wallflower Press.

Eco, U. (1979). *The role of the reader: Explorations in the semiotics of texts.* Bloomington: Indiana University Press.

Eco, U. (2009). Narrative structures in fleming. In C. Lindner (Ed.), *The James Bond phenomenon: A critical reader.* Manchester: Manchester University Press.

Edwards, R., & Dickie, L. (2004). *Diamonds and gemstones.* New York: Crabtree Publishing Company.

Fisher, B. D. (2005). *Puccini's Tosca: Opera classics library series.* Boca Raton: Opera Journeys Publishing.

Fleming, I. (1953, reprinted 2012). *Casino royale.* Las Vegas: Thomas and Mercer.

Fleming, I. (1954, reprinted 2012). *Live and let die.* Las Vegas: Thomas and Mercer.

Fleming, I. (1955, reprinted 2012). *Moonraker.* Las Vegas: Thomas and Mercer.

Fleming, I. (1956, reprinted 2012). *Diamonds are forever.* Las Vegas: Thomas and Mercer.

Fleming, I. (1957a). *The diamond smugglers.* London: Jonathan Cape.

Fleming, I. (1957b, reprinted 2012). *From Russia with love*. Las Vegas: Thomas and Mercer.

Fleming, I. (1958, reprinted 2012). *Dr No*. Las Vegas: Thomas and Mercer.

Fleming, I. (1959, reprinted 2012). *Goldfinger*. Las Vegas: Thomas and Mercer.

Fleming, I. (1962, reprinted 2012). *The spy who loved me*. Las Vegas: Thomas and Mercer.

Fleming, I. (1963, reprinted 2013). *Thrilling cities*. London: Vintage.

Fleming, I. (1964, reprinted 2012). *You only live twice*. Las Vegas: Thomas and Mercer.

Fleming, I. (1965, reprinted 2012). *The man with the golden gun*. Las Vegas: Thomas and Mercer.

Fleming, F. (2015). *The man with the golden typewriter: Ian Fleming's James Bond letters*. London: Bloomsbury Publishing.

Fruchart-Ramond, P. (2013). Facts or acts? Korean news agencies reporting on inter-Korean relations. In V. Gelézeau, K. D. Ceuster, & A. Delissen (Eds.), *De-bordering Korea: Tangible and intangible legacies of the sunshine policy*. New York: Routledge.

Funnell, L. (2008). From English partner to American action hero: The heroic identity and transnational appeal of the bond girl. In C. Hart (Ed.), *Heroes and heroines: Embodiment, symbolism, narratives and identity*. Midrash: Kingswinford.

Funnell, L. (2011a). "I know where you keep your gun:" Daniel Craig as the Bond-Bond girl hybrid in *Casino Royale. Journal of Popular Culture, 44*(3), 455–472.

Funnell, L. (2011b). Negotiating shifts in feminism: The 'bad' girls of James Bond. In M. Waters (Ed.), *Women on screen: Feminism and femininity in visual culture*. Basingstoke: Palgrave.

Funnell, L. (2014). *Warrior women: Gender, race, and the transnational Chinese action star*. Albany: State University of New York Press.

Funnell, L. (Ed.). (2015a). *For his eyes only? The women of James Bond*. London: Wallflower Press.

Funnell, L. (2015b). For his eyes only?: Thoughts on female scholarship and fandom of the Bond franchise. In C. Hines (Ed.), *Fan phenomena: James Bond*. Bristol: Intellect.

Funnell, L. (2015c). Objects of white male desire: (D)evolving representations of Asian women in Bond films. In L. Funnell (Ed.), *For his eyes only? The women of James Bond*. London: Wallflower.

Gehlawat, M. (2009). Improvisation, action and architecture in *Casino Royale*. In C. Lindner (Ed.), *Revisioning 007: James Bond and Casino Royale*. London: Wallflower.

Gill, P., & Phythian, M. (2006). *Intelligence in an insecure world*. Cambridge: Polity.

Gonzalez, G. A. (2012). *Energy and empire: The politics of nuclear and solar power in the United States.* Albany: State University of New York Press.

Gross, E. (1986). Derrida, irigaray, and deconstruction. *Left-Wright Intervention, 20,* 69–81.

Guerrero, E. (1993). The black image in protective custody: Hollywood's biracial buddy films of the eighties. In M. Diawara (Ed.), *Black American cinema.* New York/London: Routledge.

Hawkins, H. (1990). *Classics and trash: Traditions and taboos in high literature and popular modern genres.* Toronto: University of Toronto Press.

Hines, C. (2011). For his eyes only? Men's magazines and the curse of the Bond girl. In R. Weiner, B. Whitfield, & J. Becker (Eds.), *James Bond in world and popular culture: The films are not enough.* Cambridge: Scholars Publishing.

Holliday, C. (2015). Mothering the Bond-M relation in *Skyfall* and the Bond girl intervention. In L. Funnell (Ed.), *For his eyes only? The women of James Bond.* London: Wallflower Press.

Hyne, N. J. (2012). *Nontechnical guide to petroleum geology, exploration, drilling, and production.* Tulsa: PenWell Corporation.

Inkster, N. (2015). These Chinese intelligence agencies: Evolution and empowerment in cyberspace. In J. R. Lindsay, T. M. Cheung, & D. S. Reveron (Eds.), *China and cybersecurity: Espionage, strategy, and politics in the digital domain.* Oxford: Oxford University Press.

Johnson, P. (1958, April 5). Sex, snobbery and sadism. *The New Statesman.*

Jones, N. (2015a). *Hollywood action films and spatial theory.* London: Routledge.

Jones, S. (2015b). "Women drivers": The changing role of the Bond girl in vehicle chases. In L. Funnell (Ed.), *For his eyes only? The women of James Bond.* London: Wallflower.

Karlan, R. (2015). The spy who fooled me: The early Bond girl and the magician's assistant. In L. Funnell (Ed.), *For his eyes only? The women of James Bond.* London: Wallflower.

Kim, J. (2015). From Cold Wars to the war on terror: North Korea, racial morphing, and gendered parodies in *Die Another Day* and *Team America: World Police. The Journal of Popular Culture, 48*(1), 124–138.

Kramer, M. (2010). The Prague Spring and the Soviet invasion in historical perspective. In S. Karner & P. Ruggenthaler (Eds.), *The Prague Spring and the Warsaw Pact invasion of Czechoslovakia in 1968.* London: Lexington Book.

Krapivin, V. F., & Varotsos, C. A. (2008). *Biochemical cycles in globalization and sustainable development.* Chichester: Praxis Publishing Ltd.

Krebs, R. E. (2006). *The history and use of our earth's chemical elements: A reference guide.* Westport: Greenwood Publishing Group Inc.

Kunze, P. C. (2015). From masculine mastermind to maternal martyr: Judi Dench's M, *Skyfall,* and the patriarchal logic of James Bond films. In L. Funnell (Ed.), *For his eyes only? The women of James Bond.* London: Wallflower Press.

La Bella, L. (2009). *Not enough to drink: Pollution, drought, and tainted water supplies.* New York: Rosen Publishing Group.

Langfitt, F. (2015, May 18). How China's censors influence Hollywood. *National Public Radio* [Online] Available at: http://www.npr.org/sections/parallels/2015/05/18/407619652/how-chinas-censors-influence-hollywood. Accessed 11 Sept 2015.

Lawless, K. (2014). Constructing the 'other': Construction of Russian identity in the discourse of James Bond films. *Journal of Multicultural Discourses, 9,* 72–97.

Lawrence, J. S. (2011). The American superhero genes of James Bond. In R. Weiner, B. L. Whitfield, & J. Becker (Eds.), *James Bond in world and popular culture: The films are not enough.* Newcastle upon Tyne: Cambridge Scholars Publishing.

Lee, J. (2007). North Korea, South Korea, and *007 Die Another Day. Critical Discourse Studies, 4,* 207–235.

Lee, T. (n.d.). Decorating in the modern style: What is modern-style decorating? *About Home.* [Online]. http://budgetdecorating.about.com/od/designstyles/a/Decorating-In-The-Modern-Style.htm. Accessed 14 July 2015.

Levy, A. (2003). *Diamonds and conflict: Problems and solutions.* New York: Novinka Books.

Lindner, C. (Ed.). (2003). *The James Bond phenomenon: A critical reader.* Manchester: Manchester University Press.

Lindsey, B. (2002). *Against the dead hand: The uncertain struggle for global capitalism.* New York: Wiley.

Lukinbeal, C., & Sharp, L. (2014). Geography and film. In B. Warf (Ed.), *Oxford bibliographies in geography.* New York: Oxford University Press.

Lupton, D. (1999). Monsters in metal cocoons: Road rage and cyborg bodies. *Body and Society, 5,* 57–72.

Mackinder, H. (1904). The geographical pivot of history. *The Geographical Journal, 23,* 421–437.

Marks, L. U. (2000). *The skin of film: Intercultural cinema, embodiment, and the senses.* Durham: Duke University Press.

McPhail, K., & Walters, D. (2009). *Accounting & business ethics.* Oxon: Routledge.

Metz, W. (2004). *Engaging film criticism: Film history and contemporary American cinema.* New York: Peter Lang Publishing.

Mizuta, M. E. (2015). Tokyo: Lightscapes: Cherry blossoms at night and the illumination of cultural properties. In S. Isenstadt, M. M. Petty, & D. Neumann (Eds.), *Cities of light: Two centuries of urban illumination.* New York: Routledge.

Moran, C. (2011). Ian Fleming and CIA Director Allen Dulles: The very best of friends. In R. Weiner, B. L. Whitfield, & J. Becker (Eds.), *James Bond in world and popular culture: The films are not enough.* Newcastle upon Tyne: Cambridge Scholars Publishing.

Myers, N., & Spoolman, S. E. (2014). *Environmental issues & solutions: A modular approach*. Belmont: Cengage Learning.

Nepa, S. (2015). Secret agent nuptials: Marriage, gender roles, and the "different Bond women" in *On Her Majesty's Secret Service*. In L. Funnell (Ed.), *For his eyes only? The women of James Bond*. Wallflower: London.

Norman, T. L. (2009). *Risk analysis and security countermeasure selection*. New York: CRC Press.

O'Connell, S. (1998). *The car and British society: Class, gender and motoring, 1896–1939*. Manchester: Manchester University Press.

Obaje, N. G. (2009). *Geology and mineral resources of Nigeria*. Berlin: Springer.

Park, J. C. Y. (2010). *Yellow future: Oriental style in Hollywood cinema*. Minneapolis: University of Minnesota Press.

Parker, M. (2014). *Goldeneye: Where Bond was born: Ian Fleming's Jamaica*. New York: Pegasus Books.

Parks, L. (2015). "M"(o)thering: Female representation of age and power in James Bond. In L. Funnell (Ed.), *For his eyes only? The women of James Bond*. London: Wallflower Press.

Paterson, M. (2009). Haptic geographies: Ethnography, haptic knowledges, and sensuous dispositions. *Progress in Human Geography, 33*(6), 766–788.

Peacock, K. W. (2008). *Natural resources and sustainable development*. New York: Facts on File, Inc.

Petty, M. M. (2015). Hong Kong. In S. Isenstadt, M. M. Petty, & D. Neumann (Eds.), *Cities of light: Two centuries of urban illumination*. New York: Routledge.

Piotrowska, A. G. (2015). Female voice and the Bond films. In L. Funnell (Ed.), *For his eyes only? The women of James Bond*. London: Wallflower Press.

Planka, S. (2015). Female bodies in James Bond title sequences. In L. Funnell (Ed.), *For his eyes only? The women of James Bond*. London: Wallflower Press.

Purse, L. (2011). *Contemporary action cinema*. Edinburgh: Edinburgh University Press.

Rancour-Laferriere, D. (1995). *The slave soul of Russia: Moral masochism and the cult of suffering*. New York: New York University Press.

Robins, K., & Morley, D. (1995). *Spaces of identity: Global media, electronic landscapes and cultural boundaries*. Oxon: Routledge.

Rodan, D., Ellis, K., & Lebeck, P. (2014). *Disability, obesity and ageing: Popular media identifications*. Farnham: Ashgate Publishing Limited.

Rodaway, P. (1994). *Sensuous geographies: Body, sense, and place*. London: Routledge.

Rositzka, E. (2015). Random access mysteries: James Bond and the matter of the unknown woman. In L. Funnell (Ed.), *For his eyes only? The women of James Bond*. London: Wallflower Press.

Said, E. (1978, reprinted 1994). *Orientalism*. New York: Vintage.

Santos, M. (2015). "This never happened to the other fellow": *On Her Majesty's Secret Service* as Bond woman's film. In L. Funnell (Ed.), *For his eyes only? The women of James Bond*. Wallflower: London.

Schultz, J. (2008). Lessons in blood and fire: The deadly consequences of IMF economics. In J. Schultz & M. Draper (Eds.), *Dignity and defiance: Stories from Bolivia's challenge to globalization*. Berkeley/Los Angeles: University of California Press.

Scott, J. W. (1990). Deconstructing equality-versus-difference: Or, the use of poststructuralist theory for feminism. In M. Hirsh & E. F. Keller (Eds.), *Conflicts in feminism*. Routledge: New York.

Sergeant, A. (2015). Bond is not enough: Elektra King and the desiring Bond girl. In L. Funnell (Ed.), *For his eyes only? The women of James Bond*. London: Wallflower Press.

Severson, A. J. (2015). Designing character: Costume, Bond girls, and negotiating representation. In L. Funnell (Ed.), *For his eyes only? The women of James Bond*. London: Wallflower Press.

Shaw, K. (2015). The politics of representation: Disciplining and domesticating Miss Moneypenny. In L. Funnell (Ed.), *For his eyes only? The women of James Bond*. London: Wallflower Press.

Siganos, G., Tauro, S. L., & Faloutsos, M. (2006). Jellyfish: A conceptual model for the AS internet topology. *Journal of Communications and Networks, 8*(3), 339–350.

Smith, J. C. (2011). Holidays, festivals and celebrations. In J. C. Smith (Ed.), *African American popular culture*. Greenwood: Santa Barbara.

Spalding, S. D., & Fraser, B. (2012). *Trains, literature, and culture: Reading and writing the rails*. Lanham: Lexington Book.

Strebe, A. G. (2007). *Flying for her country: The American and Soviet women military pilots of World War II*. Westport: Greenwood Publishing Group.

Sturken, M., & Cartwright, L. (2009). *Practices of looking: An introduction to visual culture*. Oxford: Oxford University Press.

Tasker, Y. (2004). Introduction: Action and adventure cinema. In Y. Tasker (Ed.), *Action and adventure cinema*. London: Routledge.

Thomas, T. L. (2012). China's cyber tool: Striving to attain electronic *Shi*? In P. C. Reich & E. Gelbstein (Eds.), *Law, policy, and technology: Cyberterrorism, information warfare and internet immobilization*. Hershey: Information Science Reference.

Thompson, A. (2008, October 23). 'Solace' offers thinking person's 007. *Variety*. [Online] Available at: http://variety.com/2008/film/columns/solace-offers-thinking-person-s-007-1117994573/. Accessed 23 Jan 2016.

Tremonte, C., & Racioppi, L. (2009). Body politics and *Casino Royale*: Gender and (inter)national security. In C. Lindner (Ed.), *The James Bond phenomenon: A critical reader* (2nd ed.). Manchester: Manchester University Press.

Turner, A. (1998). *Goldfinger*. London: Bloomsbury.

Turse, N. (2013). *Kill anything that moves: The real American War in Vietnam*. New York: Picador.

Ueno, T. (2003). Japanimation and techo-orientalism: Japan as the sub-empire of signs. *Documentary Box* [Online] 9. n.p. Available from: http://www.t0.or.at/ueno/japan.htm. Accessed 17 July 2015.

Ulfsdotter, B. (2015). The Bond girl who is not there: The Tiffany Case. In L. Funnell (Ed.), *For his eyes only? The women of James Bond*. London: Wallflower Press.

Vawter, R. G. (2013). The case for development of oil shale in the United States. In D. E. Newman (Ed.), *World energy crisis*. Santa Barbara: ABC-CLIO, LLC.

Wagner, T. (2015). "The old ways are best": The colonization of women of color in Bond films. In L. Funnell (Ed.), *For his eyes only? The women of James Bond*. London: Wallflower Press.

Wakeman-Linn, J., Mathieu, P., & van Selm, B. (2003). Oil funds in transition economies: Azerbaijan and Kazakhstan. In J. M. Davis, R. Ossowski, & A. Fedelino (Eds.), *Fiscal policy formulation and implementation in oil-producing countries*. Washington, DC: International Monetary Fund.

Ward, S. (2003). Trains. In J. Speake (Ed.), *Literature of travel and exploration: An encyclopedia*. New York: Routledge.

Webster, W. (2005). *Englishness and empire 1939–1965*. Oxford: Oxford University Press.

Weiner, R. G., Whitfield, B. L., & Becker, J. (Eds.). (2010). *James Bond in world and popular culture: The films are not enough*. Newcastle upon Tyne: Cambridge Scholars Publishing.

Winder, S. (2011). *The man who saved Britain: A personal journey into the disturbing world of James Bond*. London: Picador.

Wood, J. T. (2013). *Gendered lives: Communication, gender, & culture*. Boston: Wadsworth.

Wood, A. F., & Smith, M. J. (2014). *Online communication: Linking technology, identity, & culture*. New York: Psychology Press.

Wu, J. (2015). Mao Suit. In A. Lynch & M. D. Strauss (Eds.), *Ethnic dress in the United States: A cultural encyclopedia*. Lanham: Rowman & Littlefield Publishing Group, Inc.

Zegart, A. (2008). *Spying blind: The CIA, the FBI and the origins of 9/11*. Princeton: Princeton University Press.

Zhai, Q. (2000). *China and the Vietnam Wars, 1950–1975*. Chapel Hill: University of North Carolina Press.

INDEX

Note: Page numbers with "n" denote notes.

9 781349 848812